HEADLESS
HISTORY

ALSO BY LINDA ORR

Jules Michelet: Nature, History, and Language

HEADLESS HISTORY

Nineteenth-Century French
Historiography of the Revolution

LINDA ORR

Cornell University Press

ITHACA AND LONDON

First published 1990 by Cornell University Press.

International Standard Book Number 0-8014-2379-1
Library of Congress Catalog Card Number 89-22140

Printed in the United States of America

*Librarians: Library of Congress cataloging information
appears on the last page of the book.*

♾ The paper used in this publication meets the minimum requirements
of the American National Standard for Permanence of Paper for
Printed Library Materials Z39.48-1984.

TO
Anne-Marie Bryan
Alice Yaeger Kaplan
Fabienne André Worth

Contents

Preface

My study of nineteenth-century French historiography radiates out from the trilogy of 1847 (Lamartine, the first volumes of Michelet and Louis Blanc). From there it reaches back to Cabet (1839) and Madame de Staël (1818) or up to Quinet (1865) and Taine (1875–94). That mid-century trilogy is associated with French Romanticism, so I decided to keep the word *Romantic* (and eventually the word *Jacobin*) and to expand both of them into general concepts for the purposes of argument.

Traditionally, nineteenth-century texts represent the culmination of narrative political history, although they are considered too dramatic, poetic, and biased. According to this view, the histories are curious, pre-empirical works of literature, not social science. When one reads the texts outside of that comparison with science, prejudiced in favor of science, a kind of theoretical nervousness emerges which draws attention to problems of historical knowledge. Nineteenth-century historians worry out loud about their own readership, their personal connection with the object of their history, the sneaky tactics of a rival historian, and the predicaments of the society in which they live. These are concerns later histories will clean out of their work, or disguise and repress.

Headless History begins in the experience of reading ("Long-Duration Reading"). It starts with my own relationship to the form of these histories. I describe that form, which doubles and turns against itself. Nineteenth-century histories have two stories: one emphasizes the smooth, logical texture of history and society; the other seems to con-

tradict the first one—reveals anxieties, doubt, nagging theoretical and
political inconsistencies. Like the democratic societies in which they
participate, these histories are "headless." The source of their truth or
legitimacy does not come from outside but is constituted in the process
of writing and making history (both senses of that term).

In "Repulsive Recollections" (part two of "Constituting the Corpus"), I do not go directly to my texts but to the interference that blocks
my direct relationship to them. I start with the overlay of readings which
tradition has already given us, as we cannot confront past texts without
those echoes. This interference occurs as well in the practice of history,
where almost invisible layers of interpretation obscure, if not replace,
the object.

"The Laws of Reading: Narrative Teleology and Romantic History"
plunges into the form of the Romantic texts. All too soon, in their first
pages, these texts set up expectations for development and logical results
(laws) that they admit they cannot carry out. This discrepancy between
expectations and results has consequences for the entire tradition based
on narrative history, especially when narrative is not just story or a report on research but takes an active part in the formation of our knowledge.

The third chapter, "The Problem of Legitimacy: The Popular Authority of Romantic Historiography," asks what holds together the postrevolutionary headless text and society, deprived of its logical supports.
The historian and her or his public, both professional and popular,
emerge in a mutual relationship upon which credibility depends. That
society in which the historian participates is always present in some
form or another, even by absence, but its influence is felt more and more
as my book progresses. Specifically, the situation or time and place of
writing enters into a more fully drawn opposition or dialogue with the
past where Tocqueville is concerned ("The Freedom and Terror of Un-
knowable History"). Here oppositions — past/present, object/subject,
teleology/rupture, visible or readable history/invisible or unreadable
history — struggle to work themselves out. These internal doubles and
debates make Tocqueville even more, not less, like his historian contemporaries.

In the last chapter, "The Blind Spot of History: Writing or Logography," writing literally invades the scene, but ironically for me this fore-

grounding of writing also sends me back to the archive again. I am forced to recognize the ever-powerful image of the archive. Are the texts of the logographers, those sympathetic secretaries with whom I identify too closely, literal accounts of official proceedings or fictions or already histories? The lost stenographer's text extends the image of the archive into an infinite regress, for as close as writing tries to get to speech, or language to the historical event, there still remains a divide (Zeno's Race Course) that can never be bridged. The endless layering of the archive in the last chapter stands as a framing device parallel to the layering of tradition in the first chapter. But I put what comes last (tradition) first and what comes first (the archive) last, because that is the order in which history is made.

Headless History occupies a crossroads of many worlds for me, personal and professional. It brings together the two interests, literature and history, which have most preoccupied me, at a time when the fields of literary criticism and historical studies seem finally to be coming closer together again (with the infinite divide?). For the past twenty years or so, it looked as if literary criticism was rejecting history, which had so long provided the categories of literature's own knowledge. This view was too simple, inasmuch as several currents of criticism were all the while assimilating concepts of linguistics, psychoanalysis, and semiotics into a reflection on history (in France the "sociocriticism" of Claude Duchet and Françoise Gaillard; in the United States the Marxist criticism of Fredric Jameson). And even so-called structuralism had its own way of rewriting history (e.g., Gérard Genette's palimpsests).

My background in French literary criticism and thought (all the Jacques Lacan, Jacques Derrida, and Michel Foucault I breathed in during graduate school) fed into experiences that went further back in my life than professional training. Growing up in the South, I had been obsessed with history and with history's relation to fiction. When I later read those theories about how we never say what we mean, their message sounded natural to me. As a child, I suspected that those tobacco shacks could not exist in that best of all possible worlds we supposedly enjoyed. The honey-sweet words spoken around me had a bite that undercut the sweetness. The whole culture was profoundly confusing. My situation probably resembles that of others. Double discourse thrives in the context of class or gender, as well as of race or culture. We learn it

early. Reading Paul de Man on irony brought back reading C. Vann
Woodward in Anne Scott's undergraduate American history class at
Duke. There was something Southern about nineteenth-century French
history, the way it covered up conflict and tension, which reemerged all
the more blatant.

History is now making a return in literary studies with that unbridled
energy of the repressed, and, on the other side, historians have begun to
talk again about symbolic forms, narrative, representation, and language. This rapprochement between history and literature is especially
visible in the case of the French Revolution (and its bicentennial). François Furet's *Penser la Révolution française* made legitimate again, if not
fashionable, the reading of older historical texts, especially those from
the nineteenth century. This reference to older texts is gratifying, since it
allows my own work to take center stage. But the particular contexts of
our books differ in important ways.

The reader of *Penser la Révolution française* must take into account
Furet's ongoing debate with French Marxist historians. Anglo-American scholarship influenced Furet and reinforced his "revisionist" arguments. With the help of French writing and thought (no innocent genie
in a lamp, either), my own book treats nineteenth-century texts as a contradictory, even critical, perspective on liberalism.

My reading of Furet was influenced by Claude Lefort, whose seminar
in political philosophy I attended in Paris, 1977–78. Of course I give my
reading of Furet its own twist. My book, informed by both Marxist and
"post-Marxist" work, should indicate as it goes along where I agree and
disagree with Furet.

For a long time I have appreciated the productive dialogue with historians in the United States working on France or historical theory, but
I am also mindful of the competition here between political and social
history, social and cultural history, intellectual history and all of the others. My own work has continually benefited from a range of historians,
including Lynn Hunt, Hans Kellner, Dominick LaCapra, Stanley Mellon, Carl Pletsch, William Reddy, Nancy Struever, and Hayden White. I
like to think of my book not solely as history viewed from a literary perspective but as a kind of new social history of nineteenth-century historical texts in which the study of history automatically implies a meditation on the act of writing and a fascination with language.

A shortened version of "Repulsive Recollections" appeared in *Stanford Literature Review* 6 (Spring 1989); parts of chapter 2 on Michelet and Blanc were printed in *The Eighteenth Century* 30 (Summer 1989); the French texts of "The Popular Authority of Romantic Historiography" and the chapter on Tocqueville, which have been considerably modified here, appeared respectively in *The Romanic Review* 73 (November 1982; copyright by the Trustees of Columbia University in the City of New York) and in *Poétique* 49 (February 1982); finally "The Blind Spot of History" was published in *Yale French Studies* 73 (1987). Permission to use this material is gratefully acknowledged.

My thanks go to Sandy Petrey, Nancy Miller, and Ann Rigney for getting me to finish this book; to the Department of Romance Studies at Duke University for its supportive atmosphere; to Carole Stitt for helping me bring the chapter on logography out of its miasma; especially to Susan Weiner, who worked with me for hours on end all during the last stages of this manuscript, making the hardest passages clearer. She also translated into English the original of chapter 3, "L'autorité 'populaire' de l'historiographie romantique," and the French historical texts.

My thanks also to my parents, Henry H. and Marianna Orr, who got me out for fresh air (March 1980) when I had retreated to their house to blast out the ur-book.

Thanks to the Guggenheim Foundation for a grant in 1977–78 to begin this project and to the Duke University Research Council for a research travel grant in 1980 and special grant in 1989 for manuscript preparation.

And finally, thanks to Anne Lunt, Marilyn Sale, Bernhard Kendler, and the staff of Cornell University Press; to my women's group for riding the ups and downs; and to Mary Anne Daw for her intellectual, friendly, and practical help all during the history of this book.

LINDA ORR

Chapel Hill, North Carolina

I Constituting the Corpus

Long-Duration Reading

My past experiences of reading had not prepared me for nineteenth-century historiography. After training in "close readings," I was most at ease with a dense poem. The complex language of a Mallarmé sonnet unnerved me less than what looked like the straightforward proclamations of Louis Blanc. Reading the Romantic historians was like reading Paul Eluard's poems or Lamartine's: easy to understand but difficult to write about—critically. Certainly you would not read these Romantic gargantuas for the facts or for new breakthroughs in research on the Revolution, the kind that today usually takes the form of a monograph or article. Something must have changed in our reading habits to make the Romantic historians fall from their high point of popularity. A complete set of Lamartine or Louis Blanc would have been the pride of a nineteenth-century bourgeois family. A working-class family would have been as likely to own Lamartine's history in installments as Cabet's. Now these are old carcasses in the junk lot of the library-museum. Their authors are best known for their "style." Nothing could damn them more in the eyes of contemporary historians.

I had secretly fantasized that reading nineteenth-century histories of the Revolution would be like reading novels by Dickens or Austen—the way their contemporaries did at the fireside all winter. On the one hand, I entertained a retrograde fantasy, nostalgia for a time when the middle class imitated aristocratic leisure. On the other, the very fact of reading these histories at all was a radical gesture. What I did not expect when I began was the intimacy, the personal history I would build up with the books themselves as objects and with their authors as acquaintances. Not always pleasant ones. Michelet was often tyrannical and intolerable, Blanc depressing and whiny. But the long duration of my acquaintance made for a density that I hoped to translate into my own writing about them. In the essay "Unpacking My Library," published in 1931, Walter Benjamin thought about "the whole background" of each of his books, its "magic encyclopedia" and "fate" as well as "memories of the cities . . . ; memories of the rooms where these books had been housed."[1] In my own library, the books of French history took on their own history different from the ones written on their pages.

THE PHYSIOLOGY OF READING: TIME AND THE BODY

Reading these histories is like training for a marathon. Or practicing the piano. "If I read fifty pages an hour for five hours a day for five days a week, I'll finish Lamartine in a month," I said to myself, optimistic. It was more like thirty pages an hour, three hours a day, five days a week. And I bogged down at certain "scenes." At that rate 3200 pages was more than seven months for the eight volumes of Lamartine. In the octavo edition, Blanc's *Histoire de la Révolution française* was twelve volumes. It looked shorter because I had purchased from a used-book store in Paris the more common popular edition in two quartos with illustrations. But the pages were so large that I could read only about seven an hour. The slow pace made calculations discouraging. And that edition did not have the absolutely essential notes that made up the appendix. So I stopped estimating how long it would take to finish Blanc. Years. I was aging with the books.

When I moved, across the continent, down the coast, from one house to the other, the books gained weight. Michelet alone was a blessing, in the light Pléiade edition. Lamartine was of course the most elegant, in eight scarlet leather volumes with ornate gold titles. But those two popular volumes of Louis Blanc weighed ten pounds each and started very shortly to fall apart. The dry pages chipped, the faded brown leather of

1. Walter Benjamin, *Illuminations*, trans. Harry Zohn, ed. Hannah Arendt (New York: Schocken, 1968), 60, 67.

the spine cracked into squares and dropped away. The sewing of the binding loosened. Then there was the secondary bibliography: among them, four volumes of the *Histoire de dix ans* of Blanc and miscellaneous Cabet, whose *Histoire populaire de la Révolution française* was impossible to find or available only used at exorbitant prices. The Communist became the collector's item. I took him out on interlibrary loan.

Nevertheless, when I was resettled and quiet, something incredible always happened. The books were good. They surprised me with their uncanny intelligence. Lights flashed, and ideas connected. Aphorisms danced. Take this one I found in my notebook from Thiers: "It was up to opinion to do justice to opinion itself."[2] This paradox captures the self-constituting revolutionary system in miniature. I needed only draw out what was there in the text.

The long, winding sentences were even more revealing. They played out, in miniature, how French society had in principle gotten where it was, by what contorted logic. The following sentence from Lamartine looks at first like a simple counterargument to Robespierre's, or behind him, to Rousseau's, innocent view of nature. But when you try to read it step by step, it becomes labyrinthian doubletalk that openly tries to hide the violence society uses to triumph over nature's violence: "Robespierre forgot that the state of nature was the absence or anarchy of all rights; that society alone, by triumphing, from century to century, over the brute force of each individual, created slowly, and by cutting off something from the right of each isolated being, this vast system of relationships, of rights, of faculties, of guarantees and duties which make up that social right which society then distributes and guarantees to its members."[3] Society triumphs over brutality by cutting off (*retranchant*) a part of each individual's right (*droit*): by the guillotine? In one sentence man passes from an ambiguous state of nature to an even more ambiguous social system. The trick of using the word *droit* four times raises the question of whether the *droit* as end result is superior to the original *droit* that was cut off. Is there a historical evolution from "in-

2. Adolphe Thiers, *Histoire de la Révolution française*, 6th ed. (Paris: Furne, 1837), 5:190.

3. Alphonse de Lamartine, *Histoire des Girondins* (Paris: Furne, 1847), 5:400. Subsequent references to this work will be in the text. Antoine Court (Facultés des lettres, Saint-Etienne) has written a *thèse d'état* on Lamartine's *Histoire des Girondins* which covers in complete detail all aspects of the work: sources, errors, debates around the book.

dividual" to "member," or a vicious circle, or a fundamental tautology defining modern society?

Lost in these sentences, I discovered the perverse advantages of interminable reading. The rest of life was put on hold. Nothing else existed outside of reading, and I could not possibly write because there was so much to read. Notes piled up, dossiers. Time passed, a strange time that seemed like the quintessence of time, recorded according to the hourglass of pages turned. Everything, even teaching, conflicted with this kind of reading that abolishes the days and the weeks like being sick (in Proust).

Such long-duration reading influenced the way I came to experience the content of the books. This endless reading made me take the notion of "the content of the form"[4] — to its most literal extreme. The effect of accumulation, weight, and repetition shaped a special sense of Romantic history and its double object — the Revolution and nineteenth-century society, formative mirror images of a modern struggling democracy. The plot did not hook me, nor did a main character (Madame Roland, Charlotte Corday) with whom I was supposed to identify. But I had the illusion of knowing the narrator or author. Reading these histories was like embarking upon a sensual sea of words and losing my bearings, losing the usual differentiations that keep everything straight. This impression mimed the way the historians portrayed the Revolution itself, as if the reader too is caught up in it.

Lamartine troubled me the most. His text was abstract but also zeroed in on details, symbolic and anecdotal. His narrator, I imagined, was not so much a detective hunting clues as a murderer, past or future, going over every inch of the scene of the crime. Lamartine's narrator often focuses on the royal family, the king eating chicken, the ball of yarn the couple uses to communicate in prison. Nor does this narrative close-up abate as a Swiss guard gets killed or the people mutilate a body. The pulsing pace of the language, erotic and violent more than logical, takes over the high ideas and large shapes of plot until I, the reader, enter into some unfamiliar ritual. And yet the way every detail and word, the shifting power of different words, gives that symbolic cast to the Revolution deserves reflection. These strategies, for better or worse, will be discontinued in the later, positivist histories of Aulard, Jaurès, Lefebvre.

4. Reference to Hayden White, *The Content of the Form: Narrative Discourse and Historical Representation* (Baltimore: The Johns Hopkins UP, 1987).

There is something oppressive about Louis Blanc's volumes written in exile, at the British Museum in London. The shortest historian, perhaps one of the shortest Frenchmen of his time, Blanc wrote the longest history of all. The reader gets a sense of the Revolution as much from the very bulk of the twelve volumes as from what their author says about its events. A kind of hypnotic spell is created; the text is so long that it starts to turn upon itself. Testimony of such "long servitude," alternating with bursts of hope, creates a sobering tone. Blanc's book is at once the most boring and the most poetic of the histories. At certain points, the text stops dead in its tracks, then is forced to become lyrical or to abandon language altogether. These are fragile moments when the tomes disappear, à la Dante, and Blanc stares into the enigma—the black hole of the Revolution — or the white hole, the blank page Blanc's history keeps erasing.

Michelet does not get depressed so much as desperate, unless again that sense of desperation results from so many pages flipping by and from the revolutionary rhetoric of speed and haste. The glorious eruptions of July 14, 1789, and the circle dancing of a year later wind into a "vortext" where the reader detects a terrible tension. The Revolution will not stop. Enough! seem to cry both writer and reader—but it keeps on going. Michelet himself gets captured by his most deeply ambivalent identification, Robespierre. (These histories are nothing but guilty identifications lived out on different levels of narration.) As Michelet's desired Revolution turns into its opposite, Robespierre stands there at the end as the awful consequence, Michelet's internal Terror: we all end up as scribes, or even worse, as critics slashing the speech of others. We are not always messiahs of a new dawn. We can cause harm.

If volume means time and space in Lamartine or Blanc, it means sound in Cabet. The narrator's interruptions are so insistent that the volume goes up. Besides being loud, of all the books I read, Cabet's smelled the worst. They were mildewed and moldy. His view of the Revolution was as discomforting as the others. My eyes and nose watered.

These are a few examples. Taine, Tocqueville, Thiers, Madame de Staël create their own physiology of reading history. Michelet took the concept literally and wanted to embody the history of France in his wife, in his books, in himself; he wrote his histories in tune with the rhythms of the body, his wife's and his own. There was no difference between his writing, the author-subject, and the historical object. But Madame de

Staël was someone who could occupy that privileged space of the perfect coincidence between life and history, body and event, which Michelet and Hugo could only fantasize. She analyzes the Revolution while literally registering its effects in her body. She faints in ecstasy with the crowd at her father's triumphant speech (July 30, 1789); she weaves her way among the menacing pikes as the September massacres are heating up (September 2, 1793), and she is writing twenty years later.[5]

The Romantic project seeks to dissolve autobiography and history, subject and object, form and content, text and society, history and daily life, fact and *fantasme*, theory and story, and then sort them out again. The text of Romantic history is fluid, messy, and without boundaries when judged by modern standards. Nothing had its separate place, neither sources ("references") nor debates between historians. The use of the footnote was not yet stabilized; it merely served as textual overflow.

I have not ordered my present study according to the traditional left-to-right ideology (one possible lineup: Cabet, Blanc, Michelet, Thiers, Lamartine, Tocqueville, Taine), and I have tried to avoid separating each historian into a different chapter. Suggesting, in fact, that all of these historians are Jacobin-Romantic in one form or another, I have erred on the side of blurring them together (I speak of "they" or even "it," Romantic history). They are, after all, reacting to similar, very specific sets of postrevolutionary phenomena. But I would not want them to start to sound alike — for which reason I have first depicted their narrative personalities. For each book is individual and different.

5. Madame de Staël, *Considérations sur la Révolution française*, ed. Jacques Godechot (Paris: Tallandier, 1983), 168, 285. My essay on Madame de Staël's history should be included here in my book because she inaugurates the historical tradition ("Romantic") I am constructing and studying. I presented the essay at "Women and the French Revolution," a conference at the University of California at Los Angeles organized by Sara Melzer and Leslie Rabine. Participants were asked not to publish their essays elsewhere so they could appear in a collection together (forthcoming, 1990 or 1991). We often encounter this double bind in women's studies: when a choice has to be made, should essays on women writers be grouped together or "mainstreamed" into the canon? Jacques Godechot leaves Madame de Staël out of his tradition of Revolution historiography (*Jury pour la Révolution*) because her *Considérations* ... "is more like an eye-witness account and pamphlet than history. ... Madame de Staël does not seek to be objective" (26). My own definition of history refuses an easy opposition between objective and nonobjective. However, my book will create the same effect as Godechot's since I too leave Madame de Staël out, thus cutting off my own origin, or the head of my book.

ROMANTIC HISTORY'S CRITIQUE: TEXT AND UNTEXT

We call the nineteenth century the Age of History. It was the period when historical time came into its own, in all its density and profusion. This more sophisticated history had at its disposal an object worthy of its ambition: the French Revolution. Then, as if by destiny, a line of eminent historians appeared soon after in order to meet this grand conjuncture. It was the age of Macaulay, Carlyle, Michelet, Herder, Bancroft. Who proclaimed it the Age of History? These historians themselves, with an eye to their own reputations?

Despite this moment of grandeur, the Age of History occupies a curiously ambiguous place in more recent histories of history. I would guess that the heirs of Romantic history committed that passive-aggressive act of calling the nineteenth century "the Age of History," for such a title was the eventual kiss of death. The old historians could then be relegated to the marginal status of irrelevant national monuments. The titans became neanderthals, primitives of a prehistory surpassed by new developments.

Henceforth, the Romantic historians would be considered picturesque, but not analytic; in essence they are given (back) to literature, for history, from this point on, joins with science. A present-day edition of the Larousse encyclopedia (1974) locates this epistemological break, which still rules our configuration of knowledge, as if the break goes without saying: "In the course of the nineteenth century, as a consequence of the progress of erudition and of a concern for critical rigor, there happens a reversal which is confirmed in the twentieth century: the solicitations of knowledge win out over aesthetic preoccupations, and history leaves literature in order to become an autonomous discipline."[6] History's autonomy is not so convincing since it "leaves" literature because of an unnamed someone else's "solicitations." The third part of the triangle is called "knowledge" — another name for the new lover, science? Does that imply that nothing before had any claim to knowledge?

The new configuration of knowledge — the history of its acceptance should be examined further — sits as solidly as cliché. In *A History of*

6. Alain Melchior-Bonnet, "Histoire et littérature," *La grande encyclopédie* (Paris: Larousse, 1974), 29:5939.

Historical Writing (1937), Harry Elmer Barnes (referring back to
George Peabody Gooch) points out the "handicaps" of the "Romanti-
cists" and "exuberant" nationalists. Their defects clear the way for
"The Rise of Critical Historical Scholarship," the chapter introducing,
as usual, "Leopold Von Ranke and the German School."[7] A similar historical formula even exists in the specialized area of French Revolution
historiography. Alice Gérard's indispensable manual *La Révolution
française, mythes et interprétations (1789 – 1970)* leaves no doubt as to
whom "myth" refers to (and thus who is "interpretation"). Her table of
contents tells its own story: "Contemporary Passions and Eternal Debates (1789 – 1815)," "The Triumph of Myth (1815 – 1853)," "Positivism and Demystification (1853 – 1880)," and "The Institutionalized
Revolution (1880 – 1945)."[8]

The Romantic historians would have been surprised to see themselves
described as mythic, or even more, as "Romantic." They thought they
were positivists, if not the first scientific historians. An article in *Revue
des deux mondes*, published in 1847 by Charles Louandre, sizes up the
historical profession of the first half of the century: "For the past fifty
years, in fact, the domain of history has expanded singularly. This science, lost for a long time in systems, has grown closer to the positive sciences through the strict observation of facts."[9] One has to blink and look
back at the date 1847.

I began to get defensive in my work on nineteenth-century historians
who looked like the scapegoats of modern knowledge. (For this reason,
I refuse to cordon off the term *Romantic* but allow it to be imperialist in

7. Harry Elmer Barnes, *A History of Historical Writing*, 2d ed. (New York: Dover,
1963), 239.

8. Alice Gérard's *Révolution française, mythes et interprétations (1789 – 1970)*
(Paris: Flammarion, 1970) has served for me as a storehouse of received opinions on Romantic history. These opinions are true. There is no sense denying them. But it is at this
point that the Romantic historians become interesting. My entire book elaborates on the
judgments in this one sentence, for instance, of Gérard's: "One can say, then, that romantic history succeeds in eluding the controversy: eager for unanimity, it replaces facts
with their symbols, criticism with pathos, problems with verbal solutions. As for the past,
they all end with a general amnesty: write on all those tombs, Lamartine says, 'died for
the future and the workers of Humanity' " (45).

9. Charles Louandre, "Statistique littéraire de la production intellectuelle en France
depuis quinze ans," *Revue des deux mondes* 20 (1847): 426. For a new reading of these
eighteenth-century historical "systems," see Suzanne Gearhart, *The Open Boundary of
History and Fiction: A Critical Approach to the French Enlightenment* (Princeton:
Princeton UP, 1984).

reverse, up to the present.) I considered my texts the victims of a historical conspiracy, until I enlarged my own view to see that this strategy is only a recent example in a similar series regularly repeated through the history of history. Each generation or school, in turn, draws the epistemological break at its own arrival so that everything before is "not-knowledge" while it inaugurates knowledge. Or rather, each new historical method (philosophical history, political history, social history, economic history) is considered the more truly scientific one. This new and improved practice claims to be the first, after a long line of failures and missed approximations, to reach the status of what can at last be named *history*. All the rest, historians laboring under misconceived notions, if read at all, are read as "literature."

Romantic history plays, therefore, a pivotal role in our schema of knowledge; it is the negative "before" in a history where the "after" appears as positive advancement. Moreover, everything associated with this history takes on the effect of an ideology (by virtue of this contrast) that has even more consequences for our modern definition of ourselves. Everything implied by the term *philosophy of identity* (identity of history with its object and meaning, of language with its expression, of sense with perception, of self or action with intention) seems to peak in the Romantic philosophy of history. (Does naive "identity" automatically characterize any term in the position of "before"?) In *L'historiographie romantique française (1815 – 1830)* B. Réizov sees how the notion of identity determines other aspects of Romantic history, especially its sense of universal confidence: "The characteristic trait of the new school was the idea of evolution, of the connection existing between all the eras of the history of humanity or, in other words, of its 'identity.' This is not only an idea, but an assurance, a very intense and deep sentiment."[10] Everything fits together in a growing symphony of well-being. The histories radiate, not utopia as such, but an overall faith in human beings and their institutions.

We probably need this view of at least one mythical place in recent Western memory where a society — which we see as still relatively simple, although modern and faced with revolutionary change — functions almost blithely on presuppositions of identity and human progress.

10. B. Réizov, *L'historiographie romantique française (1815–1830)* (Moscow: Editions en langues étrangères, n.d. [1950?]), 789. Also see François Furet, *Penser la Révolution française* (Paris: Gallimard, 1978), 23: "These are histories of identity."

Without the Romantics, our cultural *ingénus*, how could we describe
the more sophisticated states of our own modern life and thought, including the notion of modernity itself? Just as modern history begins
with Ranke, modern French literature (if not modern literature in general) begins with Baudelaire (Rimbaud, Mallarmé) or the realist trinity
Stendhal, Balzac, Flaubert. (Modern French literary criticism begins
with them too.) The break of 1848 or 1851 stands as a symbolic divide
between illusion and reality—even though writers like Thiers, Michelet,
and Hugo continued to be major, complex figures dominating the entire
century. Instead of separating themselves out with Romanticism coming
first, followed by Realism (or positivism), both enjoyed a mutual complicity all during the century (basic binaries in our culture?). Realism,
and positivism, knew that the Romantics were not as simple as they were
made (by the realists themselves) to appear.

The realists had it both ways. They snickered about the simpleminded
Romantics (who were not simpleminded) and appeared to make great
theoretical strides in social science and literature. Their strategy was extremely contorted. They were critical of Romantic presuppositions
(identity of thing and word, etc.), but they continued to depend upon
these same presuppositions themselves — only disguising, refining, ig-
noring them, rather than rejecting them outright. Reality became dirtier,
denser, and working class, but the "illusion" of identity supported their
theory of knowledge no less. Eventually (Carl Becker's 1926 paper) historians also came to accept that facts were no longer "hard," solid substances and that history did not speak unmediated and direct. But they
began an equally devious discourse of ever-more-sophisticated geometrical progressions toward a truth that rooted itself more deeply with
each progressive withdrawal.[11]

For this reason, much is at stake in the claim that Romantic history
embodies the philosophy of identity at the same time that it launches its
own critique. How can I describe this phenomenon of Romantic history,
which may be common to many texts in general but which has specific

11. See a more elaborate discussion of these ideas in Linda Orr, "The Revenge of Literature: A History of History," *New Literary History* 18 (Autumn 1986): 1–22. Also
see reevaluations of realism in Sandy Petrey, *Realism and Revolution: Balzac, Stendhal,
Zola, and the Performances of History* (Ithaca: Cornell UP, 1988) and Fredric Jameson,
The Political Unconscious: Narrative as a Socially Symbolic Act (Ithaca: Cornell UP,
1981). For another account of one generation's misreading of its predecessors, see Harold Bloom, *Agon: Towards a Theory of Revisionism* (Oxford: Oxford UP, 1982).

implications for modern social and historical theory? It is as if these nineteenth-century historians are telling one story out loud and, almost in spite of themselves, another one sotto voce, double entendre, between the lines, in the margins—whatever metaphor fits. As if the right hand appears not to know what the left is doing. Many configurations of this duality (that subdivides or multiplies) exist. One side or strain dominates; the other appears only in ruptures or never appears at all, except in absence, gaps. They switch back and forth. At times they act out, in the text, the discourse and counterdiscourse of society (Richard Terdiman's terms).

I want to avoid getting caught up in the different metaphors of relation and nonrelation, not stall too long at the recognition that change can be expressed only in terms of metaphor (for I know these are questions one never gets beyond), in order to follow the social and textual changes of these nineteenth-century histories. I also want to avoid talking about the multiple meanings of a text as if there is a first and second "level," surface and depth. It is more simultaneous than that. Since I am studying textual units, albeit sociotextual, that relate in many ways other than formal opposition, sometimes beyond terms of logical relation, I call this double discourse of Romantic history text and untext— like birthday and unbirthday.

Romanticism and Romantic literary criticism have long been a repository of doubles. These doubles usually take a thematic or psychological form. Romantic irony, for instance, defines the perspective a sentimental like Musset wrenched himself back into after a good cry. But irony can be bitter and deeply resonant, with implications for literature, history, and society. The extent and quality of this irony depend on how radically the Romantic split can work itself into our present historical and intellectual practices.

The problem for contemporary criticism is to figure out how something like Musset's Romantic irony is related to the more philosophical irony in Kierkegaard, Nietzsche, or even Paul de Man. In terms of this tradition of rhetoric, irony reminds us of the double nature of language (life), which cannot mean or be what it says. When a reader isolates a pair of doubles, like crying and criticism, light and dark, the pair falls into a thematic opposition. Then as the opposition evolves in the text, that symmetry eventually gets lopsided and breaks down. The text bumps up against its own "aporia" (in critical language). And the

reader is forced, even on the thematic level, to witness the other pro-
cesses going on at the same time in the language. At this point in a reading, irony can refer to the simultaneous or allegorical readings of a text
that can never be reconciled. Subversion and collapse express themati-
cally the textual breakdown of opposition. Although these moments
rarely make up a narrative whole (unless it is the Revolution itself), they
give the impression of linking together some other history within the
same history.

All during my work on Romantic history a passage from Paul de
Man's *Allegories of Reading* sounded as both a talisman and a warning:
"It could be that the so-called Romantics came closer than we do to undermining the absolute authority of this [genetic] system. If this were the
case, one may well wonder what kind of historiography could do justice
to the phenomenon of Romanticism, since Romanticism (itself a period
concept) would then be the movement that challenges the genetic principle which necessarily underlies all historical narrative."[12] The undoing
that de Man implies is heady. How can you write a history of a period
that challenges the basic premises of history, notions of both natural and
logical development, and ultimately any arbitrary divisions of knowledge, like periods, that stand in the place of explanation? Not only can
you not write about Romanticism, but you cannot write history at all,
for history is dependent on certain narrative presuppositions of explanation and sense. (What is left to write but a critique of that history, and
is that not a history as well?) De Man himself would come upon history
sideways or as a last resort after all the traditional supports had been
knocked out from underneath. But he would never go beyond a suggestive aphorism. Here is the last sentence of that cleverly titled chapter
"Promises (*Social Contract*)": "This is also why textual allegories on
this level of rhetorical complexity generate history."[13]

History was always reemerging in de Man (literally, as we now know,

12. Paul de Man, *Allegories of Reading: Figural Language in Rousseau, Nietzsche,
Rilke, and Proust* (New Haven: Yale UP, 1979), 82.

13. Ibid., 277. Multiple meanings have to be sifted out. In order to understand them,
we make a time sequence, a narrative, a history out of them, "first this, then that." The
inconsistencies of figurative language, of which we are hardly aware, produce, when magnified, an effect we translate as time and organize as history. History is a fiction that we
set up but that retrospectively takes on the authority of reality. Paul de Man's sentence
could also include this joke: a text as complicated as Rousseau's could not help but cause
trouble. We generate history, historical action or revolutions, to decide which meaning
wins the contest of intepretation transferred to another field.

World War II), a history that might look like the old one but would have been radically different. Still, he gave no easy hints. "It would be preposterous to try to state succinctly, in paraphrase, how this re-emergence of history at the far side of rhetoric can be said to take place."[14] Perhaps the only way is to show and not state this other history, which as we write, we necessarily come upon, over and over again. De Man's work as a whole might be read as the refusal to commit the preposterous while doing it all the same. He pointed the way to rethinking history while giving the impression that a book so directed could not or should not be written.

Studies of historiography, nineteenth-century in particular, have nonetheless continued. Hayden White and Lionel Gossman have pointed out specific directions for my own work. White's *Metahistory: The Historical Imagination in Nineteenth-Century Europe* (1973) demonstrated that not only the chronological developments of a writer's work turned early books against later ones, but the same text had within it conflicting formal properties. Lionel Gossman has recently described the way in which the nineteenth-century history of "identity or legitimacy" strains to take in the Other, the alien and unique, the discontinuous, the untranslatable.[15] In his earlier essay "History and Literature: Reproduction or Signification," Gossman does not disassociate his readings from their historical context (in this case imperialism), but allows them to trouble historical knowledge. He recognizes that distinctions like those of past and present, event and writing, are blurred in the work of someone like Michelet: "It is this disturbing feature—disturbing even today—of Michelet's writing that historians neither comment upon nor, apparently, wish to emulate."[16]

Nineteenth-century history holds up to us an uncanny mirror of our

14. Paul de Man, introduction, *Studies in Romanticism* 18 (Winter 1979): 499.

15. Lionel Gossman, "History as Decipherment: Romantic Historiography and the Discovery of the Other," *New Literary History* 18 (Autumn 1986): 23–57.

16. Lionel Gossman, "History and Literature: Reproduction or Signification," *The Writing of History: Literary Form and Historical Understanding*, ed. Robert H. Canary and Henry Kozicki (Madison: Wisconsin UP, 1978), 37. For that link of anxieties in nineteenth-century history, Michelet in particular, with twentieth-century practice, see Hans Kellner, *Language and Historical Representation: Getting the Story Crooked* (Madison: U of Wisconsin P, 1989), "Narrating the 'Tableau': Questions of Narrativity in Michelet" and "Triangular Anxieties: The Present State of European Intellectual History." The latter is also in *Modern European Intellectual History: Reappraisals and New Perspectives*, ed. Dominick LaCapra and Steven L. Kaplan (Ithaca: Cornell UP, 1982).

own internal difference. It provides a critique of our present thought and
social, historical practices—maybe not so much a traditional critique as
a haunting, a reminder of what we may want to hide and forget.

THE DEMOCRATIC REFERENT AND THE FRENCH
REVOLUTION

Certain characteristics of the Revolution occupied nineteenth-century history so intensely that these obsessions came to hold the status
and importance of concepts. The Revolution threw open fundamental
problems (enigmas) of social organization with barely suggested solutions.

A new (dare I use the word?) form of social legitimacy grew up
around the French Revolution. Maybe it was only the subtle displacement of old forms of legitimacy, but it produced new and astounding effects we are still dealing with today. This legitimacy depends upon a new
social referent that emerged to regulate decisions of justice and evil, normal and abnormal, down to the principles underlying the assumptions
of everyday reality. The paradoxical definition of this referent would give
it enormous power: the sociopolitical reference resides both inside and
outside the body of that society itself. It is a head—dispersed among
members. It enables society to see itself, find its identity, even a sense of
wholeness—and yet it cannot stand outside that fragile totality. Such a
notion implies yet another paradox that cannot be ignored or disobeyed
without undermining, if not destroying, the society it sets up: that referent of judgment is unrepresentable and yet must always be represented in a concrete, material form.

I have my own way of telling the story of how the new legitimacy
could have come about, using political philosophy (Rousseau), images
of the body, and linguistic theory. In *On the Social Contract* Rousseau
describes the process by which a society constitutes itself (Althusser's
Montesquieu, le politique et l'histoire has another version of a similar
process). Such a society brings about its own identity and legitimacy by
positing, after the fact or simultaneously, that which is supposed to be
its ground and foundation. Rousseau associated that indivisible, in-
alienable sovereignty with the general will. Chicken or egg: which
comes first, Rousseau's concept of the general will or popular movements (already called under the Old Regime *esprit populaire* or *opinion*

publique, in French sometimes simply called *le populaire*)?[17] Confused, groping, trustworthy and untrustworthy, this pre-formation was neither the Old Regime "nation" nor the residue of timeless folk knowledge or prejudice. It already achieved an awe-inspiring, ambiguous identity as *le peuple* (Robespierre's favorite word)[18] in the Revolution and went on to dominate the history and thought of the nineteenth century. *Le peuple* still echoes in twentieth-century power-to-the-people and popular-opinion polls.

Had the monarchy and its complex system of Old Regime "estates" and "corps" already disintegrated, emptying out to leave a power vacuum gaping for any new agency? It is easy to say (as I do for the sense of argument in chapter 3) that at least in the Old Regime there was a fixed image of society's legitimacy — even if that image did not always correspond with the fact of power. The king was at the imaginary head, and like the body of Christ, all society participated in him.[19] When the king's head fell, that society was literally left headless. Power that stood at the top, clear and identifiable, dissolved in a shape with neither center nor official hierarchy. Of course, centers and official hierarchies resurrect overnight, but they can no longer have the luxury of their own legitimacy. Even if they forget, their power is only on loan from the people.

I have stated almost as a fairy tale this extremely complicated moment of transition which historians continue to fill with their explanations. Just finding a description of the revolutionary class has led to a proliferation that makes both more and less sense of the long- and short-term events.[20] Who are the *peuple*? Peasants spreading rumors, urban artisans, the wives of these artisans, wacky aristocrats, bitter hackwriters,

17. See Mona Ozouf, "L'opinion publique," *The Political Culture of the Old Regime*, ed. Keith Michael Baker, vol. 1 of *The French Revolution and the Creation of Modern Political Culture* (Oxford: Pergamon, 1987), 419–40.

18. See the statistical analysis of a group of Robespierre's speeches in Annie Geffroy, Jacques Guilhaumou, André Salem, "L'histoire sur mesures ou pour une statistique du discours," *Bulletin du centre d'analyse du discours de l'Université de Lille III (Sur la Révolution française)*, 2 (1975): esp. 25–41.

19. Ernst Hartwig Kantorowicz, *The King's Two Bodies: A Study in Medieval Political Theology* (Princeton: Princeton UP, 1957), has influenced broader reflections on the representation of monarchy and its social consequences in the Old Regime. See Ralph E. Giesey, "The King Imagined," *The Political Culture of the Old Regime*, ed. Baker, 41–59.

20. See William M. Reddy's critique of historians' efforts to "attribute the Revolution to the intentional and purposive action of a specific group" (6). *Money and Liberty in Modern Europe: A Critique of Historical Understanding* (Cambridge: Cambridge UP, 1987).

young, self-important lawyers, salon ladies? The people implied everyone and no one particular group. Michelet was right: no one (*personne*)
made the Revolution.

So *le peuple* is a metaphor, a metaphor for reference, for the social
referent itself.[21] Though a metaphor, it still exists. It circulates in and out
of social class, professional and political groups, in and out of official or
inofficial power, both the innermost self and the common whole. It gives
justification and identity to all of the above, itself without shape or
name. But everything in which it circulates, contradictory and warring,
gives it back the effect of a most physical shape, something thick and
consistent, with adamant desires and a will.

HISTORY'S ROLE IN THE NEW SOCIETY

History occupied a privileged position in nineteenth-century French
intellectual life. Louandre's 1847 essay in the *Revue des deux mondes*,
quoted above, was itself an early empirical attempt at measuring the
"intellectual production" of his own recent past through publication
statistics. Louandre wrote that "at no other time were historians truly
worthy of the name ... more numerous or more esteemed." He proposed a list first of *érudits* (e.g., Daunou) and then of "historians" (Guizot, Augustin and Amédée Thierry, Michelet, Barante, Mignet, Gué-
rard, de Sismond). Then he emphasized the popularity of the historical
genre in general: "The books of these masters are found both in the
study of the *érudit* and the library of the *homme du monde*, and, as
proof of the popularity which they enjoy, we recall that almost one
hundred thousand copies of the works of M. Augustin Thierry have entered into circulation."[22] History attained a certain best-seller status, at
least in (male bourgeois) popular culture.

Although it is hard to compare the figures of Louandre's study, history — especially the history of the Revolution — seems to outstrip in
popularity poetry, theater, and the fledgling novel: "This year alone

21. "Where was the new center of society, and how could it be represented? Should
there even be a center, much less a sacred one? Could the new democratic Nation be located in any institution or any means of representation? . . . French revolutionaries did not
just seek another representation of authority, a replacement for the king, but rather came
to question the very act of representation itself." Lynn Hunt, *Politics, Culture, and Class
in the French Revolution* (Berkeley: U of California P, 1984), 88.

22. Louandre, "Statistique littéraire," 432.

[1847], a new historical triumvirate was constituted by MM. Louis Blanc, Michelet and de Lamartine, and the ardor, the emotion that these historians, by placing themselves each one in a different point of view, have brought to their books, the resounding reaction of the public, shows that other sentiments than curiosity, another attraction than literary beauty calls us toward the spectacle of the French Revolution. . . . "[23] Louandre himself shows a certain nervousness in view of the abundant social and political writing.

By taking on the French Revolution, history centered itself in the most controversial and charged place of its time. Oddly enough, in France there was no *Tale of Two Cities, Danton's Death*, or Hegelian philosophy theorizing the Jacobins. Was the experience of the Revolution too close, too volatile for the French to make a fictional masterpiece of it? The Revolution is a "black hole" in French literature. Victor Hugo left it as the one gap in his immense historical fresco, *La légende des siècles*. In their novels, both he and Balzac largely displaced the Revolution out to the provinces, Brittany and the Vendée. Even Hugo's astounding long, hallucinatory poem (written in 1857, published 1881) called "La Révolution" depicts not the Revolution at all but the march of the statues of Old Regime kings to the square where the guillotine has usurped one of their own. They stare at the gaping head-hole as it opens onto the abyss—"a kind of dormer window opening onto darkness."[24]

So nineteenth-century French histories threw themselves where other writers feared to tread directly.[25] They located themselves in the abyss.

23. Ibid., 433. Louandre divides history into many subcategories, each with its own count: chronologies, universal history, ancient history, ecclesiastic history, history of foreign countries, local and provincial histories, and national history. He shows the rise of ecclesiastic history (1833, 34 titles; 1838, 71; 1841, 77; 1845, 121), the fall of Empire history (1833, 47 titles; 1836, 19; 1845, 14), and the rise of local histories (1833, 128; 1836, 191; 1840s, 200 plus). The titles of history books taken all together outnumber the poetry titles (1834, 265; 1840, 444; 1842, 452; 1845, 344) and the novels (1833, 284; 1841, 185). I owe thanks to Debra Perry for the reference to Louandre and for her knowledge of the nineteenth-century book trade. For a general study of popular readership, see James Smith Allen, *Popular French Romanticism: Authors, Readers, and Books in the Nineteenth Century* (Syracuse: Syracuse UP, 1981).

24. Victor Hugo, *Oeuvres complètes*, ed. Jean Massin (Paris: Club français du livre, 1967–71), 10:243.

25. Yet almost every nineteenth-century novel and many poems approach *indirectly* the traumatic space of the French Revolution. *Le rouge et le noir* is the allegorical repetition of revolutionary history in Restoration terms: Julien Sorel plays both Danton and Napoleon. The famous country fair scene in *Madame Bovary* is also the parodic replay

No wonder they created all those images of being lost at sea in the dark.

It fell to them, however, to make sense of it all. Nineteenth-century French history shared the task of making the postrevolutionary society work. It had to write the upheavals as transitions so they looked not only possible, but already well on their way to becoming happy institutions. Nineteenth-century historians, especially Thiers or Lamartine, focused on unity and harmony and, because they had to bring about that unity, highlighted images around which their society could rally. They saw what they had to find. Over their shoulders (we forget this) there stood a living and breathing 1793 that threatened to tear French society apart again — 1832? 1834? 1848? Even if that threat was only imaginary, it seemed far more possible than the shaky, fictive unity that had to be achieved. Alice Gérard captures the intellectual and political problem of Romantic historiography: "For all of them, it is a question of succeeding there where '93 failed."[26]

In a larger sense, history is involved in the act of social bonding and reconstitution as much as it devotes itself to investigating the truth. "The political uses of history," which Stanley Mellon associated with Restoration history,[27] broadened to ideological uses in the widest sense, the formation of the society itself, its ideology and its presuppositions, its beliefs and habits. Romantic historians were open about their social project, and in fact it went along with, instead of contradicting, an emerging professional identity. Although Cabet was the only one to call his history *Histoire populaire de la Révolution française*, that is what the others were also writing all along.

The definition of history as social action may have encouraged the historians to write what appears to us today as a more "participatory" form. Michelet and Cabet explicitly address the reader with their *vous* or even *tu* and talk outright with the eighteenth-century revolutionaries as well, implicitly including the reader. Cabet confronts his rival Thiers in-

---

of a revolutionary crowd. The prefect's representative so fears that this bovine mass will switch at any minute into the Terror relived that his whole speech is devoted to stirring them up into a fear, a terror of the Terror they otherwise would have forgotten. In George Sand's *Le meunier d'Angibault*, the Revolution lurks beneath the mystery of every character's madness and ends up working itself out again, metaphorical Bastille and all.

26. Gérard, *La Révolution française*, 40.

27. Stanley Mellon, *The Political Uses of History: A Study of Historians in the French Restoration* (Stanford: Stanford UP, 1958).

side his text—Michelet and Blanc usually keep that indiscretion to notes
or prefaces. At this formative moment of historiography, the looser Cabet takes on Thiers in one breath and Tallien in the other, and us all the
while, as if they and we were all in the same room — which we are, a
paper room. Thiers does become the origin of the serious "monumental" history of the French Revolution (not de Staël or even Mignet, who
wrote too few volumes). Cabet, in his own candid style, accuses Thiers
of vituperating Robespierre while in actual practice Thiers portrays a
conflicted hero with difficult reponsibilities, much like Cabet's own
more forthright portrayal. By "deconstructing" Thiers, Cabet already
touches upon the basic schizophrenia of nineteenth-century (bourgeois
or liberal) history. If you could neither condemn nor condone completely
the Revolution, you had to appear to do both at the same time, often over
the same issues.

Historical truth in Romantic history is inseparable from professional
debates about what this truth should look and sound like; it is also inseparable from the present society and politics, where historical meanings are confirmed, changed, or dismissed as irrelevant. Michelet supports that catchall nineteenth-century concept "education" to provide
the consensus he and the other historians were engaged (*engagés*) in
making. "So the Revolution was not able to organize the great revolutionary machine: namely that one, better than law, which founds fraternity: *education*" (1:5, note). Michelet resorts to that old tactic of calling
the eighteenth-century revolutionaries "mechanistic" so he and his contemporaries can be credited with finding the real organic means of "organizing" a society. He uses *organize* not in the sense of Blanc's *Organisation du travail* but like organs of a body. Michelet does not want to
reveal that he perfected what he learned from the revolutionaries: the
strange intimacy of democratic discourse.

The competition for political and social power took place not only in
the public arena, but more crucially in the confines of each individual
heart. Madame de Staël came the closest to saying it outright: popular
consensus was a form of social (self-)seduction. Democratic society
manages its own legitimacy without arbitrary force by means of a kind
of *faire désirer*: "It is necessary to elicit desire [give it birth, *le faire
naître*] instead of commanding obedience, and even if, with reason, the
government wants certain institutions to be established, it must manage
[*ménager*] enough public opinion to give the impression of according

what it [*opinion publique*] desires."[28] Madame de Staël uses psychological, even maternal imagery in the context of writing (fiction), instead of
fighting Napoleonic wars or building certain bourgeois institutions (she
could not be a professor, professional historian, or statesman). She hints
of the necessary duplicity in a democracy where no leader must ever
openly anticipate or calculate the will of the people. If her analysis does
not reveal the hypocrisy of the system (the historian and writer as the
people's pimp), it suggests the hegemony the nineteenth century conceived of in terms of language and the body.

The historical text, then, is not exempt from those duplicities and
paradoxes that define postrevolutionary society. It must operate in the
same kind of form, both highly stable and unstable. Romantic history is
like the double-natured society in which it participates. Big, weighty
tomes, which look so sure of themselves, they narrate the fragility of
their own legitimacy.

THE THEORETICAL STATUS OF NINETEENTH-
CENTURY HISTORY

What genre should we call these nineteenth-century histories? Maybe
"theoretical fictions." I make no case for their having anything like the
self-consciousness of modernism. But they are not unselfconscious, despite the deep Romantic wish for such a state. (Or the wish of their critics to believe in such a state.) Romantic histories are too uncannily smart
to stay back in the category of the curious archive. The element of self-
reflection, even irony dissolved in the texts, does not take the same form
as in the prose of Baudelaire or Mallarmé, who seem to stand as the opposites of the French Romantics (but slip back into their own Romantic
confusions all the time). Part of the problem is, as we have long observed,
that these French historians, unlike even Macauley, did not write separate "critical essays." They did not write philosophy of history on the
side. And there was no Vico, Herder, Hegel, or Croce to do it for them.
Theory is dissolved into the narrative itself. Maybe that is where it
should be. Sometimes I wonder if the nineteenth-century historians
might not only be smart, but know something we do not know.

Who or what is smart? The author-subject, the text, the textual un-

28. Madame de Staël, *De la littérature considérée dans ses rapports avec les institutions sociales*, ed. Paul Van Tieghem (Geneva: Droz, 1959), 1:31.

conscious, the historical or political unconscious, the "something in the air"? Language? If we accused Michelet of studying the contradictions and obstacles integral to democracy, could he shrug and say, "Language made me do it; I could not shake allegory and irony from my text"? It is therefore impossible to be dumb; at least the writer transports the conflicts of the time. On the other hand, it is also impossible to be smart, because no one can reflect a total self-consciousness about the situation in which he or she is immersed, from which concepts and preconceptions come. Was Lamartine just a loose wire in the social noise, or a wise man? And what is the status of the critic who tries to add to that wisdom or noise?

The minimal sign of critique is a difference in discourse from the object of study. And that is perhaps all we can ask. As I try to explain a Lamartine sentence, I only get in deeper. I am not sure I ever get out of the danger of miming the discourse I am trying to read — just as nineteenth-century historical texts mime revolutionary or Jacobin discourse. My book, then, is also both Jacobin and Romantic.

Repulsive Recollections: Postrevolutionary Writers and Their Misreaders (Marx, Baudelaire, Flaubert)

Historical writing of the nineteenth century either had to swallow the distasteful, the disgusting parts of the Revolution or cough them up. It had to excise or assimilate into the logic of history the cup of blood, heads bobbing on pikes, and the slash of the guillotine that leveled everyone and everything including thought itself. But the repulsion of nineteenth-century historians looking at the French Revolution is not that convincing. That they are attracted — flip side of repulsion — to what repels them shows in the energy of the writing. Michelet enhances Marat when he casts him as a slimy toad. Lamartine's style is at its trembling best when he describes Mademoiselle de Sombreuil saving her father: "She dips her lips into a glass filled with aristocratic blood" (3:354).

It is more likely that the nineteenth-century historians are less repulsed by the Revolution than we are by them. These historians appear to us as sappy, verbose, preachy, silly, dull, and windy. As I was trying to read these works, I realized that I couldn't escape facing this strong re-action coming from both their contemporaries, on up through the canon, to mine and to me. So I will use it. Repulsion serves, then, as a minimal, if not negative, handle on this body of literature that incarnates the social body in which it also sinks and disappears. Repulsion makes what I'd call the nineteenth-century discursive nebula emerge. Repulsion also represents for me the core of a theory of history in which a violent turning away makes the first distinction between past and present.

I need to evoke the three histories of the Revolution published around 1848—Lamartine's, Michelet's, and Louis Blanc's[29]—and to link them to their historiographical tradition, including Madame de Staël, Thiers, Mignet, Cabet, Quinet, Tocqueville, and Taine. They are only the tip of the history-iceberg. And they also represent a conglomerate socioliterary discourse that has sunk into oblivion. I'll give an incantation of names to erect that space: historians Barante, Thierry, Guizot; social thinkers Proudhon, Enfantin, Leroux, Considérant, Abbé Constant, Flora Tristan, Lamennais; epic writer Ballanche; eclectic philosopher Cousin. The literary historian can keep them in separate categories, but they overlap, many not definable by any categories at all. Whereas Rousseau published separately a social contract, novel, and autobiographical meditations, Michelet's *Sorcière*, Hugo's *William Shakespeare*, Chateaubriand's *Mémoires d'outre-tombe* are all of these and more: what I've called the omnigenre.[30]

I would not have seen the coherence of this massive discourse without the repulsion that may finally provide its only clarity. Marx, Baudelaire, and Flaubert emerge paradoxically as masters of nineteenth-century literature and thought. It is no accident that they are repulsed by a multitude of writers, and they lump these writers together and dismiss them at the same time that they establish their own authority—as they convince themselves of their superiority over the others. For their work is successful only insofar as it distinguishes itself from the discursive nebula that threatens at any moment to subsume it again.

29. See Leo Gershoy, "Three French Historians and the Revolution of 1848," *Journal of the History of Ideas* 12 (1951): 131–45.

30. Linda Orr, "The Romantic Historiography of the Revolution and French Society," *The Consortium on Revolutionary Europe, 1750–1850: Proceedings, 1984* (Athens, Ga.: The Consortium on Revolutionary Europe, 1986), 242–47.

I am analyzing here passages from Marx, Baudelaire, and Flaubert. But the chapter is meant as well to be about historians like Michelet, Blanc, Lamartine, about why we are repulsed by them, why we cannot read them. I am, as we say, constituting my corpus — but by dissolving it first and focusing on the smoke screen in front of it. I have chosen to do history in this way. (Do other ways end up here as well?) But it leads into that labyrinth of layered interpretations that delay and obstruct any direct relationship with the historical object. To say that Baudelaire and Flaubert are the Jacobins of modern literary history is too strong. Suffice it to say that I am concentrating on one instance where the repressed violence of interpretation, only visible in a telltale repulsion, makes it impossible for anyone coming after to read a whole mass of nineteenth-century writers except through writers like Baudelaire and Flaubert. The practice of history for me means the study of one specific instance of historical misreading. Instead of depending only upon an illusory direct relationship between present-day historians and primary sources, this practice seeks to restructure the invisible, unrecognized or repressed labyrinth of many traditions and social formations of knowledge.

Out of Marx's, Baudelaire's, and Flaubert's repulsion and anger I have constructed a loose formula for the nineteenth-century discursive nebula. First, a distorted French Revolution is absent/present throughout the entire century. Second, genres are mixed indiscriminately; history and literature especially become indistinguishable, and that collapse further breaks down the difference between reality and language or illusion. And third, the mobile monster of a discourse will admit of no outside, no rising above it, no crawling beneath it. A strange kind of historical object, it is one of the most important discoveries or creations of nineteenth-century France. Metaphors churn from it and help construct it — mostly the physiology of digestion seen from both ends of the body. It was given names, identities, concepts. The names can be literal, such as socialism, democracy, communism, to describe the postrevolutionary phenomenon of communality. The nineteenth-century term *le peuple* sometimes seems close to seizing it, or the term *public opinion*. *Bourgeois* has also been used to capture that effect of homogenizing society. The French might call it by that catchall *la chose sociale*, the socioliterary thing. And at this point you rightly conjure up the grade B horror film the nineteenth century falls into. The blob and the zombies.

The forms evolve from the familiar to the horrible, or, in reverse, the horrible becomes absorbed more and more into everyday life. Flaubert called it *la bêtise moderne*; it gave Gramsci his theory of hegemony.[31]

As the reader moves from Marx through Baudelaire to Flaubert, the elements of the nineteenth-century discourse spread out and jumble more and more, while becoming both more autonomous and real.

Marx's *Eighteenth Brumaire of Louis Bonaparte* repeated the image the nineteenth century held of itself: ghosts wandering in a fog fated to repeat the order of the Revolution. Caussidière reincarnated Danton, Louis Blanc was Robespierre, the Mountain was the Mountain, and Napoleon came back as the sleazy nephew. And we remember Marx's famous opening sentence in which he comments on Hegel's remark about how all history occurs twice. "He forgot to add," writes Marx, "the first time as tragedy, the second as farce."[32] A sequence of disguises and ghostly figures culminates and, in fact, prepares the devious return of

31. I have made this leap in logic, using Jacques Guilhaumou's essay "Première partie: Le rapport des forces (1792–1794), Sur le jacobinisme à la lumière de quelques remarques de Gramsci," *Dialectiques* 10–11 (1975):34–44.

In various passages from *Prison Notebooks*, Gramsci constructs a complex genealogy leading from the eighteenth-century Jacobins through their contradictory nineteenth-century offspring down to the Second Empire, World War I, and modern France. Gramsci follows the history of the word *Jacobin*: "The term 'Jacobin' has ended up by taking on two meanings: there is the literal meaning, characterized historically, of a particular party in the French Revolution . . . and there are also the particular methods of party and government activity which they displayed, characterized by extreme energy, decisiveness and resolution, dependent on a fanatical belief in the virtue of that programme and those methods" (*Selections from the Prison Notebooks of Antonio Gramsci*, ed. and trans. Quintin Hoare and Geoffrey Nowell Smith [New York: International Publishers, 1971], 65–66). One might say that the linguistic sign "Jacobin" split, and signifier and signified migrated all over nineteenth-century politics and historiography, both of which share the same discursive milieu—which is why Gramsci likes *porte-manteau* words like *politico-historiographic* or *juridico-political*.

The fanatic belief in program and methods (signifier) had two different offspring: the juristic obsession of the nineteenth century and the infantile proletarian philosophies (Cabet, Proudhon). The "literal," realist meaning (signified) continued the tradition of a national populism and the project of a permanent revolution in the form of working-class praxis. But there is a broad ground where Gramsci allows ambiguity. Restoration historicism and "byzantine" constitutional law tradition combine both realistic and illusionary elements of Jacobinism and create a very clever mechanism of control and consent which Gramsci calls hegemony. Not only does Gramsci's analysis not bypass nineteenth-century French thought and history, but it makes nineteenth-century France the crux of his important theoretical insights.

32. Karl Marx, *The Eighteenth Brumaire of Louis Bonaparte* (New York: International Publishers, 1963), 15. Subsequent references to this work will be in the text.

Louis Bonaparte as his uncle: "From 1848 to 1851 only the ghost of the old Revolution walked about, from Marrast, the *républicain en gants jaunes*, who disguised himself as the old Bailly, down to the adventurer, who hides his commonplace repulsive features under the iron death mask of Napoleon" (17).[33] The false elation of 1848 and the literal inebriation of 1851 are followed by Bonaparte's rule, which turned into "a long crapulent depression" (*ein langer Katzenjammer*, Eng. 19, Ger. 101). The German *Katzenjammer* characterizes the period as a prolonged hangover; the English and French (Latin *crapula*) include the cause, drunkenness, along with the effect, so that the cycle keeps recurring.

In Marx's *Eighteenth Brumaire*, both the eighteenth-century Jacobins in their Roman disguise and their nineteenth-century clones were living out history's unavoidable double time. But the Jacobin double corresponds with history and the new, whereas the nineteenth-century neo-Jacobins miss history because they are stuck in the old. "Thus the awakening of the dead in those [18th-C.] revolutions served the purpose of glorifying the new struggles, not of parodying the old; of magnifying the given task in imagination, not of fleeing from its solution in reality; of finding once more the spirit of revolution, not of making its ghost walk about again" (Eng. 17, Ger. 98). Both revolutions, then, have in common their basis in imagination and spirit, but one is a proper double and the other an improper one. The Micheletist phrase "spirit of the Revolution" is reframed in Marx but comes out of French discourse of the 1840s.

In the *Manifesto of the Communist Party*, also published in 1852, Marx and Engels separate out the categories of French political and socialist writers as reactionary, bourgeois, and utopian. Literature progressively contaminates each category: the reactionaries fight "a literary battle alone" and the bourgeois led by Proudhon become "a mere figure of speech."[34] Marx implies that they try to impose artificial "literary" plans onto history instead of working within its deeply determined structure. Finally the utopians, unnamed except as disciples of Saint-

33. "Commonplace repulsive features" translates "der seine trivial-widrigen Züge." *Der 18. Brumaire des Louis Bonaparte, Gesamtausgabe (MEGA)* (Berlin: Dietz, 1985), 11:98.

34. Karl Marx, *Manifesto of the Communist Party* (New York: International Publishers, 1948), 32, 39. *Manifeste der Kommunistischen Partei, Frühe Schriften*, ed. Hans-Joachim Leiber and Peter Furth (Darmstadt: Wissenschaftliche Buchgesellschaft, 1975), 2:844, 853.

Simon, Fourier, and Owen, operate in pure fantasy. "In proportion as the modern class struggle develops and takes definite shape, this fantastic standing apart from the contest, these fantastic attacks on it, lose all practical value and all theoretical justification" (Eng. 41, Ger. 2:855). The repetition of the word *fantastic* confirms again the climate of ghosts. The utopians and communists loop back, then, and link up with the reactionaries, handmaidens all of the emerging bourgeoisie, captives all of illusion.

A particularly brilliant phrase from *The Eighteenth Brumaire* encompasses a broader range of social elements that will be ripe for collapse as exercised in the *Manifesto*. Notice the word *it*, which refers to "Socialism" but engulfs, in order to wipe out, a half-century of French thought: "It sentimentally bewails the sufferings of mankind, or in Christian spirit prophesies the millennium and universal brotherly love, or in humanistic style twaddles about mind, education, and freedom, or in doctrinaire fashion excogitates a system for the conciliation and welfare of all classes" (Eng. 66, Ger. 135). Blanc and Proudhon are perhaps the sentimental writers Marx has in mind, then come all the thinkers mixing Catholicism and socialism from Buchez and Roux to Lamennais, and then the anti-Jesuit humanists like Michelet and Quinet; finally the pun on the word *doctrinaire* includes Guizot and his school, so they go under. No one is left but Marx.

The last section of the *Manifesto*, on the unnamed utopians and communists, mentions Cabet through the metonymy of his "Little Icarias." Marx and Engels had chosen the word *communist* for their pamphlet instead of socialist because the term *socialist* was already too contaminated and they could more easily create a difference between themselves and French communists. When Marx like Heine came to Paris as a young man, he lived in the city of the Revolution. Those past events were always present to him, making him like "that mad Englishman in Bedlam who fancies that he lives in the times of the ancient Pharaohs" (Eng. 17, Ger. 98). Like Baudelaire and Flaubert, Marx wanted to hide the traces of this past enthusiasm. His writing was constantly haunted by the paradox of translating the old language (of French political philosophy and history) into the new (of the workers). For all were contemporaries competing for the future of history, which is never decided once and for all.

Through their willingness to conform, Baudelaire and Flaubert sense the doubling on both the vertical plane of history (eighteenth for nineteenth century) and the horizontal plane of society (literature and history), all of which combine to form the social *sottise, la bêtise moderne*, that soup of stupidity. They are bothered not so much by the return of the Revolution in stages as by the perversion of equality and fraternity, the slippery legacy of the Jacobins, murky Robespierre and his shadow, Rousseau. In his diary Baudelaire has Saint-Marc Girardin, his most despicable bourgeois — scribbler, politician, and history professor — mouth an adage of Robespierre in its twisted nineteenth-century form: "Saint-Marc Girardin made a statement that will last: *Let's be mediocre*. Put this next to Robespierre's: *Those who don't believe in the immortality of their being do justice to themselves*."[35] Not only the left, like Blanqui, but, more surprisingly, a bourgeois majority also descends from Robespierre. The Jacobins' ideology of equality, their use of rhetoric, and their strategies of public opinion were adopted, whether they liked it or not, by almost everyone in postrevolutionary public life and political writing — Michelet, Hugo, all of them included. The Jacobin legacy is diffused like a guilty secret throughout nineteenth-century French society — if not twentieth as well.

In a passionate open letter to the *Figaro* in 1864 Baudelaire analyzes nineteenth-century discourse unsystematically, through his rage. He is furious that what he calls "messieurs the factotums of democratic literature" organized a motley but symbolic gathering of the most petty elements of France in order to celebrate Shakespeare. This gathering included unknown *petits humanitaires* and Villemain, Guizot, even Victor Hugo selling his new book. Baudelaire is also upset that he is not invited. The poet blames a specific historical conjuncture where literature fused with politics: "You know, sir, that in 1848 an adulterous alliance was made between the literary school of 1830 and democracy, a monstrous and bizarre alliance" (797). This cultural intersection of Romanticism and democracy or this adulterous crime created a minotaur, a social monster: nineteenth-century society. The letter culminates in a fictive toast. In this tragicomic primal gesture, a society makes and cele-

35. Charles Baudelaire, *Oeuvres complètes*, ed. Y.-G. Le Dantec and Claude Pichois (Paris: Gallimard, 1961), 1290. Subsequent references to this work will be in the text. I have translated all the quotations from Baudelaire and Flaubert.

brates its unity through common speech. The archetypal moment refers back to the republican banquets of 1847, if not the grandiose but empty oaths of the eighteenth-century Revolution. (Can it contaminate forward to Mallarmé's use of the "toast"?)

Baudelaire works himself up to performing the toast he imagines will take place; he in fact gives the toast in a kind of free indirect discourse: "Then, according to the circumstances and the particular *crescendo* of idiocy in the crowds assembled in one place alone, you give toasts to Jean Valjean, to abolishing the death sentence, to abolishing poverty, to *universal Fraternity*, to the spread of enlightenment, to the *true* Jesus-Christ, *legislator of Christians*, as one used to say, to Mr. Renan, to Mr. Havin, etc., finally to all the stupidities that belong in this nineteenth century, where we have the tiresome good fortune to live, and where each is, as it seems, deprived of the natural right to *choose his brothers*" (798). This one sentence dissolves history, socialism, religion, the hero of Hugo's novel, two writers of the day, all in the same steamy brew, and holds it up in a glass to drink, or rather to spit out. While we could trace each phrase to a specific literary or political movement, Baudelaire's point is that it's one mishmash.

What Baudelaire wants to forget, wants us to forget, is that he had drunk deeply of this discourse himself. In the part of his diary where Robespierre comes up, Baudelaire also speaks of "my drunkenness in 1848 ... a literary drunkenness; the memory of reading" (1274). It would not be so bad if this reading had only consisted of Robespierre, but it was made up as well of Robespierre's shameful legacy: the Proudhons, the Michelets. The terror was wandering or erring in the nineteenth century in the form of these misreadings, as errors that produced this gooey mess, worse than the Terror itself as far as Baudelaire was concerned. In fact, he fantasized resorting to his own terror as the only way of getting out of the twisted legacy of the Terror. In the prose poem "Assommons les pauvres!" the narrator says that sixteen or seventeen years ago (1848) he read "books treating the art of making the people happy, wise and rich in 24 hours." He writes: "I had then digested — swallowed whole, I mean — all the *elucubrations* of all these entrepreneurs of public happiness" (304–305). It leaves him in a state of "dizziness and stupidity" (305). The narrator-poet then rushes out (in 1848) and pummels a decrepit old man in order to give this pauper a sense of true equality. He hits his victim until the poor man finally gets angry enough to fight back.[36] Dumb or old men, like the seedy clown or the figures in "Seven Old Men," ghosts and specters fill Baudelaire's work with repulsive recollections. Sometimes they represent the crowd or just stupidity itself, and the poet appears to turn on them arbitrarily. Here is another typical encounter: "For me, I was suddenly caught up in an unmeasurable rage against this magnificent imbecile, who appeared to concentrate in himself all the spirit of France" ("Un plaisant," 233).

Michelet, author of the *History of the French Revolution*, shows himself to be one of these disgusting old men when he publishes *L'amour* (1858). Baudelaire goes out of his way in his 1859 essay on Gautier to attack the dirty lecher and nursemaid. Baudelaire's poetic stomach is turned when Michelet advises his reader: caress the ugly cancer in your love's breast and give your wife the pleasure of a little whipping if she wants it. Furious, Baudelaire responds: "And what punishment will he let us inflict on an old man without majesty, nervous and feminine [*un vieillard sans majesté, fébrile et féminin*], playing the baby doll, rhyming madrigals in honor of illness and rolling with delight in humanity's dirty linen" (688). Baudelaire of all people, author of "The Metamorphoses of the Vampire," is repulsed by Michelet's rooting in humanity's underwear. And the poet comes up with a suitable chastisement in more light verse: "*Ridicule* is more cutting / Than the blade of the guillotine" (688). It is not an accident that Baudelaire imagines punishment in the image of the Terror, and its nineteenth-century literary version in terms of a farce. But Baudelaire's revenge links him to Robespierre or, worse, to his disgusting nineteenth-century descendants, the very ones the poet rails against.

Still, Baudelaire's image of Michelet is nothing in comparison to his image of George Sand, *grosse bête* (1281) of the century, queen of the democratic quagmire. In his diary, the poet writes: "She has the famous *runny style* [*style coulant*], dear to the bourgeois" (1280). She has, he continues, the moral sophistication of a concierge or a kept woman. "That some men could go gaga over this latrine, it's indeed the proof of

36. See Richard Terdiman, *Discourse/Counter-Discourse: The Theory and Practice of Symbolic Resistance in Nineteenth-Century France* (Ithaca: Cornell UP, 1985) for a political reading of this Baudelaire poem. Terdiman's concept of discourse and counter-discourse highlights conflicts in nineteenth-century society and texts similar to those in my book. I concentrate on how the division between the two oppositional terms switches according to both contemporary and historical perspectives, a phenomenon Terdiman also recognizes, differently.

how low the men of this century have sunk" (1280). What terrifies Baudelaire is that he may be no different from what he despises. His irritable smugness — naïve to think he can pull himself out where others are trapped—may make him the most imbecilic of all. "You forget each second that throwing insults at a crowd drags you into the dregs too [*c'est s'encanailler soi-même*]" (678). The more one scrambles out, the deeper one sinks.

This bit about giving up his old democratic reading binges is a front for his continuing addiction to the *foule* (crowd). "The walker, solitary and pensive [*le promeneur solitaire et pensif*], gets drunk, oddly enough, on this universal communion" ("Les foules," 244). Baudelaire protests that he is an aristocrat of art, but he knows, as Vigny did before him, that the only language possible is the one that is steeped in Rousseau and the Jacobins, twisted by contemporary "democratic literature." He is the ghost of Rousseau's *promeneur solitaire* and his word for that nineteenth-century communality, *communion*, fuses society and religion no less than the Catholic socialists did. Only the finest distinction separates this communion from "a prostitution," which, as Baudelaire writes nervously, "I could call *fraternitary*, if I wanted to speak the lovely language of my century" ("La solitude," 264). Baudelaire succeeds in making us forget the degree to which his words are saturated with the ubiquitous discourse of his century. But maybe the first and last words of the famous opening poem of *Les fleurs du mal* regain some of their thickness when we lower them back into the social context. *La sottise, l'erreur* begin the list of torments. *La sottise, l'erreur, le péché, la lésine / Occupent nos esprits et travaillent nos corps* (Stupidity, error, sin, avarice / Fill our spirits and torment our bodies). And think of the resonance of *mon semblable—mon frère*. These are no longer idealist, religious, or psychological words, but fully politicized and acculturated.

Flaubert, more than anyone, congealed the nineteenth-century socioliterary nebula around his rage and repulsion. He carries the blend of elements to an extreme where they take on a frightening autonomy. Fog and seamy underside, all of it runs together and thickens into a social glue, both imaginary and real, that measures everything according to its own mediocrity, which can itself be neither measured nor encompassed. Flaubert lashes out at the bourgeois, the republicans, the socialists, for desiring this mediocre society, the "fruit of the democratic stupidity" (*fruit de la bêtise démocratique*),[37] and he finds and pours his disgust into those blatant examples of the puddle or pile: Lamartine and Thiers.

As he tries to make sense of his own century, Flaubert thinks back on the Revolution. For him in 1852, the prolific language of the Terror, imitating Roman oratory, was behind present problems: "The rage of the *discourse* of rhetoric and the mania for reproducing ancient types (badly understood) pushed mediocre natures to excesses not really excessive."[38] Flaubert means by this paradox that excess served to rule out all excess, in politics and society as in art. "Robespierre and [the critic] M. de LaHarpe rule us from the depths of their tomb" (2:514, Jan. 23, 1854). Flaubert uses the verb *régenter* for rule, which suggests regency and the Old Regime. It is not just politics, then, that is to blame. It is politics mixed with political writing, literary criticism, and history. Flaubert sounds off to Louise Colet in 1852: "Republic or monarchy, we won't get out of this so soon. It's the result of a long evolution [*travail*] in which everyone took part from de Maistre to old man Enfantin. And the republicans more than the others" (2:91, May 15 – 16). Right and left collaborate with the mass of middle.

Flaubert's references to his own stupefying readings, like the ones in Baudelaire's prose poem, multiply until he regurgitates them all in his unfinished novel *Bouvard et Pécuchet*. He confesses in a letter of 1853 to having loved "the theories, the symbolisms, Micheletteries, Quinetteries (I was there too, I know them), comparative studies of languages, gigantic plans and mostly empty mumbo jumbo [*charabia*]" (2:249 – 50). He complains, as do both Baudelaire and Marx, that the republicans' plans or grand social designs are "factitious." Later, preparing *Bouvard et Pécuchet*, Flaubert, as his two characters do, flees in exasperation from one history of the Revolution to the other. In 1868, Flaubert is reading Buchez and Roux: "I just swallowed the first ten volumes of Buchez and Roux. The clearest thing I got from it was an immense disgust at meeting up with the French" (14:447, Oct. 17). Bouvard and Pécuchet then literally play out Flaubert's disgust. *Dégoût* progresses to nausea: "But the pathos of the prefaces, this amalgam of socialism and

37. Gustave Flaubert, *Correspondance, 1859 – 1871, Oeuvres complètes*, ed. Société des études littéraires françaises (Paris: Club de l'honnête homme, 1975), 14:391, Dec. 15, 1867. Subsequent references will be in the text.

38. Gustave Flaubert, *Correspondance (juillet 1851–décembre 1858)*, ed. Jean Bruneau (Paris: Gallimard, 1980), 2:170, Oct. 7, 1852. Subsequent references will be in the text.

Catholicism turned their stomachs (*les écoeura*); too many details kept
them from seeing the whole. They resorted to Thiers."[39] But they were
only plunging deeper into the abyss of revolutionary history.

I have culled from Flaubert's correspondence an existential thematics
of nineteenth-century discourse that coheres especially around Lamartine and Thiers, both important political figures of the nineteenth century. Who is to decide whether it is worse or better that Thiers has more
consistency than the liquid Lamartine? The Romantic school of the latter wrote sentences with no spine, no breath, no muscle, says Flaubert,
"inane." "They drool their poetry of sugary water. ... I'm frothing
[with rage] [*j'écume*]!" (2:310, Apr. 20, 1853). Then he takes images
from both ends of the body: "[Lamartine] he's a eunuch-head, no balls,
he's only pissed clear water" (2:299, Apr. 6, 1853). Flaubert finds all the
varieties of water imagery to describe the socioliterary dissolution:
"Can't you tell that everything is dissolving now, in *looseness,* in the hu-
mid element, tears, gossip, milk products. Contemporary literature is
drowned in the menstrual periods of women" (2:508 – 509, Jan. 15,
1854). This sentence comes like many others from a letter to a woman,
his mistress, Louise Colet, about whose literary loyalties Flaubert was
always complaining: "I knew you as a pure democrat, admirer of
George Sand and Lamartine" (2:317, Apr. 26, 1853). Before Sand was
Flaubert's friend, she was ridiculed as much as in Baudelaire. Her style
"oozes," Flaubert writes, "and the idea flows between the words, as between flabby thighs" (2:177, Nov. 16, 1852).

Lamartine and Thiers's common penchant for running or lumping
everything together infuriates Flaubert. The poet is Flaubert's target in
the 1850s: "These [writers for the *Revue de Paris*] are indeed men of
Lamartine's poetry in literature and his provisional government in politics. ... Their cerebral activity, with no fixed goal or direction, treats,
with an equal temperament, political economy, belles-lettres, agricul-
ture, alcohol legislation, the linen industry, philosophy, China, Algeria,
etc., and all that at the same level of interest" (2:371, July 2, 1853). By
the 1860s, Thiers is far ahead of all the others in eliciting Flaubert's total
repulsion. In a letter addressed in 1867 to George Sand Flaubert sits
Thiers, the stinking fruit, the bulbous growth, on top of a compost that

39. Gustave Flaubert, *Bouvard et Pécuchet*, ed. Jacques Suffel (Paris: Flammarion,
1966), 142.

has been fertilizing his victorious return: "Can you see a more triumphant imbecile, a more abject old scab [*croûtard*], a more turd-shaped
bourgeois! No, nothing can give the idea of vomiting that this old dip-
lomatic melon inspires in me, rounding his stupidity on the dunghill of
the bourgeoisie. Is it possible to treat with a more naïve and inept nonchalance philosophy, religion, whole populations, liberty, the past and
future, history and natural history, everything, and the rest! He seems to
me eternal like mediocrity! He's crushing me" (14:392, Dec. 18 – 19,
1867). Here is the paradox. Thiers, embodiment of the old *tiers état* now
made one, has managed the democratic miracle. He is a model, even a
mountain, of mediocrity where nothing must stand out. The other
Mountain rose up too high and had its heads cut off. Lamartine's history of the Revolution was a best seller in 1847, but Thiers's had the
longest run with the most reprints. Could the authors and readers have
been that dumb? No. They are involved in a social bonding and political
and historical experiment crucial for the century.

Since Flaubert's figuration of nineteenth-century culture does not
stop here, the two writer-politicians seem only to have represented in
Flaubert's work what also goes beyond them. The historical and historiographical mix will produce a monster that Flaubert's fears material-
ize: "Isn't the ideal of the state, according to the socialists, a kind of vast
monster, absorbing in itself [himself?] all individual action, all person-
ality, all thought, and which will direct everything, do it all?" (2:90,
May 15 – 16, 1852). Another, more obscene version of this figure is in
the feminine: "humanity, monstrous with obesity" is propped up in a
niche, rocking on her sex, drunk, dumbfounded, digesting lunch and re-
lieving herself. Or humanity is a stomach in which history and ideas and
injustice churn: "The adoration of humanity for itself ... (which leads
to the doctrine of the useful in art, to theories of public safety and reason
of the State, to all injustices and all narrowing, to the sacrifice of rights,
the leveling of Beauty) this cult of the stomach [*ventre*] I tell you, engenders wind [*vent*] (my turn for a pun) [*passez-moi le calembour*]" (2:334,
May 26, 1853). The French Revolution circulates as a phrase, "public
safety," but has no more identity than anything else being digested, Hegel or utilitarian art.

These astounding metaphors spring up where postrevolutionary society reaches the limit of its self-representation. Not even the loaded con-

cept of the people works anymore: "Up till now we respected that idea
[of *le peuple*]. Those of royalty, authority, divine right, nobility have
been swept aside. The people alone remained standing. They have to
drag themselves down low in ignominy and brute stupidity so we can
pity them in turn.—And so we can recognize in fact that nothing is sacred" (2:104, June 13, 1852). There is nothing or no leader to give shape
and sense to this amorphous moving substance but passing masters in
mediocrity. "We have no foundation or echo [*ni base, ni écho*]" (2:538,
March 19, 1854). There is no ground, no repetition, nothing but these
sensations—mud, a whitish grease, a cud or paste—that one swallows
but wants to spit out, where the same glutinous element forms and de-
forms external reality.

Flaubert, like Baudelaire, knew that he too was stuck up to his throat.
"Humanity has a passion, a rage for moral abasement. And I'm mad at
her, because I'm part of it" (2:437, Sept. 22, 1853). His rage itself raises
the level of social viscosity: he matches Lamartine's syrup with his own
milk foam (*J'écume* ...). Flaubert asks how difference is possible in
such a mess: "What form must one take in order to express sometimes
one's opinion on matters of this world, without the risk of sounding like
a fool?" (14:393, Dec. 18–19, 1867). What form would not be gobbled
up by the omniform as soon as uttered? No wonder Flaubert refuses to
give a narrative "opinion" in his famous novels of *impassibilité*; no
wonder the narrator is supposed to be like God to keep from being
sucked up by the free indirect discourse of public opinion. But is it,
equality or fraternity, the opposite of freedom? Flaubert feared a Terror
like a fat whore or a cosmic gassy stomach, and he dreamed of writing
tough macho sentences to separate himself from it, but he also had vi-
sions of writing "a formidable humanitarian symphony" (2:151).
"Maybe," he thought as early as 1852, "this great confusion will bring
Liberty" (2:152, Sept. 4, 1852). Out of the great confusion of modern
democracy, always ambiguous, liberty emerges, as well as its multiple
perversions and totalizing opposite.

This reminder, however repulsive, that we do not have it figured out
brings us to the possibility of thinking freedom. Nineteenth-century discourse, especially those histories of the Revolution, very graphically performs life in a society where social legitimacy has to be reinvented at
each instance from inside, from what is often invisible or a guilty secret,

unsayable but the minimal coherence of the sociotext.[40] Nineteenth-century historians and political writers are digesting, often poorly, the Revolution, where a present and future society is working itself out. Sometimes it's revolting.

On the other hand, they never had much of a chance to be read after what contemporaries like Marx, Baudelaire, Flaubert, Vigny, Leconte de Lisle wrote about them. Who would ever work seriously on Big Mama Sand, the prissy and fishy Lamartine (there were always jokes about his name), the old lech Michelet, or the putrid Thiers? It's hard to imagine anyone being afraid that the social designs of these Romantic writers might stick to history. It's hard to imagine Marx or Flaubert defending himself by calling those rivals irrelevant, blind, and delirious. It is frightening how the freest forms totalize so quickly in unpredictable ways and make everything else around them uniform. But it is enlightening how the uni-form tears and starts to diversify freely again. Baudelaire and Flaubert were right to be terrified by the implications of a confused nineteenth-century discourse. It is dangerous to blur distinctions of class, gender, region, race, and unique desiring subjects, but equally dangerous to exaggerate to the point of drowning a projected fear of losing one's own footing.

The nineteenth-century discursive monsters induced in me a state of discomfort that proved useful for thinking about social, historical, and literary practices and theory. They made me suspect our notions of social constitution, our reliance on the word *constitution*, its root for stability, through laws, practices, contracts, traditions. At most, society forms itself in a kind of consistency. Hegemony is perhaps already too orderly a notion. A sticky mass without a name, it is destroyed when named and no longer works. That collective metaphorical space attracts all manner of specific desires and shames (in Lamartine revolutionary tradesmen are already contaminated by a fear of the modern worker). Blanchot might call that furtive social coherence the inadmissible community, *la communauté inavouable*.[41] A history that responds to this

40. My common use of this word comes from French *sociocriticism*. See Claude Duchet and Françoise Gaillard, introduction, *Sub-Stance* (special issue on sociocriticism) 15 (1971): 2−5. Instead of paralleling, reflecting or opposing society, the text, as it works out complex social hierarchies and manipulates ideologies, is producing or performing the society that will in turn appear to explain the text.

41. Maurice Blanchot, *La communauté inavouable* (Paris: Minuit, 1983).

kind of social constituting works as much on principles of repulsion as
of sympathy, difference as of identity. That violent turning away, often
not even acknowledged, as illusive as the shift of a sign, the turn of a figure (a "prefigure," to use Hayden White's word), is an insignificant gesture that can have lasting repercussions. Call those repercussions the
differential mark of sense, the minimal beginnings of a story, the point
that divides past and present or future and so demands the order of history.

Or the gesture of turning away is no more than that, an instinct about
repression, a funny feeling to follow because something does not fit. For
me, an overreaction to my work made me suspicious that there was more
to it. The predictable grimace whenever I mentioned my authors and
texts. They were telling us something about our Western representative
societies we did not want to hear, giving us back a shameful part of ourselves. Then too I was drawn by my own Romanticism to the underdogs
of present literary history (had they ever really dominated in the past?),
the *canaille* of history, the *femmelins*, the little women — Prudhon's
category, himself castrated by Marx. And sometimes I admit in quiet
moments that their dismay, their struggle with illusion and ungrounded
suffering moves me until their exaggeration disgusts me again.

It would be dazzling to turn the masters under and raise this dark
continent up, letting it laugh and carouse in its articulate, inarticulate
way. As Michelet wrote about the first Bastille Day, "the people's rage
was inexpressible." But I am not sure whether I have gotten more energy
from the repulsion I feel lifting the allergenic, moldy tomes of Cabet or
the disintegrating ten-pound brick of Louis Blanc — or from my anger
at Baudelaire and Flaubert. Or maybe what irritates me the most is the
support system that maintains the latters' mastery — including this
chapter. At most I would like to pull the ones up down and the crowd a
little higher.[42]

42. See also Claude Mouchard and Jacques Neefs, *Flaubert* (Paris: Balland, 1986),
and Mouchard, "Déchirer l'opinion," *L'arc* 79 (1980): 69–76. See also Pierre Pachet,
Le premier venu: Essai sur la politique baudelairienne (Paris: Denoël, 1976), and Sima
Godfrey's forthcoming book on Baudelaire.

II The Laws of Reading: Narrative Teleology and Romantic Historiography

Cette idole ... sans parents ni cour, plus noble que la fable
— Rimbaud, "Enfance"

In nineteenth-century historiography, narrative appears to correspond to a teleological view of time. History lines up from a beginning through the present to an ultimate end. We have come to associate this history in particular with the political event, with *histoire événementielle* in which the dates are points that organize the whole. If the eighteenth century set history on its course of progress, Romantic historiography laid down not just any beginnings and ends but the origin and culmination of modern history, if not human time. The French Revolution was often the crux of this historical system. Christian metaphors, words like *messianic* and *evangelical,* described the Revolution, reinforcing even more the teleological apparatus of Romantic history.[1]

The Romantic period marked the height of narrative development in the historical form. The Romantic historians had their own ways of solving the age-old challenges of history. The historical enterprise grows out of a basic moment when nothing happens until a single element, hovering still between likeness and a new identity, reproduces itself (two points). Two moments, objects, events, they can only become opposites or stand related in time as before and after or in logic as cause and effect. And the historical system keeps building from that initial difference so

1. See Alice Gérard, *La Révolution française,* 42: "The Romantic vision of history was supposed to stop, fascinated, in front of the Revolution: marked as a sign of the absolute, it became the pole of attraction of universal history, and a microcosm that foretells the future. From this comes a finalism (revolution: revelation) which no historian of the time escapes from." See also Jean Guéhenno, *L'évangile éternelle* (Paris: Grasset, 1927).

animilitory the march tend

that all three—opposition, narrative, analysis—have to work together
to come up finally with the desired persuasive overall result.

The latter two, narrative and analysis, must also find a way of inter-
acting. (Have they always existed simultaneously? When and why did
history as pure story feel the need to invent the discourse of analysis?)
Analysis and explanation do not necessarily sustain the teleological impulse of the story (the line drawn between two points) but hinder and
halt it. The trick to writing history is setting up a moment of difference
that then becomes an opposition like cause and effect, analysis and narrative. Difference is not such an easy proposition to bring about. Yet creating difference is crucial if truth, which is an effect of these differences,
is to succeed in the historical text, or at most any social scientific endeavor.

François Furet, while uncovering the rhetorical and ideological bur-
den of Romantic narrative, brings under greater scrutiny the notion of
teleology that functions in these texts. In *Penser la Révolution française*,
Furet considers the special relationship in French Revolution history between narrative and analytic functions. Analysis was associated with the
"origins" or "causes" of the Revolution. Then the narrative per se began
with the "effect" or "events," usually in 1787 or 1789, and finished on
the 9th of Thermidor or the 18th of Brumaire. Analysis and narrative
are superimposed on cause and effect. This device produced the following mechanism: "as if, once the causes are set out, the play went on by
itself, propelled by the initial upheaval."[2] Furet implies that such an internal distinction of "genres" is rhetorical and does not necessarily represent a distinction between explanatory and narrative modes of discourse. But he does not pursue just how significant for history writing
this rhetorical gesture of division is. Nor does he consider the consequences for the status of explanation itself.

The section Louis Blanc literally calls "Origins and Causes" in his
Histoire de la Révolution française does not depend on explanation as
much as it simply prolongs the narrative backward. The farther back in
time, the better. According to this liberal strategy, practiced already in
Restoration history, the Revolution gained a momentum of legitimacy
by assimilating the march of time. Blanc began with the sixteenth-cen-

---

2. François Furet, *Interpreting the French Revolution*, trans. Elborg Forster (Cambridge: Cambridge UP, 1981), 18; *Penser la Révolution française* (Paris: Gallimard,
1978), 34.

tury religious wars; Michelet with the medieval Church; Cabet with the Roman conquest of Gaul. No matter how far back the explanation reaches, it concludes and steps aside, as Furet observes, so the dramatic story can begin. The differentiating, rhetorical gesture — which corresponds as well to periodization — distinguishes narrative from analysis and thus draws the distinction upon which the meaning of that history depends.

When the revolutionaries manage to split history in two — Old Regime and Revolution — they reactivate the mechanisms for remaking national history. All sorts of oppositions and rhetorical sequences reshuffle into place — cause and effect, developments, hierarchies, and various other images found in histories. Their act is a creation, a re-creation at this mythical rebirth of time that pretends to found new origins but is always in midtime and from within a complex social order. The arbitrary but necessary differentiation between cause and effect, analysis and narrative, old and new, completes the installation of a rhetorical system of truth. This small, almost automatic linguistic and politico-historical move constitutes our temporality from which we make our categories of reality, along with the category of reality itself. We posit that reality from the fields of knowledge and objects organized in ever greater metonymic or synecdochic refinements.[3] And the process does not stop, since neither history nor society is ever ordered once and for all.

Periodization, the structure of historical narrative, is not then simply a matter of organizing data but of producing them. The rhetorical dif-

---

3. See Hayden White, introduction, *Metahistory: The Historical Imagination in Nineteenth-Century Europe* (Baltimore: The Johns Hopkins UP, 1973), esp. 35 – 36. "And, by such reductions, as Vico, Hegel, and Nietzsche all pointed out, the phenomenal world can be populated with a host of agents and agencies that are presumed to exist *behind* it. Once the world of phenomena is separated into two orders of being (agents and causes on the one hand, acts and effects on the other), the primitive consciousness is endowed, *by purely linguistic means alone*, with the conceptual categories (agents, causes, spirits, essences) necessary for the theology, science, and philosophy of civilized reflection."

This quote should also be read in the context of discussion around *Metahistory*. See "Metahistory: Six Critiques," *History and Theory* 19 (1980), esp. Hans Kellner, "A Bedrock of Order: Hayden White's Linguistic Humanism" (1 – 29). Also see Fredric Jameson, "Figural Relativism, or the Poetics of Historiography," *Diacritics* 6 (Spring 1976):2 – 9; and David Carroll, "On Tropology: The Forms of History," *Diacritics* 6 (Fall 1976):58 – 64. Finally see Dominick LaCapra's chapter on White's *Tropics of Discourse*, in *Rethinking Intellectual History: Texts, Contexts, Language* (Ithaca: Cornell UP, 1983), 72–83.

ference between explanation and narrative that engenders Romantic history is reactivated throughout these texts. The end or beginning of a chapter or section is often entitled "jugements historiques" or "critiques historiques" (see Blanc, Lamartine). As summaries, no more or less moralizing than the rest of the narrative, they provide a place of rest or of paralysis from which the entire edifice can supposedly be viewed, if not yet understood or explained. The central plot revolves around Parisian politics, more specifically Parisian parliaments, i.e., the speech and language of politics. Two major subplots — military and provincial history or the foreign and civil wars — shuffle in at conventional "frequencies"[4] so that the reader can always juggle the whole. Macrohistories (economic, geographical, cultural) and microhistories (the press, the judicial system) are also interspersed at regular intervals. These ingenious structures could compete with Proust in architectural complexity. And they also have practical consequences: intricate sociotexts, these histories are working out social and political hierarchies as well as hierarchies of knowledge and meaning.

The largest order of these narrative structures is tripartite. The trinity emerges, as subtitle and section head: Assemblée constituante, Assemblée législative, and Convention, like a syllogism or dialectic.

If the numerous possibilities for the origin already dim that origin's prestige, its narrative and explanatory authority, then the end and culminating event presented, still presents, even more difficulty. Furet participates in that important tradition of revolutionary historiography that wants to "end the Revolution" — an ever renewable tradition, keeping the Revolution more alive perhaps than those who want to continue it.[5] The latter make up a tradition that was evident as early as Babeuf and continued with Cabet, Guizot, Michelet, et al. to Soboul, Mazauric, and Vovelle. For them, the Revolution barely misses its mark each time, but is always eagerly awaited: 1830? 1848? 1870? 1914? 1936? 1968?

Not so purely teleological after all, Romantic history is constructed upon a paradox or even a tautology rather than upon logic and the affir-

4. See Gérard Genette, *Narrative Discourse: An Essay in Method*, trans. Jane E. Lewin (Ithaca: Cornell UP, 1980), ch. 3. A more thorough and strictly technical narrative analysis of a historical text would be fruitful. See Ann Rigney, "Toward Varennes," *New Literary History* 18 (Autumn 1986):77–98, and her forthcoming book.

5. The first half of *Penser la Révolution française* is titled "La Révolution française est terminée." See also François Furet, *Marx et la Révolution française: Textes de Marx présentés, réunis, traduits par Lucien Calvié* (Paris: Flammarion, 1986), 88, n. 1.

mation of progress. Such a historical system constitutes its own origin and end, its own referentiality and legitimacy, its own conclusions. Operating within an autonomous homogeneity, it establishes its own points of difference, defending them against the numerous other possibilities where none is definitive. So the crux or historical center of revolution, stabilized in principle by the points of origin and end, is susceptible to a continual reordering.

These self-generated beginnings and ends imply, first, that the history known for its dependence on events (those differentiated points of a spectrum) leaves the very notion of event unmotivated, putting into question the idea of a telos. Second, and more serious, these Romantic histories turn within their own undifferentiated narrative space (just as, according to Furet, Jacobinism turned within its own imaginary sociopolitical space), from which emerges, nevertheless, a possibility of critical perspective, but into which this critique is submerged again. Although our models of knowledge and history still work from the genetic, teleological tradition, the contradictory tendencies within this tradition become so disruptive that we must ask whether these disturbing elements are not constitutive and necessary to such a model? Must one modify or relinquish the model per se? Are we speaking about another kind of history?

I want to read the system of (Jacobin) Romantic narrative as if it represented neither a defect, an accident in historical practice, nor the neglected leftist political tradition of France, but rather the condition from which historico-realistic literature is written (and where it cannot help but end up). Furet draws a crucial distinction between two modes of history writing, which — for the sake of polemics — he attaches to the figures of Michelet and Tocqueville:

> It seems to me that historians of the Revolution have, and always will have, to make a choice between Michelet and Tocqueville. By that I do not mean the choice between a republican and a conservative interpretation of the French Revolution, for those two kinds of history would still be linked together in a common definition of the problem, which is precisely what Tocqueville rejected. What separates Michelet and Tocqueville is something else: it is that Michelet brings the Revolution back to life from the inside, that he communes and commemorates, while Tocqueville constantly examines the discrepancy he discerns [*l'écart qu'il soupçonne*] between the intentions of the actors and the historical role they played. Michelet installed himself in the visible or transparent Revolution; he

celebrated the memorable coincidence between values, the people and
men's action. Tocqueville not only questioned that transparency or coincidence, but felt that it actually masked the nearly unbridgeable gap [*opa-
cité maximale*] between human action and its real meaning that characterized the French Revolution, owing to the role played by democratic
ideology.[6]

The two "sides" become caricatures by virtue of the comparison. Michelet, the priest, communes mystically—that is, uncritically—with the
spirits of the Revolution, whereas the always-questioning and suspicious
Tocqueville alone "thinks. ... " But Furet intends, in this way, to shift
the debate from the context of ideology (whether liberal conservative vs.
republican, republican vs. socialist; Girondist vs. Babeuf, non-Marxist
vs. Marxist), from the question of political content, to the relationship
of the historian to his object, his text. In essence, this debate is shifted to
the question of form.[7] If these texts are taken seriously, it may be difficult
in the end to isolate the "Tocquevillian" alternative from the contradictory "Micheletist" history that covers up the opacity of revolutionary
discourse by celebrating its transparence. The nineteenth-century historians reanimate or repeat Jacobin strategies, for the Jacobin problematic conveys a basic gesture of history, or at least of our Western history so wrapped up in the Revolution. Nineteenth-century historians
advertised loudly their own lucidity, which in large measure depended
upon making the break of periodization stick and thus constantly having to make it anew. Such internal tensions only muddied that ever proud
lucidity.

It is not only possible but necessary for these histories both to pro-
mote adamantly the origins per se and to panic, hesitate, cover up, dance
around an infinitely postponed gesture that would fix that teleological
system of truth. Each postponement and provisional reordering create a
discrepancy between actions and intentions, means and ends, practice
and ideal that is more endemic to the historical process than the one Furet (reading Tocqueville) recognizes. This *écart* is the gap within mean-

6. Furet, *Interpreting the French Revolution*, 16; *Penser la Révolution française*, 30
-31.
7. Furet's own book gets to a study of the French Revolution through the accumu-
lated blindness of historiography. Perhaps without meaning to, Furet locates the practice
of history in competing readings of historiography, rather than in truth claims of the archive.

ing and language or within any means of self-expression, not between two separate entities. Does Tocqueville's capacity to focus on the *écart* in revolutionary practice provide him, in turn, with that *écart* or distance necessary for the practice of analytic history? The discrepancies integral to revolutionary ideology, accumulating in historiographical practice, may contribute to that more visible impression of a confusion between action and intention or action and consequences, that is, between action and its meaning. Or maybe the discrepancies show up first in historiography and are then projected back onto the political practices of the revolutionaries. Those paradoxes or duplicities à self-representation within politico-historiographical practice, less clearly identifiable than the more traditional oppositions (action/intention etc.), interject an element of slippage that plays havoc with the teleological system while not being able to do without teleology.

My basically structural and thematic treatment of Romantic narratives concentrates on Michelet, since he provides the institutionally acceptable[8] edge from which to pass into less familiar territory, and on Louis Blanc, since he best incarnates the neo-Jacobin tradition.[9] Like his contemporaries (e.g., Cabet), Blanc has been studied, if at all, only in terms of social or political history, or even more rarely, in histories of history. And who fills in the nineteenth-century blank of Furet's category when, in the end, Furet saves Michelet from the category he defines? Generalizing from close readings, I hear a "new" history emerging that these historians can perhaps not express and that they connive with us readers to represent. However, I am also aware that this chapter should be about how hard it is to separate "old" from "new" and to generalize in the first place.

8. As well as Furet, see Albert Soboul: "progressivist tradition of revolutionary historiography, from Michelet to Lefebvre, through Jaurès, Aulard and Mathiez, . . . — the only one which, in its methodology from the first, was and remains scientific." Avant-propos to Claude Mazauric's *Sur la Révolution française: Contributions à l'histoire de la révolution bourgeoise* (Paris: Editions sociales, 1970), 6.

9. I am extending the term to define an inseparable element of nineteenth-century French society, as Gramsci does, instead of limiting it to the context of Isser Woloch's *Jacobin Legacy: The Democratic Movement under the Directory* (Princeton: Princeton UP, 1970).

Michelet's Genealogies of History: The First
Part of His Introduction

In the introduction to his *Histoire de la Révolution française*, Michelet immediately considers the problems of relationship — that is, of historical periodization, which he discusses, awkwardly and brilliantly, in "logical" and "historical" terms at the same time. Revolution and Christianity are a first antagonistic couple, upon whom are superimposed Justice and Grace. The constant antagonism of these concepts manifest in material history (Revolution vs. Christianity, Justice vs. Grace) does not exist, according to Michelet, at the beginning of this history and dissolves at the end.

The famous sentence of the introduction and its rewritings provide an aphorism or enigma, instead of a definition, to which the introduction and the history keep referring in order to give it the effect of a definition:

> I define the Revolution, the advent of the Law, the resurrection of Right, the reaction of Justice.

> The Revolution is nothing else but the delayed reaction of Justice against the government of favors and the religion of Grace.

> What is the Revolution? The reaction of fairness, the late arrival [*l'avènement tardif*] of eternal Justice.[10]

While Michelet first uses Christian metaphors, such as *advent* and *resurrection,* he finally settles on the more neutral or polyvalent *reaction.* The Revolution not only rises as if from nowhere, but does so in response to another system, called Grace. But *reaction* does not clarify that response: Justice might be a return to an anterior state, might always (atemporally) oppose Grace, or represent, as in the chemical connotation of the word, any interchange between two substances. The creeping insistence on the word *tardy* implies not only that Justice is late in declaring its eternal dominion but that Justice is eternally late — that the only eternal quality Justice possesses is its lateness.

The enigmatic definition leads quickly to the question: "Is the Revolution Christian, anti-Christian?" And just as quickly, the historian,

10. Jules Michelet, *Histoire de la Révolution française,* ed. Gérard Walter (Paris: Gallimard, 1952), 1:21, 30, 76.

without limiting the importance of the question itself, acknowledges the strategic or theoretical significance of being able to answer or pose that question in the first place. "This question, historically, logically, precedes all others." The question has two simultaneous branches. First Michelet asks how the new principle, Revolution, can be described in relation to the old one, Christianity: "The person who will recount the crisis of the new principle that arose and made a place for itself [*se fit sa place*] cannot do so without asking what this principle is with regard to its predecessor, in what way it is a continuation of the former, in what way the new principle goes beyond it, dominates or abolishes it. Serious problem that no one has yet confronted face to face" (1:21–22).

The question of principle can also be restated as a practical one. Simply: What verbs does the historian use to shape his periods: *continue, go beyond, dominate, abolish?* Do these proposed solutions contradict the fiat (*se fit*) of a "rising up" of the "new," ex nihilo? Somehow no one else ever seems to ask this basic question that Michelet alone always uncovers. Others either act as if it has already been resolved or as if it is merely "une question accessoire" (1:23). On the contrary, writes Michelet, no history can be written until this problem has been reckoned with. The other part of the question concerns whether there are one or two historical objects (one or two questions?): "As historian of the Revolution, I cannot, without this research, take even one step.... The miserable connivance in which these two parties linger, is one of the main causes of our moral weakening. It is a combat of the *condottieri*, where no one is combative. ... As long as the basic questions remain unconfronted, there is no progress to hope for, religious or social. ... Never, not in forgery, trickery, or treaties of lies, can faith begin" (1:24).

It was convenient for the *condottieri* (Italian mercenary soldiers), as Michelet refers to both the political (parlementary) and religious (Jesuitical) orders of the day, to connive with each other. Although a political and social Revolution was supposed to have happened, Michelet asks if the event simply reshuffled (political) structures already developed by the Church, and if the Church still held the "historical base" of power. The word *connivance*, frequently privileged in both the introduction and Michelet's work in general, evokes the image of eyes half-closed (trying to stay open or closed?) with the added connotation of the wink. Connivers have one eye open and one closed, for they pretend not to see the wrongdoing they sanction by this very pretense, and they conve-

niently cannot be accused of this (inadvertent?) sanction. Finally, the
transition that Michelet brings off at the end of this paragraph between
historiographical strategy and historico-political (or moral) strategies
appears less naïve when one considers that both practices respond to
similar questions, summarized perhaps too broadly as what makes
modern society cohere. Whatever gives the historical narrative its sense
may also be working to keep the sociohistorical institutions in operation.

A rather astounding passage follows in which Michelet resolves, with
near sleight of hand, that "serious problem" no one had heretofore even
posed:

> If the Revolution was that and nothing more, it would be indistinguish-
> able from Christianity.... It would be nothing in itself. In this case, there
> would not be two actors, but only one, Christianity. If there is only one
> actor, there is no drama, no crisis; the struggle we thought we were seeing
> is pure illusion....
> But it's not like that. The struggle is only too real. This is no simulated
> combat between two sides that are really one. There are two combatants.
> And one should not say that the new principle is only a critique of the
> old, a doubt, a pure negation.—Who has ever seen a negation? What is a
> living negation...?
> So, there are two things... the old, the new....
> One has to get beyond misunderstandings [*il faut sortir des malenten-
> dus*], if one wants to know where one is going. (1:24–25)

The circular reasoning embellishes a tautological syllogism. It is almost as simple as saying that if the Revolution was an extension of
Christianity then it would not exist, but it does exist, and therefore it is
not an extension of Christianity. The circularity is troubling since the
decisive factor—whether there is drama, crisis, battle, that is, actual antagonism, or not — represents what was previously being questioned:
the *combat de condottieri*. He uses as the turning point in his argument
the denial of the original question: How can we tell a simulated from a
real combat, a simulated from a real Revolution? In fact, the very out-
rageousness of the reasoning implies that it hardly matters how one
breaks through an unresolvable question, this rhetorical barrier, before
beginning a history (or society based on faith); what matters is to state
that there are two objects and to get on with it. The process is somehow
reversed in that the initial presupposition appears as the consequence:

"Il faut sortir des malentendus." In order to get out of the cycle of arbitrary misunderstandings in which we cannot distinguish between two
conniving parties, we posit the possibility, even the necessity, of the distinction between the two, one of which is named the "old" and the other
the "new": one Christianity, the other the Revolution; one Grace, the
other Justice. With this distinction made (as the process of signification
arbitrarily differentiates signs that we take for granted, or as metaphorical language is resolved into the two terms of comparison in order to be
explained), the historian can then proceed to build his argument upon
that unquestioned cleavage of comparison itself: "There you have the
complete resemblance. And here is the difference" (1:25). History can
then be written.

But Michelet's text also connives with itself because it both is written
and yet never gets beyond the question it sets out to answer. After trying
to work out his "grave problem" through a syllogistic logic, Michelet
will appear to turn toward different manifestations of "story" in order
to provide a form of explanation (aphorism, genealogy, fable, the long
historical narrative). The first part of the introduction begins with the
aphorisms encapsulating the relationship of the concepts or principles,
then extends the aphorisms into a genealogy and finally a little allegory
or historico-moral tale. These forms, unusual for history, actually cover
the Roman and medieval periods. The second part (not treated here) appears to approach history proper by examining the monarchy and
causes of the Revolution. And, as usual, narrative history finally begins
with the main body of the text. But as early as the first part of the introduction it is hard to say in the progression of forms where timeless
aphorisms and moral tales end or flow into story and history. Each
seems equally inadequate without the others. The (logical) principles or
aphorisms of Michelet's introduction can only be explained in the main
body of the text, the long narrative, which would not make sense without the frame of aphorisms — even if they are paradoxical and difficult.

One might also conclude, with some regret, that the mode of discourse does not in fact change when it passes from the fables (or even the
"logic") of the introduction to the seven-volume history of events. The
reader learns nothing in the seven volumes he or she does not know from
the introduction. And yet these volumes, besides telling the story in a
long form that was conventionally pleasing to the audience of that time,
are necessary to the success of the project. The weighty body of the text

retrospectively proves the logic of the introduction by erecting an undeniable Revolution, by miming the monument it constructs. Even at this outlandish proportion, this history keeps telling the story of how the (real) Revolution has not arrived, perhaps cannot arrive. That is, it is still not sure if it can tell the difference between the Old Regime's false revolutions and the promise of the new. History—in both senses of the word—still cannot take that first step.

Michelet's *Histoire de la Révolution française* performs the very historical problematic whose repetitions keep it moving, for the historian must define the (new) Revolution within the (old) prevalent Christian system; he must find the material equivalent of the teleological narrative form. Is this why readers dismiss Michelet too easily, read him too literally? One can no more extract those Christian figures from his language than one could extract figure itself from language, Hegel from Marx, Roman virtue from eighteenth-century revolutionary discourse.

Consider now the genealogy of Grace and Justice that follows the first pages of Michelet's introduction. The intricate, almost devious logic parallels the question of whether there are one or two historical objects, Christianity and Revolution. At first the story appears to coincide with the familiar biblical and Romantic myth of the fall like Hugo's *Fin de Satan*, but a closer look shows Michelet's typical twists. The first part of the introduction is, after all, titled "On the Religion of the Middle Ages." As usual, Michelet maintains in his discussion a strict identification of logical principles (allegory) with specific concrete historical events.

Once upon a time, associated with the teachings of Saint Paul, a mythical fall or separation occurred in which man threw Justice or liberty out the window "like a useless piece of furniture" and "blindly entrusted himself to the hands of Grace" (1:31). Saint Paul made the mistake of subordinating justice to faith; humanity was saved by the blood of Christ, not by individual or collective will and action: "Saint Paul, by laying down this principle of salvation by faith alone, expelled Justice from the court. From then on it was nothing more than an accessory, a result [*suite*], one of the effects of faith" (1:26). *Court* can refer both to the divine court of justice (from which the Archangel was ejected) and to the court of kings, already proleptically suggesting the corrupt court of Louis XIV. But Paul brought about the impossible, a miracle in reverse. Separating Justice from its own court is like emptying a word of its very meaning. The clever Paul does not chase Justice out of Paradise; he renders it impotent, then keeps it around and simply acts as if it is no longer important, an accessory, an old chair, junk, one of the many side effects of another first principle. Justice is a courtesan in the court of Grace, which is now and henceforth sovereign. Justice tags along as one of its "suite." But the consequences of this slipup or ruse are fatal:

> Once outside of Justice, we must keep going, descend into the arbitrary.
> Believe or perish! ... [Michelet's ellipsis]. When the question is asked that way, one finds out with terror that one will perish. ...
> The arbitrary need go no further. The system is complete. (1:27)

Almost before (Michelet's) history begins, it appears to have already been decided. He has already in fact prefigured as well as he ever can the terror that will be literalized as the Terror.

The Council of Trent (1545–63) took Saint Paul's doctrine to its logical, if not contorted, conclusion: "If *Grace,* says [the Council of Trent], with the Apostle [Paul], was not *gratuitous,* as even its name shows ... it would be Justice, and no longer Grace, (*Conc. Trid.* sess. VI, cap. viii)" (1:27–28). The only way one can define Grace is to repeat its name in another form — "gratuitous," for instance. For Grace is by definition what can have no motivation, no cause, no way of being arrived at or even understood, except through this kind of negative definition. If Grace is at all explainable, it becomes Justice, its other; it is no longer itself.

A human institution like the Church is forced to make decisions and operate in the world. Believers are rewarded for sheer faith, for a unity in the blood of Christ. Others are shunned, punished, killed. And these judgments are supposed to appear logical and just, but there is no principle of explanation at all. According to Michelet, this procedure is no different from the long rule of Old Regime privileges inherited through blood alone. The contradiction of a Grace that judges produces an untenable duplicity at the logical origin of history. As a result, Grace can only be read masked as a Justice that is always false: "That puts into many things something false and wrong; one only gets out of this double position through hypocritical means. The Church judges and does not

judge, kills and does not kill. ... Terrible Comedy where Justice, false
and cruel Justice, puts on the mask of Grace" (1:28).

A kind of history, evolving spirals of repetition, unfolds from the original tautology — Grace is gratuitous. In such a history, according to
an ironic retribution, Grace, which is all powerful, must always appear
masked as Justice, as its "other," and never itself. (Which only Michelet
detects.) Robespierre culminates the series of displacements from Paul.

Such a form of history does not reduce into a flat monotony because
the repetition is each time displaced by the promise of Justice, and Justice is both illusory and convincing each time it resurrects the entire system, which is neither cycle nor strict repetition. Michelet's introduction
takes seriously the enigma of why the people keep self-destructing in regime after regime of continued repression. A kind of *peuple-Candide*,
whom he often compares to the child, keeps resurrecting with each Infant, each *bon roi* who is always recognized at first as the *adorable en-
fant,* one of them. Then when "the king, that god, that idol, becomes an
object of horror" (52), the *peuple-Job* takes more abuse. As in Sade's
cycles of *Justine*, psychology inadequately explains such a process in
which learning seems impossible. How does one write a history when
true history is conceivable only as the story of the infancy of the revolution — always already turned into an idol? It is odd that Rimbaud uses
the word *idol* in his poem "Enfance" to describe the child who has no
history: "That idol, of black eyes and yellow mane, without parents or
court, nobler than fable."

Justice and Grace are supposed to be united at the beginning and end
of history, but meanwhile they are engaged in a *mortelle bataille* where
the sides do not appear equal — although maybe they really are. Grace
lies forever on its deathbed, its *lit de justice*, but also keeps reviving
enough so history cannot know Justice except in the folds of these turn-
overs, revivals, revolutions.

On the one hand, it looks as if Justice is the very term precluded by the
system (of Grace), which works by definition on the exclusion of Justice
and cleverly bars its eventual return by perverting all of its possible forms
of expression. One cannot get there from here, to Justice from Grace.
"Since it began as arbitrary, this system must remain within the arbitrary, it cannot take even a step away" (1:29). And yet, on the other
hand, Justice has only to be itself to reverse the mock sovereignty of
Grace: "So that Justice ... ventures to raise its head, something difficult

has to be done (since common sense is so stifled by the weight of pain and centuries), Justice must begin again to believe that it is just, to wake up, remember who it is and become aware again of what is right" (1:30).

Justice simply has to recognize itself for what it is: just. But does that not mean that Justice is gratuitous, because it is defined only by identity with itself, in tautology? But this definition is supposedly that of gratuitous Grace. So, following this hairsplitting logic, Justice is really a form of Grace. And Grace is (false) Justice. Such paradoxes would keep history turning into its other and (never) starting over again: something other than teleology or ontology. Unteleology? Untology?

If the reader has not yet understood the (new?) form of history, the first part of Michelet's introduction ends with a last version in the encapsulated story of the Roman slave. It serves as a *petite allégorie* (Hugo's term) for the whole history of the French monarchy, foreshadowing as well the Revolution and the Terror. These couple of pages (39 – 41) might be called Michelet's historical fable of error. He also calls it a "sublime and terrible farce."

A poor slave, "convulsing" with dread, balancing a very symbolic egg on his hand (not a spoon), makes his way through a group of satiated and sleepy lions, to the raucous joy of the corrupted people in the Roman Coliseum. As ever, the scene is also at the same time riveted to chronological history ("this spectacle was renewed toward the end of the Middle Ages") and moves up through the kings. Michelet gives the key to his allegory: the slave represents the genius, all incarnations of the people ("O mes pères, ô mes frères, Voltaire, Molière, Rabelais") who suffer the ridiculous disguise, the "deformed martyrdom" of "buffoons of fear" in order to place ultimately that fragile life of liberty on the altar of history.[11] But just as the symbolic slave gets ready to pose the egg, at the high point of the fable, allegory of the Revolution, a tiny noise of

---

11. The passage in which the slave progresses through the history of the Middle Ages and the monarchy to the eventual Revolution is typical of Michelet. "Who will give us the power to follow, from the depths to the surface, the rising of a thought: ... How from instinct to dream to musing, and from there to poetic chiaroscuro, the idea has wound its way up!" (1:40). This is the allegory of the Revolution digging through the mountain of the Old Regime toward the light of Bastille Day, and it is the natural history of all creation, from rock to plant, man and bird toward the idea. See a similar passage in *La montagne*, *Oeuvres complètes*, ed. Paul Viallaneix, vol. 20, ed. Linda Orr (Paris: Flammarion, 1987), 131–32. Also see Edward K. Kaplan, *Michelet's Poetic Vision: A Romantic*

warning is sounded: "Only one thing worries me . . . " (Michelet's ellipsis). As if it is nothing really. "So what is the place of refuge where they
are going to hide these goods [*cacher ce dépôt*]?" (1:41)

This simple question will resonate in each attempt at democracy
throughout Western history — but rephrased in Michelet's terms, it
merely asks where Justice can be sheltered for the night, and that includes asking how Justice can be seen or read in the first place, in what
shape or form, in what language or symbol. What does the genius do
with this "he knows not what" that is sacred, this invisible hot potato
he cannot seem to put down anywhere? Michelet then continues to harp
on his one message that we, like Justinian or Justine, never hear: be careful that this fragile egg, this infant (in-fans),[12] does not become an *idole*,
is not already an idol: "Watch out for human idols, avoid gods of flesh
or wood, who, far from protecting others, cannot protect themselves . . . "
(Michelet's ellipsis, 41).

Going beyond Rousseau's theoretical distrust of any representation
of popular sovereignty, Michelet makes a history of this warning cry: "I
see all of you, from the end of the Middle Ages, from the thirteenth to
the sixteenth century, build up, enlarge this sanctuary of refuge: the altar of Royalty. To destroy idols, you put up an idol, you offer it everything, gold, incense, myrrh . . . [Michelet's ellipsis]. For this idol, gentle
wisdom; for it, tolerance, freedom, philosophy; for it, the final reason of
society: the Law" (41).

There is no clear accusation here, no simple conspiracy theory, because the well-meaning genius or the people as a whole imperceptibly
turn into their horrifying other. One sinuous lineage runs from Rabelais
to Louis XIV. After Saint Paul the priest gets to him, "in the name of liberty . . . sometimes a child kills" (38). The instant the infant, tired, discouraged, stops to put fragile freedom down somewhere, she or he has
laid the first stone of the new Bastille.

Michelet's history therefore must be read both teleologically and un-

---

Philosophy of Nature, Man, and Woman (Amherst: U of Massachusetts P, 1977). There
is, however, a constant hitch in the ascension toward light: "The truth that is found is not
clear enough yet" (1:40).

12. The word *infant* comes from the Latin *in-fans*, "one unable to speak." For the
word in a context of historical theory, see Michel de Certeau, *L'écriture de l'histoire*
(Paris: Gallimard, 1975), 8.

teleologically. He keeps trying to reestablish the "line" (between the "Old" Regime and "new" Revolution, between Grace and Justice) that slips, multiplies, and keeps being effaced before he can begin to secure it. Curiously enough, Tocqueville works toward a similarly duplicitous history from the other direction. He keeps trying to erase the lines, especially that all-important one of 1789, that he must nevertheless continue to draw elsewhere in order to make sense of his narrative. One must be careful to follow the differences as Michelet's break keeps slipping away from him and as Tocqueville's erased line keeps reappearing, but one can also see a similarity in the historical systems that both imply. "Here you have the complete resemblance." Michelet's system of Grace transfers itself: (1) from the medieval ecclesiastical courts of law, (2) to the monarchy's arbitrary justice, and (3) to the Terror's false Revolution. The Old Regime system of centralization and homogeneity is constantly displaced in Tocqueville: (1) from the emergence of Roman law in Europe, (2) to the growing central administration of the monarchy, and (3) to its extension in the "imaginary" Revolution. For both, Justice or liberty keeps escaping to the limits of a system in which it can only be read as what is excluded and yet whose promise and reality keep that system in constant circulation. Both try to refer to a historical precedent from which they can predict the possible return of Justice or liberty (for Michelet, the Roman tradition of Justice; for Tocqueville, what is supposedly just the opposite: the common-law tradition). But both define Justice or liberty precisely by the impossibility of getting from the one system to the other logically, by links, by cause and effect although both recognize that the "antagonists" are strangely interdependent, they connive with each other. Both historians spend, therefore, most of the space of their histories, nonetheless permeated with the desire and poetry of liberty, with a similar analysis of the tenuous and yet resistant strategies of the system in place. These are, oddly enough, the same strategies its competition, liberty, uses too. For both historians, the reversals, which are prepared "ecclesiastically" in Michelet and like a subterranean supplanting in Tocqueville (like Marx's grubbing mole), can never be read until they are already complete.

But despite the affinities of structure (and differences of content)[13] be-

---

13. Sometimes, however, their content and very words are similar; the following description from Michelet, lamenting the disappearance of local traditions, anticipates Tocqueville's: "No more feudal system or city life—it is lost in royalty. No more religious

tween Michelet (his Jacobin-Romantic colleagues) and Tocqueville, why
do we naturally perceive them as opposites? "And here is the difference." Is the difference purely rhetorical? Michelet's discourse sounds
crazy to us, while Tocqueville's is analytical and lucid. Besides consid-
ering the ideologies of reading, we might also entertain the hypothesis
that Michelet's "madness" (as if Tocqueville's excruciating logic is any
less mad) serves as strategy. You have to take the risk of being a buffoon
to carry that unnamable something through the lions in front of the betrayed and betraying public to the evanescent refuge of freedom. Does
Michelet think he will get away with his outrageous ambition of inscribing Justice or the Revolution (within the linguistic and historical system
of Grace) by appearing to speak folly (obviously common sense if we
would only wake up)? Or does he invite our devastating criticism and
a kind of sadistic mockery, himself a masochist?[14] Both Michelet and
Tocqueville, along with their contemporaries, wanted to right the Revolution of liberty, instead of reinstituting its idolatry, and yet neither one
could predict with what violence he might be read.

Louis Blanc and the History of Anticipated Dis-appointment

Louis Blanc's *Histoire de la Révolution française*, a stereotype of (Jacobin) Romantic historiography, not only fits — too well — Furet's description of the genre but prolongs a discourse alternating between

---

life — gone out with the clergy. Alas! not even local legends, national tradition, no more
of those happy prejudices which make up the life of the infant people. They have destroyed everything that was the people's, even its mistakes" (1:55).

14. In Michelet's introduction, as in Hugo's *Quatrevingt-treize*, there is a troubling
passage in which books are violently destroyed. Justice, like smoke from the pyre, is finally and ironically freed from its own oppression (inside books) and *grâce aux* (thanks
to the) ferocious actions of Grace taken against it. "This holy house of study four times
forced, pillaged, its books profaned, thrown about, its manuscripts irretrievable, heritage
of the human family, dragged through the gutter, destroyed. . . . They did not destroy Justice; the living spirit, penned up in these books, was freed by the flame, then spread, and
entered everywhere; it penetrated the atmosphere, so that, because of the murderous fu-
ries of fanaticism, the only air one could breathe was the air of fairness" (1:38–39). For
the scene in Hugo, see Jeffrey Mehlman, *Revolution and Repetition: Marx/Hugo/Balzac*
(Berkeley: U of California P, 1977), 66–69; and Sandy Petrey, *History in the Text: "Quatrevingt-treize" and the French Revolution* (Amsterdam: John Benjamins B.V., 1980), 92
–94.

paranoia and pathos, hysteria and lyricism, for twelve volumes: the record for this nineteenth-century corpus (except for Buchez and Roux's forty volumes of "documents"). Supposedly simplistic passages, wheeling out the clichés of Romantic history, especially the binaries of cause and event, of idea and material history, are made more bothersome by categorical pronouncements that exaggerate the usual didacticism and by a plot held together with the milky consistency of melodrama.[15]

In a short preamble to his introduction, Blanc, applying something like Hegel's dialectic, announces that history is structured according to three "principles" (thus differing from the more binary divisions of Michelet or Tocqueville): "Three great principles share the world and history between them: AUTHORITY, INDIVIDUALISM, FRATERNITY."[16] First, Authority, established through obedience to Church and lord, developed a unified society in which the subjects ultimately had no identity apart from that solidified homogeneity. Then Individualism sprung up as a reaction to that total conformity: people used their own reason to define themselves for their own profit in opposition to those repressive institutions of the past. The bourgeoisie was born. But Individualism or rationalism "pushed to the limit, denounced itself" in the form of intellectual anarchism. Society would fall apart unless Fraternity again provided individuals with a sense of community—without using the methods of Authority. After setting up these three principles in his introduction, Blanc refers back to them later but does not mechanically apply them. He would not necessarily have had to read Hegel to adopt this tripartite order, since Hegel's dialectic was well known at the time (after Victor Cousin's lessons). Another structure, more reminiscent of Michelet and Tocqueville, also emerges in Blanc. The rise and triumph of the bourgeoisie (like Michelet's monarchy or Tocqueville's Old Regime-centralization-&-equality) leave little room on either edge for Authority or Fraternity. The monarchy is interesting only as the site of the "silent ... struggle" in which the bourgeoisie is already benefiting from whatever maneuvers the monarchy thought enhanced its own power.

15. It is no accident that nineteenth-century history is imbued with melodrama; both popular genres gained impetus from the Revolution and attained importance in the first half of the nineteenth century, extending beyond that. Theater and history are as interrelated as narrative and history. See Peter Brooks, *The Melodramatic Imagination: Balzac, Henry James, Melodrama, and the Mode of Excess* (New Haven: Yale UP, 1976).

16. Louis Blanc, *Histoire de la Révolution française*, 2 vols. (Paris: Maurice Lachâtre, n.d.), 1:xxix.

And Fraternity is the desired, perhaps impossible, element of Blanc's history, like Michelet's Justice and Tocqueville's liberty, present already in the unreadable future: "Beneath this surface, the immortal idea, the irrepressible idea of France follows its course, and when this idea reappears, it is surprising to see how far it has gone, when not a visible sign, not the slightest noise, gave away its movement" (1:562).

The predominance of one principle, challenged by nothing visible yet, presents again a dilemma for the historian. He does not want to celebrate the (bourgeois) system already in place nor to lament, while charting, its incredible survival, but rather to reveal the necessary coming of the (second) Revolution. Less explicitly than Tocqueville, Blanc also suggests that perhaps the historian has no other alternative than to mirror the present authority, whose repetitions as past or future, as "surface glacée," block or freeze the future or past one would rather read. Is Blanc's frustration, exacerbated at times to hysteria, more understandable when one sees him running again and again into this surprisingly resistant surface?

The rhetorical or generic division of Blanc's history into "Origins and Causes," followed by the supposedly motivated events of the narrative, should correspond as well to a shift in the evolution of the three principles. His "Origins" traces the rise of bourgeois Individualism from within ecclesiastical-monarchic Authority, and the body of the narrative recounts the parallel emergence of Fraternity from within bourgeois Individualism. However, Fraternity fails to emerge. The two parts of Blanc's history might instead be described as, first, the playful logic of prerevolutionary history, followed by a classless, or homogeneously bourgeois, unprincipled state called the *noir imbroglio* of the Revolution.

The problem comes from living that frustrating paradox in which no one can read what retrospectively will have already taken place without a sound, to appear perfectly logical only years later. Blanc expresses, then, opposing points of view on this history that appears or is made to appear both capricious and methodically systematic. On the one hand, he, like Michelet, incorporates a conspiracy into the logico-historical beginning of his narrative. On the other hand, also like Michelet, he presents the story of the conspiracy as a way of illustrating a less-determinable, constitutive problem in history. Just as for Michelet Grace had slipped into the guise of Justice, for Blanc Individualism triumphs by committing inequities in the name of liberty. When one looks more closely, the three principles, "arid" as Blanc thought their definitions were, already inscribe a snagged development, despite the effect of their syllogistic logic. "Freedom! Luther had said, freedom! the eighteenth century *philosophes* repeated in unison; and it is the word freedom which, today, is written on the banner of civilization. There are lies and misunderstandings written here; and, since Luther's time, this misunderstanding and this lie have filled history; it was individualism arriving, and not freedom" (1:xxix).

In the beginning was an ambiguous takeover; mistake or ruse? This substitution of *liberty* for *individualism* creates a kind of logical impasse: How can the true proponents of liberty declare the advent of their principle when people think that they have been living in liberty all this time? What can they call *their* principle? How can they know it? It was a little absurd to accuse the bourgeoisie (Richelieu or Louis XIV) of maliciously plotting to get where they did not know they were going. "The bourgeoisie itself, in its heated course toward complete domination, had only a confused sense of what it was doing, and the bourgeoisie was far from believing that making the royalty independent would abolish it. But, I repeat, men are almost always the puppets of what they accomplish. Societies live on an eternal misunderstanding [*malentendu*]."[17] In this passage from Blanc's *Histoire de dix ans* (1842), the word *malentendu*, whose recurrence in his work will become more obvious, generalizes the predicament—while still including the possibility of lies. From one point of view (its own?) the bourgeoisie was muddling around, while from another (history's) it was racing toward absolute domination. Blanc pauses at this striking aphorism—societies live on (according to, on the basis of) an eternal misunderstanding. They are founded, curiously, upon a condition of impaired hearing. They cannot be sure of exactly where they are as they nonetheless rush there as if driven by an order.

The result is the *noir imbroglio* of the Revolution as narrated in Blanc's remaining eleven volumes, for the bourgeoisie already drops out around 1789 (with Lafayette, Mounier, Bailly, Sieyès, Lally-Tollendal). Does it drop out because everything is now bourgeois? The class analysis, presented with relatively sophisticated definitions, falls away. And

17. Louis Blanc, *Histoire de dix ans, 1830–1840* (Paris: Pagnerre, 1844), 1:79–80.

the "utopian-socialist" historian must fill the dark space between that completed empire and the invisibility of the new one. It can be argued that Blanc, at this point, gives us a Revolution from the inside or even from the point of view of his own characters, including the well-intentioned Robespierre, for no one can read what is going on. From the winding syllogisms, Blanc resorts to the repetitions of parody and farce as if not even absurd syllogisms can be unraveled from the mêlée anymore. Both ridiculous and tragic imitations of the desired system—liberty, democracy, the people, fraternity—pile up: the Girondists, "artists gone astray in politics," donned red bonnets and promoted the joke *sans culotte*, while Hébertists dressed up (*affubla*) their doctrine "in rags" and "gave it the language of the streets [*halles*]" (1:363). And, all the time, each manifestation of the mask accuses the others of disguise: "There was a moment when Paris became the city of costumes, calling all the while: 'Down with your charades!' " (2:367). The chapter titles in Blanc outdo even Lamartine in their evocation of trickery, mystery, blindness, confusion, madness, and titillating horror: Imitation Riot, Simulated Frights, Fraudulent Steps of the Riot Instigators, False Rumors, The Blindness of Two Opposing Parties, The Trumpet of the Last Judgment Sounded . . . , Delirious Paris, Monsters Created by the Reign of Murder, . . . What Came out of this Abominable Coupling." So how could the Revolution avoid making mistakes and errors? "Wrapped in intrigue and betrayal as if by a dense night, and forced to fight enemies that most often it [the Revolution] only noticed in glimmers of light, what undoubtedly happened was that its blows strayed onto innocent victims, but even they were only struck because it had the misfortune to believe they were guilty" (2:383). The obsessive thematics of the Revolution's errancy — where it went wrong, went off course,[18] got lost, strayed—returns in the verb *égarer*. The Revolution, *égarée*, lost control of its own defensive blows and struck itself.

When the revolutionaries are blinded by their own experience, the historian calls himself in to see clearly: "And this is what makes so delicate, better yet, so formidable, the task of History, called upon to see

18. See ch. 5, "The Revolution Blown off Course," François Furet and Denis Richet, *French Revolution*, trans. Stephen Hardman (New York: Macmillan, 1970). The verb *égarer*, which returns so often in histories of the Revolution, recalls the predicament of Michelet's buffoon-slave, who had no refuge, no garage for his unnamable treasure. The French *garer* comes from the Frankish word meaning to dock, to guard, to protect (cf. warranty, guarantee, garrison).

clearly in this black imbroglio, and to unravel" (2:525). While Blanc, like his contemporaries, undertakes this task, does he not, also, write the more feasible novel of the national nightmare? "This is the task to be completed in order to make us understand a revolution that would only appear to us, if we did not do that, as the bloody dream of a country's delirium" (1:cxlvii). When the principles and the class distinctions disappear, Blanc is left with the parody of that repeated delirium.

Blanc's *Histoire de la Révolution française* further breaks the illusion of eighteenth-century history speaking itself[19] by referring to contemporary, nineteenth-century events. In so doing, his history appears to anticipate solutions for eighteenth-century impasses, and yet it also turns those solutions back into the problems that called for them. Does that mirror effect set up, nonetheless, a kind of tautological explanatory system?[20] The Revolution, was, therefore, blind to what *Organisation du travail* (1839) promises to provide (and fails to?) — the Revolution. Then the *Histoire de dix ans, 1830 – 1840* (1842) repeats, more profoundly, the blindness of the Revolution and the same unanswered call for social remedies: "Would the overthrow of royalty be enough to make capitalism's tyranny over the workers impossible in social relations? ... Questions such as this one were too lofty at that time, and more than one storm had to break before people thought of resolving them. In 1830, people were not even thinking about asking them" (1:348).

Even 1848 (and Blanc's *Histoire de la révolution de 1848*, 1870–80) represented no progress, which, in an odd reversal, the post-1848 volumes of the *Histoire de la Révolution française* laments. "One knows what happened after the Revolution of 1848. It would have been necessary to organize work: people only knew how to regiment misery" (1:214). Blanc may well be referring to his own disappointment when the Luxembourg Commission got no support from the provisional government of 1848 that set it up, so it failed to change the workers' situation significantly. The more one tries to bring about that magic formula, to organize work, the more one produces its other, a kind of inorganic, mechanical, or even military reordering of the same poverty, the same

19. See Roland Barthes, "Historical Discourse," *Structuralism: A Reader*, ed. Michael Lane (London: Jonathan Cape, 1970), 145 – 55, trans. of "Le discours de l'histoire," *Social Science Information* 6 (August 1967), rpt. in *Poétique* 49 (February 1982).
20. For a study of this strategy as represented in Flaubert's *Bouvard et Pécuchet*, see Françoise Gaillard, "An Unspeakable (Hi)story," *Yale French Studies* 59 (1980):137–54.

travail.[21] On the one hand, Blanc predicts the second (socialist) Revolution and the new (social) history of the Revolution (Soboul et al.), that he knew himself not to have the equipment to accomplish. And Blanc the politician strives constantly to bring about that prediction. But on the other hand, he keeps inscribing in all of his histories a metaphorical space for future error: neither utopia nor dystopia ("utropia" perhaps).

So why does Blanc's text (and history) not come to terms with itself?

His *Histoire de la Révolution française* does pause to reconsider itself at certain strategic moments. These places, including the end of the second volume (of the original twelve-volume edition, published in 1847), and a reflection on the Terror (vol. 10) can be identified by a list of rhetorical questions or even exclamations that gesture toward a radical redefinition of history. But the question is hardly formulated when Blanc either answers it (rhetorically), represses it, or postpones it, implying that the answer depends upon the successful performance of his own book — the one answer his book cannot give.

This passage on the Terror most blatantly closes the opening that it has just made:

> Nevertheless, if, under the pretext of the public good [*salut public*] you punish Themistocles with ostracism; if you banish an evil prince's family for life; if you strike an innocent person because he seems dangerous to us, where will the compass of the moral universe be? Where will the refuge from iniquity be, that has suddenly become justice, by virtue of the PUBLIC GOOD [SALUT DU PEUPLE], which will have been understood in this or that way and arbitrarily defined by transition governments, infallible as long as they are standing, accused of imposture as soon as they fall to the ground? ...
>
> The problem is that there weighs a fearsome misunderstanding on this debate, and woe to the one who would not point it out, thinking he had discovered it! ... In practice, the PUBLIC GOOD always means THE GOOD OF ONE PUBLIC. ... So do not say, then, THE PUBLIC GOOD IS THE SUPREME LAW: say: THE GOOD OF HUMANITY IS THE SUPREME LAW. From then on, no more darkness. (1:487)

21. The pun made possible by the different meanings of *travail* in French and in English ironically underscores Blanc's point. Cf. "Blanc's historical studies aroused within him a sense of travail, of bewilderment, and a fear of those too simple formulas that lure men into fatal action." Leo A. Loubère, *Louis Blanc: His Life and His Contribution to the Rise of French Jacobin-Socialism* (Evanston, Ill.: Northwestern UP, 1961), 34.

Blanc analyzes the disfiguration of that most promising of phrases: salvation of the people. If Blanc avoids appearing to defend the enemy (Vergniaud? Philippe Egalité?) by using the ancient Greek example of Themistocles, he brings up the problem his contemporaries (and ours) have cast in the same metaphor: if this sacred phrase can be used as the excuse for such crimes, "where is the moral compass?" Are we a ship tossing at sea or a walker lost in the dark woods? Michelet's genius-people made the mistake of seeking refuge, symbolic incarnation, but is the alternative of perpetual errancy and *égarement* any more acceptable? We are back in the fable of Justice and Grace. Iniquity appears in the guise of justice, by virtue (that loaded word in the context of the eighteenth-century Jacobin Revolution) of these magic phrases whose prestige gives protection to the wrong camp. *Salut du peuple* is captive to each succeeding government; it is defined "arbitrarily" by each passing authority that appears to know all until the next Revolution, when the preceding one is said to have been wrong and criminal.

Consequently, when we read the first sentence of the second paragraph, we expect a justification on the order of the "eternal misunderstanding." In fact the phrase "thinking he discovered it" suggests the irony that only a naive researcher could believe he has "discovered" something so recurrent. But perhaps Blanc is not ironic at all. He continues by recommending, or rather ordering, the substitution of one word for another, as if the whole problem hinges simply on that. The figurative generality of "people" too easily covers up each nation's egotistical desires. Blanc predicts that the frightful (terrorizing?) misunderstanding would not subsist if the word *humanity* was used in its place. One feels the relief that follows this historical and rhetorical impasse, as if the doors of narrative swing open again (reminding us of Michelet's "one has to get beyond misunderstandings, if one wants to know where one is going"): "From then on, no more darkness." It is hard to believe, in the constantly reenveloping night of Blanc's plot, that this conclusion is definitive.

In the passage closing the first two volumes of his *History* and published in 1847, Blanc adopts the other tactic. He suggests that he cannot answer the rhetorical questions except by postponing them, but he ends, in fact, by establishing another imperative that is this time more problematic, if equally authoritarian in tone.

But the moment came when the misunderstandings would become evident. Individualism had just revealed its formula: already Brotherhood's was almost visible.

That is why . . . a second revolution was inevitable. . . .

What! Didn't a sovereign law, a terrible law, attach evil to good as an absolute, irrevocable condition? What is this universe that we live in? . . . What is truth? . . . In nature, species only subsist by the destruction of inferior ones . . . .

Do not rush to conclusions! The ardent, invincible protest which comes out of the depths of human conscience, is what shows that the NECESSITY FOR EVIL is a lie. Man's dignity consists of believing this, his power will be to prove it. (1:182)

In such passages, Blanc often asks literally if there is a "law" to be deduced from the history that keeps writing itself in his book, despite himself.[22] The only way he can express the pattern he keeps reading, if it is even that systematic, is in Christian terms (evil inseparable from good) or in fatalistic terms, cast here in uncannily Darwinian metaphors.[23] But no hypothesis really satisfies him, as he runs through the gamut yet another time. Here, Blanc does not have a quick solution, and he cautions against the practice of hasty conclusions that he, of course, in turn adopts elsewhere.

But leaving history in suspension is not the same as setting out to write, as realizing that you've written a history of suspended suspension, a history that would be constitutively inconclusive. The strategy arrived at in the last sentence could, however, only apply to a history whose results are not in yet. Lies, like truths, are constructed after the fact, rather than after or according to facts. The Necessity of Evil is not an a priori metaphysical hypothesis but the result of a syllogistic proof the historian or anyone makes history fit into. The problem with this a posteriori interpretation is that history is continually up for grabs. The only way that Blanc can finally prove the Necessity of Right in history is to bring about, by virtue of his history, the new society he inscribes as inevitable. His book must "perform" the Revolution it predicts. Such a paradox comments on the aphorism Michelet rephrases in his famous 1869 pref-

22. "Did he [Robespierre] wonder about the law, frighteningly mysterious, which, since the beginnings of the world, honors the artisans of iniquity?" (2:552).

23. *The Origin of Species* (1859) was translated into French in 1862. See Ivette Conry, *L'introduction du darwinisme en France* (Paris: Vrin, 1974). Where could Blanc be getting this language in 1847? (Malthus?)

ace to the *Histoire de France* ("Man is his own Prometheus," "Humanity creating herself") as well as on similar statements by Marx that do not necessarily contradict his determinism.

The closing pages of the long introduction to the *Histoire de dix ans* give the impression that Blanc has resigned himself to reading two histories that are mutually exclusive: the repetition of death and poverty and the cyclical promise of progress that somehow keeps replenishing its continuous exhaustions. Is one history any more or less narratable than the other? The usual rhetorical questions ("what" is now followed with an exclamation point, not a question mark) build again to, not a letdown, but another attempt at some kind of impossible logic with which to understand history.

> What!... what! All that in order to lead to who knows what kind of miserable variants in the history of great sufferings and great crimes! In these eternally varying forms, what have I seen up till now? An eternal tyranny. And in the diversity of objects I have only discovered the stubborn lie of words. A strange and cruel mystery! What stormy end are we headed for? Such endless efforts! Since the beginnings of society, such energy lost on earth! Would the people be condemned to toss and turn without relief in the darkness, like those blind horses, hard-working creators of a movement they are unaware of? For in the end, what are the evolutions of humanity worth in history? Anticipated deception is hope. (1:140−41)

The striking image of the blind horses sets up again an oddly intertwined, paradoxical history, a diabolical dialectic. In this instance, the horses or people, whose story is unnarratable since it goes nowhere, "create," in contrast with simply being the victim, the "movement" they cannot know. What movement? The false progress going on in the Assemblies as if over their heads or separated to the side of them? The legitimacy and energy of postrevolutionary history depend on what that history cannot know and what cannot even know itself — the people, language, the language of the people. And when Blanc weighs all this evidence, he comes up with the following balance sheet: "Anticipated deception is hope." The word *deception* synthesizes or figures the element that keeps throwing off Blanc's principled history, whether some untraceable errancy or simple misunderstanding or lies. The Old French meaning joins the English: to deceive, to trick by making one believe something false. But in modern French the word corresponds rather to the English *disappoint:* to take away something, rather than to take someone in. Etymologically, to disarrange the points, disturb the teleology. In order not to be dis-appointed, we can expect from history not the corrections of past errors in a perfectible future, but the undoing of our perceptions in the certain anticipation of continued misperception. The aphorism implies not that one can anticipate how one will be deceived — there is nothing disappointing in that — but that one will always be deceived in unpredictably diverse ways.

In the last paragraph of this same introduction, Blanc leaves the reader with yet another pithy enigmatic formula: "What do we know in the end? ... Every revolution is useful, at least in the way it absorbs deadly [*funeste*] eventuality" (1:144). First, Blanc simply implies that a revolution prevents a greater future evil. But this aphoristic sentence means that revolution exists to anticipate a future disappointment or lie — and not a visible disappointment but a conditional one, not a specific "event" but an "eventuality," the possibility of something's becoming an event. Which comes close to reinscribing the Terror's paranoia. Focusing on that subtle difference between "event" and "eventuality," one might also read Blanc to mean that revolution absorbs the nature of history as uncertainty (eventuality), anything that has the potential of bringing harm (*funeste*). Then history would be knowable and benign. And, more than that, to do away with eventuality, that is, the general concept of what defines the event, suggests going beyond event-history itself. All this exercise, mine and Blanc's, in the end serves to preserve the usefulness, if not necessity, of revolution in the midst of enigma.

Romantic historiography rediscovers in its own arguments and language simultaneous forms of history that should not be able to coexist. Historical time continues to appear as sequence and logic, as the statement of problem and solution, as cause and effect, as teleology, but it also enters into strangely reversible complicities where the ever-secure totalizing power has been undermined without showing it — may never show it — or where through an imperceptible transgression one element has already become its opposite, its unthinkable other. In such histories, lining up a dialectic of thesis, antithesis, synthesis is impossible, for all three are more likely to be going on at once. And Michelet's question remains: Are there one or two objects after all? Let us say that one irresolvable enigma exists as well as many difficult, finite questions that call for pragmatic and immediate action.

So what happens to that Tocquevillian alternative if we cannot escape the Jacobin-Romantic moment of sharpness attached to confused tirades of truth? Analysis continues to return to narrative and vice versa in the attempt to extract a point of view from the self-legitimating and self-destructing process associated with history and other forms of cultural self-expression. But it is risky to hang onto and rely upon the glimpses of critique, especially self-critique. They turn as quickly and as dangerously into another suggestion of how better to institute the proper history and society. Almost pretentious advice, this suggestion serves again to rejuvenate the system of Grace—and maybe, eventually, Justice along with it.

Quinet—a Coda, Almost a Synthesis

> They [these downfalls] are therefore not an accident, but an element of our new society.
>
> —Edgar Quinet

Edgar Quinet criticizes the Revolution for adopting and reinforcing habits of the Old Regime, but his criticism is intended to preserve this historical experience as the central meaning of French history. He agrees then in part with both Tocqueville (1856) and Michelet (1847–53), but *La Révolution* (1865), coming later than the books of his colleagues, has its own unique perspective, its own advantage and disadvantage. Quinet begins his history where Blanc stops short and where Michelet turns away (although what Michelet avoids returns to trouble him constantly). Quinet takes as his starting point the phenomenon, the fact, of repeated frustration produced by what he called the "aborted" Revolution.

La Révolution confronts from the outset those rhetorical questions that structure Blanc's history. Quinet (thank goodness) does not have to go through twelve volumes to work up to and back from them. He, unlike the others, identifies recurrent disappointment as the object of his historical and philosophical analysis: "What then is there left to say? What is left to discover and show is why such immense effort, so many total sacrifices, such a prodigious expense of men, left behind results that are still so incomplete or shapeless."[24] It sounds as if there cannot be much left to say after all the voluminous histories, but really everything is still left to figure out.

It would be tempting to let Quinet, as the third historian after Michelet and Blanc, serve in my dialectical ordering as the historian who finally expresses self-consciously the paradoxes and doubles of the French Revolution and of his own difficult status as postrevolutionary historian. But I would be erecting my own hierarchy after trying to avoid the traditional ideological ordering from left to right or Furet's similar privileging of the analytical (Tocqueville) over the celebratory (Michelet). If I privilege more apparent self-consciousness over that disguised Romantic semi-consciousness, I might well undo the effort I have made to give credence to the latter.

Quinet does impressively manage to keep the tension of the Revolution always before the reader, there where it regresses or turns in the ruts of the dangerous past and there where it makes incredible conceptual and practical political leaps into the open future. He allows for a simultaneously teleological and unteleological text and history. His text, again like Tocqueville's, gives more recognizable space to what we today consider theoretical discourse, along with straight narrative — if that distinction can continue to hold up. Quinet found a balance. But the same question underlies the litany of other questions that troubled his Romantic colleagues (about all this frustration and tragedy and the status of repetition in history). Without a preordained head, what gives postrevolutionary society body? What unity does the acephalous society create for itself so it can move on?

Right from the beginning Quinet was not fooled by the Revolution. Michelet let his hopes fall, and with such sorrow, at the September massacres; the socialists Cabet and Blanc thought the Revolution was on track, especially after 1792, until it missed its mark on the 9th of Thermidor (1794). Quinet is also disappointed, but from the beginning. Still, he does not share Tocqueville's ambivalence; he is genuinely grieved. The other republican and socialist historians play out the stages of repetition as if, as Furet states, from within the temporality and con-

24. Edgar Quinet, *La Révolution* (Paris: A. Lacroix, Verboeckhoven, 1865), 1:1; (Paris: Belin, 1987), 65. Subsequent references to the original edition are given in the text.

sciousness of the revolutionaries themselves, in surprise, shock, horror
—Candides, Justines. But Quinet anticipates the repetitions before they
happen, from the beginning integrates his critique after the fall, after the
fact, into the ongoing texture of the narrative: "The political constitution ... will be erased at the same time as it will be composed"(1:36).
The building and erasing take place simultaneously in this strange history. "The first oath of freedom! ... Soon oaths will wear away other
oaths" (1:58).

After a few of these observations, at only a tenth of the way through
his history (two volumes in the original octavo, 1000 pages), Quinet decides already that it is time to take stock. He pauses to repeat the questions with which he began his book but this time with the added perspective of seeing, not horrifying accumulation without sense, but some
kind of sign, if not pattern: "In this silence everything disconcerts me;
such astounding contradictions, such heroic beginnings, such magnan-
imous promises and such misjudgments, how can they all be reconciled?
Maybe if these downfalls had only occurred once—but several like them
can be counted [*compter*] in half a century. They are therefore not an
accident, but an element of our new society. What is their cause?" (1:147
−48).

Quinet loses none of the passionate pathos of his predecessors. First
the silence of incomprehension greets each fall and miscalculation. The
echo of *compter* emphasizes that the repetitions are mounting up. They
are too numerous to be ignored or simply deplored. Quinet takes the
next step and says, okay, so let's assimilate these abortive promises into
our general understanding. They are no accident but an integral part of
our new democratic society.

I keep letting this arresting sentence resonate backward and forward
through Quinet's history. Maybe I privilege it too much. But it recalls the
doubles and tension when the reader almost forgets the pattern of mistakes, is almost convinced later when a more confident Quinet, in a different discourse still his, promises that he can fix the very problem he has
just identified as central to postrevolutionary society and history. Because of this sentence, even what can be learned from the Jacobins, from
their Terror, is also an element of our new society. Quinet was one of the
nineteenth-century thinkers who came down the hardest on the Terror,
and he was the strictest about adapting his action and life to his beliefs.
The Michelets enjoyed the social seasons of Paris despite their wander-

ings, Nantes, Italy, Le Havre, Hyères, while Quinet and his wife lived until the fall of the Second Empire in Veytaux, Switzerland, where the
Michelets visited as summer tourists.[25]

Quinet is not content—who is?—with arriving at the sentence that
articulates the contradictions of modern revolution. He has to know as
well "what then is the cause of all this?" Then not only does he proceed
to answer, but he provides the solution from within his own terms, to
the challenge of democracy. If the historian, like Quinet, finally articulates the main problem of his project and offers a solution, that solution
will then appear to be the only one possible. That too must be "an element of our society," of our reasoning. We cannot raise a problem and
rest secure until we know how it arose and how we can fix it. Such an
impulse—does language itself push us on?—regenerates the narrative
and history, the narrative of history. Not accidentally, the question that
keeps regenerating these histories as well as the society itself—one that
evades answers and solutions—asks, what is it that regenerates our society, keeps it integral and productive? So the question—what generates
history/narrative?—may be its own answer.

Quinet answers that the cause of all the frustration, failure, endless
attempts, and suffering is "an eternal misunderstanding." He selects one
of those charged places of modern origins, Rousseau, as his archetypical
example of where things went wrong and would continue to do so, culminating in the Terror. Recall that Rousseau stated the problem this
way: "Man was/is born free, and everywhere he is in chains." What
happened along the way? Quinet focuses on Rousseau's Savoyard vicar
as the place of error. Not ostensibly out of spite or even pretention and
pride, the vicar, like one of Unamuno's characters in modern literature,
with the best of intentions wishes to spare his flock from too brutal an
exposure to the Revolution he nonetheless lives and breathes and talks
into their lives. "For each word, a contradiction," writes Quinet. "As a
result, total confusion thrown into human awareness [*conscience*] and
so, no real innovation at all" (1:133).

Innovation is another way of stating that desired goal of a dynamic
society that constantly regenerates itself, avoids repetition, does not fall

25. See Simone Bernard-Griffiths, "Rupture entre Michelet et Quinet à propos de
l'histoire de la Révolution," *Michelet cent ans après* (Grenoble: Presses univ. de Grenoble, 1975), 145–65. See also Claude Lefort, preface to Quinet's *Révolution* (1987),
15.

back into reaction. The opposite of innovation would be continuous self-destruction, like the Revolution that keeps undercutting itself. Then Quinet reproduces the same phrase that obsessed Blanc: "Here then is a religious revolution that would occur without anyone realizing it! An eternal misunderstanding would be its base" (1:133).

Extending from his analysis of this fundamental duplicity, *un malentendu éternel*, Quinet presents one of the most developed critiques of the Terror. In a surprising twist of logic, he accuses the Jacobin revolutionaries of being too timid when it came to the real religious revolution (complete religious freedom and all it implies about free choice). In order to hide this lack of courage, the revolutionaries overcompensated by resorting to irrational repressive violence that threw them back into the ruts of Old Regime practices. While appearing to be radically different, they ended by repeating the mistakes of the past. Quinet adds, as well, the more common criticism of the Jacobins — that they constructed an abstract vision of their own constituency, *le peuple*. In so doing, like the Savoyard vicar, the revolutionaries missed the chance of reeducating their public in a profound and lasting way. They only left the people confused and frightened, terrified.[26]

For Quinet the "religious revolution" does not refer to institutionalized religion. He has, however, a predilection for Protestant moments in history (influence of his second wife?). Thus, his history appears as the flip side of the interpretations of Blanc and especially Buchez and Roux, who see the Revolution as culminating Catholic values. Quinet treats his Protestants with ambiguity. Blanc's history is also ambiguous: he privileges John Huss over Luther at the same time that he values the Catholic League of the sixteenth century. Quinet needs a minimal model for his religious revolution and chooses the Protestant Reform, just as the eighteenth-century revolutionaries looked back to the Roman republic for some precedent. If we keep Quinet's notion metaphorical, then it comes to mean something that galvanizes a society into realizing its identity, realizing what gives it coherence, energy, faith in itself, promise for its future. In its most general sense, the idea of religion pulls together all the

26. I am summarizing Quinet's critique of the Terror, which is analyzed in more detail by Claude Lefort in "Edgar Quinet: La Révolution manquée," *Essais sur le politique (XIXe–XXe siècles)* (Paris: Seuil, 1986), 140–61. Also see François Furet, *La gauche et la Révolution au milieu du XIXe siècle: Edgar Quinet et la question du jacobinisme (1865–1870)* (Paris: Hachette, 1986).

standards, values, historical awareness that society creates for itself (and that serve paradoxically as internal points of reference), constantly modifying and questioning them. After peeling away what Quinet's religious revolution does not mean, Claude Lefort arrives at a definition that preserves the conceptual content: "the pure meaning of a transcendence, which lives in people; the need within them for a creation that is assumed, without any outside guarantee, both in moral life and the experience of democracy."[27]

But can Quinet guarantee this configuration of meaning that defines *religion* without its being contaminated by the other meanings or connotations attached to the word throughout its long history? Michelet, his best friend, first fell into the trap of reading the word literally, or at least arguing that the word with its accepted meanings was no longer useful in describing the new society. Religion had already been irreparably linked to a history of repression. It was no accident that Michelet insisted on reading/misreading Quinet, on literalizing Quinet's construct, even though he and Quinet were equally aware that the Revolution depended on keeping meanings fluid, on balancing the principle of social representation very delicately between metaphor and practice. Remember that Quinet's *Révolution* (1865), a mere two volumes, threatened to unseat the monument of Michelet's *Histoire de la Révolution française*, which was supposed to stand as the definitive national history of France.

Both Quinet and Michelet associated the tradition of a repressive Catholic monarchy with the loss of certain basic human rights, including in particular the freedom of religion. But agreement stopped there. Michelet argued that the spirit of the Revolution itself was religion enough for society, that social self-definition could never be institutionalized or literalized. But Quinet pointed to the vacuum in that revolutionary society which threw up far more dangerous and ludicrous substitutes, like Robespierre's famous *Etre Suprême*. At a particularly ambiguous moment in Quinet's critique against the Terror, his solution for historical frustration and disappointment approaches, is drawn to that edge where solutions turn into (worse) problems. In a couple of

27. Lefort, preface, 27–28. If I qualify Quinet's uniqueness and connect him with the rest of my Romantics, I appreciate the figure he represents for Lefort, one I would like to see associated with other Romantics: "Quinet dismantles the religious sentiment of the quest for certainty; he adds to this a well-thought-out restlessness, a constant debate over rights" (28).

chapters rife with Quinet's irony, he complains that the poor eighteenth-century French were just not cut out for being terrorists. They did not have "the true temperament for Terror" (chapter 5 of the section "Theory of the Terror"). The Venetian Republic or Czar Nicolas; now, there were regimes that operated in silent denunciation and secret without the messy spectacle of gossip and speeches. Quinet suggests that his thoroughgoing religious revolution would require no gratuitous violence because there would be no more duplicity, no *malentendu éternel*. History without duplicity and foiled intentions avoids the false terror but leaves the way for Quinet to posit a true terror with different forms of persuasion. Quinet implies that one can know, that he himself knows, what is the *innovation véritable*, the real religious revolution as opposed to the illusory ones. This self-assurance makes him as Romantic as the others. He too writes a double discourse. The difference is that his abortive history of repetition and disappointment dominates while being ever so carefully jolted by the call for the true revolution, instead of vice versa.

Still it must be said that Quinet states sharply, perhaps more sharply than the others, the irony integral to the Revolution. But is his own text ironic at this point? It does not sound as if it is: "In no revolution have the leaders acted in a way that was directly contrary to their goal; all their power, they made it work against their own intentions. This is what gives the French Revolution a character of fury that human affairs to this point have never shown" (2:151–52). The French Revolution, in particular the Jacobin experience, has become one of the most symbolic examples of how history turns into what its agents least expect or desire. Revolutionary furor may well come from such disappointment. For Marx the Jacobins demonstrated a strange mix of realism and illusion. In *The Holy Family* he echoed the dismay and horror of the French Romantic historians, not just socialists, who saw in the Jacobin double bind the tragedy of history. "What a terrible illusion it is to have to recognize and sanction in the *rights of man* modern bourgeois society, the society of industry, of universal competition."[28] The more the Jacobins tried to practice their program, both realistic and theoretical, the more they came up with the opposite result from the one they started out with — whether that result was the eventual rise of the railroad and textile mag-

28. Karl Marx and Frederick Engels, *The Holy Family; or, Critique of Critical Criticism: Against Bruno Bauer and Company*, trans. Richard Dixon and Clemens Dutt (Moscow: Progress Publishers, 1975), 144.

nates of the nineteenth century or the more immediate nightmare of more tumbrils passing on their way to the guillotine. Somewhere between a cynical theory of complicity (the Jacobins invented invasions and enemies for the sake of gratuitous violence) and a blanket impunity (they knew not what they did) lies the problem of historical action.

As their histories run to keep up with each missed opportunity, each aborted rendezvous, the historians defend their own solutions to the problem of historical slippage. Although the solutions can shift between concrete, practical, political content and metaphorical content, all end up predicting real history somewhere, if far into the future, and all maintain a quotient of conceptual thinking. Cabet, one of the earliest historians in the Romantic corpus, introduced a concept that would become much more literal than he ever imagined: communism. *Histoire populaire de la Révolution française* (1839) charts the zigzag of disappointment the notion of communism describes in Cabet's attempt to link it to something comparable in the French Revolution — which would give it a logic for commanding future French society.[29] Blanc's socialism also

29. Etienne Cabet, *Histoire populaire de la Révolution française de 1789 à 1830* (Paris: Pagnerre, 1839) represents another subversion of teleological history; that is, of the Revolution that, as Robespierre said, missed its goal. Robespierre's aphorism could also have served as an epigraph to my chapter: "Whether one is too close or too far from the goal, one misses it all the same [*le but est également manqué*]" (Robespierre, speech, Dec. 25, 1793). Here are some ideas on Cabet translated from a previously published essay.

Cabet wanted to make a tradition coincide, really to invent a tradition that would link him to Robespierre through Babeuf. Robespierre went as far as speaking of "the equality of goods," which Cabet wanted to move closer to the "Community of goods," Babeuf's expression. Each metonymy, "commodities made communal," "portion of goods equal to its placement," "common resources," led Cabet to announce that the Revolution was "almost the Community of goods."

Yet the idea of the "Community of goods" did not assure a bridge from 1796 to 1839 either, for Cabet recognized that his own ideas did not exactly correspond with the "Community of goods." He joined to it at the same time an expression overdetermined by the context of the years 1830 and 1840: "social organization." Cabet's history thus had to be legitimized by resulting in something that, still unnamed, nevertheless stood out in the history of the Revolution by its absence or approximations. Yet what most discouraged Cabet was the inconceivable distance between Robespierre and these fragments, metonymic ones, of a new social order. The signifier "Robespierre" was in place, but lacked a sociopolitical signified: "One goes as far as ... the equality of fortunes, a sort of agrarian law, or rather a Community of goods, without anyone, however, presenting a clear-cut idea of this sort of social and political system, almost entirely unknown" (3:151). Another problem: the Girondist and Hébertist enemies were already starting to stammer ideas that were supposed to belong solely to Robespierre.

hovers as the place the Revolution cannot get to. And that ever-promising *Organisation du travail*, which became a rallying point for the 1840s, is hardly a practical manual. Read it and you see how it continues to delay the promise amidst all kinds of frightening calamities that will befall society if it does not manage to apply that program of organization right now. Quinet had his religious revolution to point to; Michelet his (spiritual) Revolution of 1789; Tocqueville the phantom remains of local custom and habit. All pointed to their own books.

Each solution represents a risk — the risk of state control (Blanc, Cabet) or ever more subtle social unification (Quinet, Michelet) and the risk of elaborating impractical abstractions. Yet a history that risks no solution at all opens itself up perhaps to the greatest of dangers.

In so rethinking the structure of history ruled by this utopian place, Cabet ended up wondering if the tradition he so very much wanted to trace should not perhaps skip over Robespierre entirely, passing directly from Lycurgus, Mably, and Rousseau to Chaumette or Hébert, or even if it should not jump over the Revolution altogether and land at Babeuf, who still did not represent Cabet's communism. As in Michelet's text or Madame de Staël's, what must mend history fractures it. Finally, history retracts to the point of the sole enunciator, the historian and his or her act of writing history. Linda Orr, "Le discours jacobin de l'historiographie romantique," *Sédiments 1986,* ed. Georges Leroux and Michel Van Schendel (Québec: Hurtubise HMH, 1986), 141–42. See also Christopher Johnson, *Utopian Communism in France: Cabet and the Icarians, 1839–1851* (Ithaca: Cornell UP, 1974).

III The Problem of Legitimacy: The Popular Authority of Romantic Historiography

Historical authority has traditionally been determined according to that infamous distance (*écart*) of the text from the real. But aside from the issue of the *écart*, history is always implicated in a relation of power. The elements of narrative are constantly regrouping themselves in changing hierarchies: reality, author, reader, narratee, narrator, and text. If the status of the author is ambiguous and open to question, so is the system of authority that flows from it.

Seen from the "mimetic" perspective by which the representation of the real gets its legitimacy from a possible coincidence (word with object, word with signification), the author assumes a position of authority second only to reality, which occupies the sovereign position. In the beginning a simple mediator of the real, the author eventually seizes all power, since the real in question appears only by his or her doing. But let us invert this mimetic view of representation. Without looking any different on the outside, the once-established hierarchy of power is really turned inside out. (Roland Barthes's short essay "Historical Discourse" serves as a good example of this exercise.) If the hypothetical center is now the text, no matter how unstable, upon which the characters, both narrator and narratee, depend, then author and reader also assume an identity by the effect of the text. They occupy a position whose insignificance is exceeded only by the real itself, a projection both phantasmatic and material, that derives its legitimacy from rhetoric and language. The figure of the author, after the exercise of inversion, refers then to a space opened up by the narrative. It is a metaphorical space that this narrative, however, cannot grasp — but that gives the author ostensible authority, parental authenticity.

Romantic historiography inscribes, actively constitutes, almost simultaneously a tenuous coherence that is both textual and social. The society that seems to lose its author in the Revolution regroups around a new notion, no less symbolic, of the "popular." The problem arises when the political and literary representation of this now fundamental function turns out to be impossible or constantly re-placed. The author undergoes the same decapitation as the king and must be eclipsed, like a good democrat, behind the author-reader who is the people. The final result may not look any different from the realist narrative, also the traditional form of history. The author, who is effaced behind either the real or the people, simply reorients this disappearing act and keeps as much power, may even increase it. (Recalling the etymology of the word *author, augere*.) But in migrating and expanding, does the available power ever let itself be read? Is this process what we call revolution?

Among nineteenth-century historians, it is often Michelet who maps the strategies of an entire historico-literary production, because he exaggerates them. (Roland Barthes and Lionel Gossman choose Thierry specifically because he does not exaggerate them.)[1] The way Michelet establishes his authority can be summarized in this doubly paradoxical relation: I am not an author, but I am the origin (understood, therefore, the author) of the possibility of all history of the Revolution, really of modern history.

An effacement or confusion traditionally makes the historical narrative function — Genette (in *Figures III*) already calls this setup "perhaps legitimate."[2] In a progressive confusion, the author is first lost (loses himself) or fades into the narrator, who himself in turn fuses with the characters in the plot — let us say the history — which, thanks to the ambiguity of the French *histoire*, ends up turning into History, capital H. History or the real, then, is what speaks all by itself, alone. The events seem to write and read themselves: a headless history. The preface of 1868 of Michelet's *Histoire de la Révolution française* (whose seven volumes were published for the first time between 1847 and 1853) provides

1. Lionel Gossman, "Augustin Thierry and Liberal Historiography," *History and Theory* 15 (1976):1–83; Barthes, "Historical Discourse," 155.

2. Gérard Genette, *Figures III* (Paris: Seuil, 1972), 226.

an example of this double discourse, in which the author must be
eclipsed in order to return as a more authoritative figure. Moreover, the
text of the history or the narrative of the events can exist only insofar as
it succeeds in repressing this preface where Michelet goes on talking too
much about his own shady activities. The preface has to be separated
out, decapitated from the body of the text, but, once read, its disclosures
keep returning.

Michelet considered his book *Le peuple* as the ideal model of a history, which would blend author, narrator, object of study, narratee and
reader in, not a book, but a person listening to him or herself speak, lov-
ingly. The first stage of this progressive fusion, which moreover Michelet
will never move beyond, is contradictory: while repeating the thesis of
his book — whoever writes is irrevocably separated by definition from
the category of the people — he tries to repair this fatal rupture himself
by integrating it into the story of his family and of his own life. At first,
embodying both people and infant (*in-fans*), the young Michelet is a
compositor in his father's printing office before otherwise composing
books. He then chooses the teaching profession — "a real job [*un vrai
métier*]" he says, rather than that of writer.

Less literal in *Histoire de la Révolution française*, the contact of the
historian with his object of study must also be immediate:

> Have not I lived with them, have I not followed each one of them to the
> depths of each one's thought in its transformations, as a faithful compan-
> ion? Eventually, I was one of them, a favorite of this strange world. I gave
> myself the ability to see among these shadows, they knew me, I believe....
> The dust of time remains. It is good to breathe it, to come and go, through
> these papers, these dossiers, these registers. They are not mute, and all
> this is not as dead as it seems. I never touched it without a certain some-
> thing emerging, awakening ... [Michelet's ellipsis]. It is the soul.
>
> In fact, I was worthy of this. I was not the *author*. I was a hundred
> leagues from thinking about the public, success: I loved, and that was all.
> I was fierce [*acharné*] and avid as I went here and there; I aspired toward,
> I wrote this tragic soul of the past. (1:14–15)

I will stop at the fictive character of the author-historian because this
mythological descent into the archives, always enriched by the poetry of
dust, is repeated throughout Western narrative tradition: in Tocqueville's *Ancien Régime et la Révolution*, where one would expect it less,
or in Vigny's "Esprit pur": not even modern historians like Foucault

are exempt from it. This character has to surface, has to be invented in order to fulfill the declaration that follows: "I was not an author." Such is the goal of the historian's strategies, the ultimate gesture of legitimation. This sentence is even more surprising when it is contradicted at the end of the paragraph: "I was not an author. . . . I was writing." To be the author means more than the fact of writing or the person writing, and takes form only through the process of assuming authority.

Michelet extracts himself from his author-body, which is profane, wheeling and dealing in a marketplace world; after this split, the purified self is ready to go underground for his initiation. He is metamorphosed, by a long ritual, into something both heroic and troubling, always ambiguous, neither dead nor alive. Moreover, the paraphrase of the uncanny *le familier étrange* appears in the passage. In this liminal zone, the historian encounters other beings no less ambiguous than himself, neither dead nor alive, neither speaking nor mute subjects. Such an in-between identifies the possibility or the impossibility of the narration, a place where neither author nor characters should be allowed to enter, or else a mediation between them.

The atmosphere of myth and fairy tale—Orpheus in the underworld, the Prince and Sleeping Beauty—comes to an end, however, in the metaphor of the final sentence. While the I-character affirms that it is good to breathe, to come and go among the spirits in the first paragraph, in the long run this coming and going becomes frenetic. The word *acharné* especially marks this progression from the faithful companion who lived among them, was close to them, to the hungry seeker of knowledge. If he is not the trained predator to whom the taste for meat was given in order to chase game, he is even more sinister—ambiguous image of the man who seeks the warmth of another, of the half-dead man eager for flesh, eager for truth, who is himself finally metamorphosed into one of these zombie-vampires whom he is now obliged to live with forever. This narrative that tells the history of how archives are formed, a kind of *hors-texte* ("insert" or outside-text) in the text, preface or note, claims to make the primordial material coincide with the text in an intermediate space that rejoins the very voice of truth.

But since everyone is pulling at it, this object of truth which fades immediately into the mute shadows, the criterion for arriving at truth becomes very different from a simple search for certainty or facts. Rather, an intertextual struggle, a discursive competition, the reference to which must be silenced at any price, decides the place where truth will be forced to give itself up as readable. And yet another complication: this competition (like the one between Michelet and Blanc) shows up in a pseudointertextuality that is really intratextual. Two separate texts are not competing for the upper hand. Each text recasts the struggle in its own terms. Historical truth results not from constructing authority on the validity of proofs, but from occupying a place that is not really a place at all, this *symbolique* or trope of authority never arising where it should.

Is the order of the definitions of the word *authority* significant? The Littré dictionary defines it, first, as the "power of making oneself obeyed" and, second, as "credit, consideration." In fact, the definitions of the word do not confuse belief in the truth with the actual possession of it. Possessing power does not necessarily mean possessing the qualities to be worthy of it. Nor does credibility mean one is right. Credibility relies on a promise—of money sometimes—in which we voluntarily or involuntarily believe. A real sense of reference, the promise of referentialities, does come out of the textual and social struggle, if only as an effect of credibility and power.

Now the stakes go up more. Michelet, more naive or audacious than the others, explains the strategy, which will be the same for history and for historiography. First he takes over not only the archives but the central archives, often the only original documents that can clinch the matter. Everything else necessarily falls back to the status of the copy, and even the miscopied copy of the already miscopied (*falsified*) copy. Next, he plays down the first step, adding that once accepted, the authority of these sources need not be reinvoked at every moment. Finally, he substitutes his own narrative for the fact itself, even for the historical event, and in that way usurps all the prestige of the origin. From then on, one goes back to the past and up to the future from this point, his point:

> A word on the way in which this book came into being.
> It was born from the midst [*sein*] of the Archives. . . .
> Armed with the acts themselves, with original and manuscript documents, I was able to judge this printed matter, and especially the *Memoirs*, which are defenses, sometimes ingenious pastiches (for example, those that Roche made for Levasseur).
> I judged day by day *le Moniteur*, that Messieurs Thiers, Lamartine and Louis Blanc follow too closely.

From the start, it is rearranged, corrected, each evening by those presently in power. Before September 2, the Gironde alters it, and the 6th, the Commune. The same in every great crisis. The manuscript proceedings of the Assemblies illustrate all this, contradict *[démentent] le Moniteur* and its copyists, the *Histoire parlementaire* and others, which often chop off more of this already chopped-up *[estropié] Moniteur*. (1:13)

Michelet's book arises, therefore, from the matrix of history, the *sein* or lap of the archives. Only the legitimacy of this matrix, which must appear as a given, will assure the denegation/denigration of all other archives. Michelet, whose preface is directed, above all, against the history of Louis Blanc, asks: "Can one [read: can one dare] in London write the history of revolutionary Paris?" (1:17). The historian does not discover this matrix; he or she invents it, institutes or rather institutionalizes it, and not without the compromising aid of the centralization of the state —and Michelet boasts, like Tocqueville, the advantage of having had the chance to work at the Préfecture de police.

In order to be true, the archive must be essential and complete, giving the historian a panoptic perspective on the event. This totalizing viewpoint doubles the central perspective of the State, and of what back in the seventeenth century, as bureaucracy was growing, was called the "authorities." Michelet (who can continue to stand in here as the archetype of the character of historian or author of the realist narrative) defends his archives and repeats the litany of the profession: "I found and gave the inestimable and capital document of September 2" (1:18). In the meantime, he slips in an apology to explain his nonchalance toward his sources, when he has just given his reader the impression that they were sacred. "What gives the narrative authority," he avows in passing, "is its narrative logic [*suite*], its cohesion, more than the multitude of small bibliographical curiosities" (1:14). Still depending on the proletarian physicality of his work as a non-author, Michelet finally assumes the place that he just constituted as authentic: "For such a central fact, my narrative, identical to the acts themselves, is as immutable as they are. I have done more than to extract passages, I have copied out by hand (and without employing anyone else) the scattered texts and have brought them together. A light resulted from this, a certitude, which no one will change. It is fine if they attack me on the meaning of the facts. But they will have to recognize first that they get from me the facts they want to use against me" (1:14).

This metalepsis puts the practice of history back on its feet, summarized by this verse of "L'esprit pur," by Vigny: "If I write their history they will descend from me." In a sort of lapsus that better shows this logic of authenticity (the one that comes after or at least during the constituting activities) Michelet reinforces the impossibility of deviating from his own interpretation, now and forevermore fixed in the immutable position of his facts: "As for the events of the 31st of May, . . . I put religious care into reading and copying the registers of the 48 sections. These copies furnished me with the immense, detailed narrative that others will read, a narrative, henceforth authentic, of these funereal days we scarcely knew about" (1:18). The copies of which we must forget every echo, Michelet's own note-taking as well as all reworkings of the documents, and even the documents themselves—all of these only attain the status of authenticity at the moment of the narrative's constitution. The historian ends up "authorizing" his own text.

The strategies for capturing the place of historical truth repeat, with a striking resemblance, practices we associate with the Jacobins during the Revolution. François Furet follows the steps that led to the triumph of the Jacobin or revolutionary ideology. The Jacobins claimed not only to usher in the "new" but that the new corresponded with the origin of society's identity. This origin is not a fixed place one can defend like a rock. It is self-constituted by the social contract, so it moves around: "The Revolution only needed to shift that founding image [*représentation fondatrice*] onto itself in order to legitimate its claim to constitute the matrix [*la place matricielle*] of the social and national contract."[3] This founding matrix of society coincides as well with the will of the people and comes to represent that decisive, potent combination Furet calls the "revolutionary *symbolique*" (symbolic system). Furet's analysis in *Penser la Révolution française* joins with Furet and Richer's earlier image of the Revolution blown off course.

The displacement of the origin, that original shift, starts an infernal process that seems unstoppable. Whereas 1789 set history *adrift* (Eng. 46; Fr. 69 *une période de dérive*), by 1793 that migrating symbolic goes awry. It is, in linguistic terms, a dangerous free signifier any content can come along and fill, or (keeping the psychoanalytic body metaphor) a floating womb (*matrix*) that everyone wants. The accelerated *dérive* or

3. Furet, *Interpreting the French Revolution*, 33; *Penser la Révolution française*, 53. Subsequent references in this chapter will be given in the text.

dérapage (skidding) of social meaning progresses to the nightmarish state of delirium or madness: "This delirium [Fr. *délire;* Eng. *figment*] proves to be infinitely malleable [*d'une plasticité presque infinie*]" (Fr. 79; Eng. 54). When Furet refers to Marx's phrase for the Jacobin moment, "the political illusion [*l'illusion de la politique*]," the word *illusion* seems to refer to the opposite of reality. That is, the Jacobins imposed their abstract *fantasmes* onto political and historical situations to which they were blind. Jacobin discourse, implacably opaque, announced itself as transparent.

Certain Marxist historians (Régine Robin, Jacques Guilhaumou), influenced by Foucault, analyze the Jacobin moment in terms of "interdiscursive" strategies of hegemonic struggle.[4] Neither purely opaque nor transparent, this Jacobin interdiscourse twisted meanings in its own sense, used disguise, absorbed and mistranslated the interpretations that threatened its own dominance. In order to retain power, Jacobin discourse had to appear unified and transparent; it had to hide its opacity, the fact of internal struggle going on within. Guilhaumou summarizes the definition of the hegemonic, democratic discourse: "Any discursive formation hides within the thread of its discourse the very existence of the interdiscourse."[5] In turn, Jacobin language was subject to subversions (Hébert) and misunderstandings the Jacobins themselves

4. Issue no. 2 (1975) of the *Bulletin du centre d'analyse du discours de l'Université de Lille III* is titled "Sur la Révolution française." In the avant-propos, Régine Robin and Jacques Guilhaumou define discourse as "the place of a complex relationship among multiple historical determinations: the dominant ideology, the apparatuses in which discursive practices are inscribed, the rhetorical constraints of these apparatuses" (6). "Interdiscourse" becomes a more precise way of talking about these complex relationships. These historians justify their study of discourse in terms of their Marxist formation: "What this means is that it is not a question of a simple articulation between one internal analysis (obtained with the help of linguistic procedures) and its conjuncture (obtained with the help of concepts of historical materialism). The problem is to get at the inscription of these determinations and in particular the inscription of the conjuncture within discourse" (8–9). See also Robin, *Histoire et linguistique* (Paris: Armand Colin, 1973). Also: *Langage et idéologies: Le discours comme objet de l'histoire* (Paris: Editions ouvrières, 1974), rpt. of *Le mouvement social* 85 (Oct.–Dec. 1973). Finally: an overview of this research in *Annales historiques de la Révolution française* 51 (1979):510–12, and *Bulletin du centre d'analyse du discours* 5 (1981), "La rhétorique du discours, objet d'histoire (XVIIe–XXe siècles)."

5. Jacques Guilhaumou, "Deuxième partie: Premiers jalons pour une étude des discours révolutionnaires," *Dialectiques* 10–11 (1975):45. Also see his *Langue politique et la Révolution française: De l'événement à la raison linguistique* (Paris: Méridiens Klincksieck, 1989).

could not anticipate or control. In the context of these definitions, which throw another light on Marx's *Holy Family*, Jacobin discourse corresponds with popular expression by virtue of the political illusion or credibility the Jacobins created — which, as an effect, made them the people's mouthpiece. When both conscious duplicities and unconscious historical ironies no longer work to produce the collective discourse, the Jacobins fall from power.

Jacobin discourse is subject to the "tragic illusion" of at least two basic doubles in its (ironic) language. These doubles transport an internalized past and future-to-be whose consequences cannot be calculated. The Jacobins conceived of the French Republic through metaphors of Roman history, and civil and social rights came in a package with economic development that perverted those rights while supporting them.[6] Furet observed how the nineteenth-century historians mimed Jacobin discourse. Sometimes the repetition is shockingly literal. But the Jacobin interdiscourse is a complex phenomenon whose conditions are hard to avoid in any competition where truth no longer stands self-evident, outside the mix of cultural formations.

In his preface of 1868, it is not enough for Michelet to constitute the symbolic of truth and then to settle his own work within it. He must disqualify anyone else from occupying that sacred spot like the king on the movable mountain. In that preface Michelet took sideswipes at rivals Thiers, Lamartine, and Blanc for following the incorrect and touched-up *Moniteur* too closely. Here is Thiers again, showing up as the first in the emerging line of historians to be reckoned with. Does Michelet choose Lamartine and Blanc because they started publishing their his-

6. Marx hints at being able to "vindicate the illusion of the Terrorists historically" while analyzing their errors. In *The Holy Family*, he criticizes Bauer for simplifying the relationship of the Jacobins to the "popular community" as a "contradiction" between abstract rules and a vulgar, self-seeking people. Marx writes that, instead, the Jacobins miscalculated the kind of popular community they connected with. The Jacobins confused the real slavery of ancient Roman society with the "emancipated slavery" of modern society. The sentence quoted in part at the end of "The Laws of Reading: Narrative Teleology and Romantic History" in this book is more complex than that initial irony: "What a terrible illusion it is to have to recognise and sanction in the *rights of man* modern bourgeois society, the society of industry, of universal competition, of private interest freely pursuing its aims, of anarchy, of self-estranged natural and spiritual individuality, and at the same time to want afterwards to annul the *manifestations of the life* of this society in particular individuals and simultaneously to want to model the *political head* of that society in the manner of *antiquity!*" (144).

tories when he did? Does he ignore Tocqueville (1856) on purpose and find it convenient to read Quinet (1865) publicly as a repetition of his own ideas? The preface of 1868 narrows its opposition down to the one Louis Blanc who will represent them all. While Michelet uses every authorial tactic at his disposal, low-level and high, he accuses Blanc of being authoritarian: "In his democracy, he is authoritarian" (1:17).

Michelet was scandalized by the little Louis Blanc who "triumphed at his leisure, sprawled out as far as he wanted, and finally found himself to have really written a big book on my book. ... I am the man, after Robespierre, who has certainly most occupied [Louis Blanc]" (1:15, 17). France's premier historian is also surprised by the misunderstandings between himself and Blanc:

> Nothing was easier than consulting my manuscripts. Men of letters understand each other. . . . If I had been told, I would have very willingly given mine to Louis Blanc without asking if he intended to use them for or against me.
>
> I was sharp in my short reply. It had less to do with me than with the Revolution itself, so narrowed, mutilated, decapitated, in all its different parties except the one Jacobin party: to reduce it to this point is to make a bloody stump of it, a terrible fright [*épouvantail*], for the joy of our enemies.
>
> It is to this which I must respond, this I must oppose as best I can. No less than this duty was needed in order to arouse me from my peaceful habits. I do not like to break the unity of the great Church [*Je n'aime pas à rompre l'unité de la grande Eglise*]. (1:19–20)

A surprising metaphorical displacement occurs in the second paragraph: historiography remakes the history of the Revolution; history remakes the event. The writing of history becomes the actual performance of the Revolution. Such a strategy seeks to, has to, not just safeguard but reconstitute the unity of the Church, which is constantly to be recreated.

In the second paragraph, Michelet confuses Blanc's insults and attacks with the castrations of the Revolution; through metaphor, he draws a parallel between his rival's practices and those of the September massacres. If Blanc is identified with Robespierre and his party, is not Michelet suggesting that his rival is also responsible for revolutionary violence? Whatever the case may be, now Michelet, more than Blanc, uses metaphorical violence comparable to Robespierre's strategy, for he and the Jacobins were successful at monopolizing all discourse. Moreover, the energy of Michelet's history comes from this ambiguous identification with Robespierre that he must repress. Michelet acts—rather, he *must* act—as if public opinion and he were synonymous. Democratic rewriting of the phrase: "*L'état c'est moi.*"[7] He accuses Blanc and the Jacobins of narrowing the Revolution to one party, one bloody stump, although they said it represented everyone. But Michelet's reading also understands that there is no place for anyone outside the Church. Michelet-Robespierre must, therefore, decapitate metaphorically those texts he judges guilty of having decapitated France. A discursive competition arises around this symbolic whole each group wants to possess—however, they must not be caught brandishing the Phallus (in the Lacanian and literal senses) on the pike, because the person who vaunts having this power meant for no one party or church in particular will be decapitated next.[8] That person's history will be ripped apart, another chopped-up copy for the archives.

Mutilating the words of rivals is a primal scene in both history and historiography, whose parallels flip and merge in nineteenth-century texts. Exaggerating the words of allies is, likewise, just as prevalent among historians. The metaphorical, but no less lethal, violence seconds, if not drowns out, the revolutionary violence that accompanies it. Michelet yells in horror at Robespierre's henchmen, who practice all kinds of tortures on Danton's speech so that in no way can any historian coming after get back to the real, effective defense. "The treachery of the mutilators is palpable here. They cut up the speech, struck out this living word" (2:799). They did worse (*chose perfide!*)—turned Danton's "obviously ironic" words into shameless confessions. Thus, the only account of this crucial historic moment comes to us "by the sole testimony of the very one who snuffed out" the resistance that might have existed (7:790).

After all this indignity, Michelet turns around and does the same thing to Robespierre's speech of the 8th of Thermidor. Michelet is Danton's revenge. Since Robespierre's speech is so long, the historian summarizes the points, interrupting with fervor — "odiously ridiculous statement" or "this obvious duplicity" (2:940). Michelet is like a member of the Convention shouting from the benches whose outburst must

7. Like "Madame Bovary c'est moi."
8. See especially Quinet, *La Révolution:* "Democracy considers, in fact, any of those inside it [*les siens*] as the enemy as soon as they rise up out of nothingness; the merit of having served democracy or suffered for it is what democracy pardons the least" (1987 ed., 535–36; 1865 ed., 2:244).

be noted in the record. Finally, after building his own emotions and argument, Michelet concludes that Robespierre's speech is the mark of a man who has lost his mind (*aliénation de l'esprit*, 2:943). Those speeches, those scenes of interrupting and mutilating speeches, never seem to end. When Cabet jumped into the discursive fray, it was to defend Robespierre, to make that final speech, so terribly lacking at the time, that would have saved Robespierre's life, and the Revolution: "For us, we will say to his conquering enemies: You accuse him of being cruel. . . . No, it is you instead; . . . of being the main cause of the Terror. . . . No, he is less so than you are."[9] These historians are literally the incarnations of Danton, Mirabeau, Robespierre, Babeuf. Each one wants to have the last word and overcome foreseeable objections—including the unforeseeable ones of the future. For besides having the best methods, the central documents, and the only possible objective overview, this uncanny foresight is required to capture the symbolic space. The battle for this coveted position is never finished because past, present, and future must all three be won again, with new historical interpretations. A kind of literary history of historical interpretation always, whether implicitly or explicitly, accompanies the researched accounts of the past. Louis Blanc saw this endless task of history rise before him in his already lengthy footnotes. The thought of having to take on all of Michelet's excessive injustices, much less Lamartine's, made his head swim: "we do not have enough space . . . ; it is a mountain of errors to lift up."[10] Blanc's twelve volumes begin to seem like the epitome of efficiency and discipline, or even represssion.[11]

9. Etienne Cabet, *Histoire populaire de la Révolution française*, 4:136.

10. Louis Blanc, *Histoire de la Révolution française*, 12 vols. (Paris: Langlois et Leclerq, 1847), 7:214, 216.

11. The apparatus of the *hors-texte*, especially the preface and footnotes, has its own history. In these Romantic texts, the footnotes serve as overflow for the text or for the internecine quarrels. The modern, scientific footnote has yet to be perfected. In *Les origines de la France contemporaine* (Paris: Hachette, 1906), 5:13–14, Hippolyte Taine appears to use a more modern form of footnote, except that he includes Flaubert's novel *L'éducation sentimentale* along with his archival references. The footnote developed a textual space that mimes the outside to which the text refers. It provides an apparent link between the past reality and the text, covering over that slippage from nondiscursive practice into discourse. By placing the text in relationship to its "references," the notes represent the referentiality of the historical text. For a discussion of this connection between "references" and referentiality, see Stephen Bann, *The Clothing of Clio: A Study of the Representation of History in Nineteenth-Century Britain and France* (Cambridge: Cambridge UP, 1984), 32–53, and Linda Orr's review essay in *History and Theory* 24 (1985):307–25.

The symbolic space of sociohistorical[12] truth, however, cannot be judged by historians alone, among themselves: this unspoken rule was something all who wrote history in the nineteenth century understood. Such a judgment would close the circuit of truth in an absolute self-referentiality whose legitimacy is doubtful. Nineteenth-century historians conceive of what was lacking in their authority by means of the postrevolutionary terms of their own society. Everything depended on the reader, who occupied the same position in historiography as the people in democratic society. Authority came first and last from the popular reader, defined no less paradoxically than that enigma, *le peuple*. Michelet illustrates the steps of the formula: first, I am not an author, a writer-intellectual, but a man of the people. *Le peuple, c'est moi.* Therefore, the people are writing my history book. Vigny, not so aloof from the competition as he seemed, has the ready aphorism for the new theory of history in his preface to *Cinq-Mars*: "History is a novel of which the people are the author."[13]

If the people read your book, that very act proves that the people have written it. The historian or writer embeds a narratee in the text along with the narrator, or at least the metaphorical space for a reader who cannot be held by that narration. Just like the people, the reader by definition cannot be represented — unless, as some would say, by the impossibility of representation, political and linguistic. Michelet kept trying all of his life to write popular books, *Le peuple*, the naturalist reveries, *L'amour*, and he sometimes included in this group the *Histoire de la Révolution française*. His competition is not "cold history," he knows, but the novels of Balzac and Sand (the tradition of Walter Scott).[14] Michelet aspires to the audience of *La femme de trente ans*. But Michelet's *oeuvre* remains split between the upper bourgeois male reader of his history books and the (female?) reader of his books that sold for Fr3.50. I suspect that Michelet was worried most about competition in (warm) history from Thiers, Lamartine, and Blanc because all three came out with cheaper installment editions in 1865 — and no one could beat the number of editions in which Lamartine's and Thiers's

12. See the nuance of the term *socio-historique* in Cornelius Castoriadis, *L'institution imaginaire de la société* (Paris: Seuil, 1975), 148.

13. Alfred de Vigny, "Réflexions sur la vérité dans l'art," *Cinq-Mars, Oeuvres complètes* (Paris: Gallimard, 1948), 2:22.

14. See Linda Orr, introduction to Michelet's *La montagne, Oeuvres complètes*, 20:65–66.

work appeared.[15] As Michelet wrote in *Le peuple*, "the people ... are difficult to find in the people,"[16] that is to say, any literal translation of that symbolic spot was destined to fail. The very moment someone takes on the name of the people, that usurpation is a sure sign that the people have been lost to the cause. If too literal, the reader too no longer fills that legitimizing metaphor of sociohistorical practice.

It is important to understand all that is at stake in this notion, by now overused, of the people, who, as Claude Lefort writes, refining Furet's ideas, can only be represented through the symbolic system of language (if they can be represented at all):

> Power emigrates from a position both fixed, determined and hidden, which it held under the Monarchy, into a position paradoxically unstable, undetermined, which only shows up in the incessant workings of its enunciation; it is detached from the king's body in which society's central organs were located so it can then join the impalpable, universal, and essentially public element of the word. A fundamental change which marks the birth of ideology. Certainly using words, modeled after the founding word, had always been linked to the use of power, but where the language of power reigns, there comes to reign the power of language.[17]

15. The same Romantic authors wanted to be read by scholars, by the growing bourgeoisie (who could afford the more expensive octavo sets of books), and by a less affluent class of petits bourgeois, who either went to the *cabinets de lecture* to read or purchased the inexpensive but sometimes ultimately costly installments or *livraisons* — brilliant marketing idea of the publishers. Maybe among these were artisans of the working class —those highly literate workers, of whom we know very little, who wrote poems or prose narratives. In order to appeal to this commercial version of *le peuple*, history books had to look like that bible of the people, the republican almanac (about 50c.). Or at least the *livraisons* resembled the form of the *feuilleton*, so popular in the new, more widely distributed press of the time. History was its own serial, extracted from a magazine. (For the example of Lamartine, see Fabienne Reboul, "Histoire ou feuilleton? La Révolution française vue par Lamartine," *Romantisme* 52 [1986]:19–33.)

Talvert and Place illustrate in their study of Lamartine's editions why he was the most popular of all. *Histoire des Girondins* was published first in March 1847 by Furne in the eight-volume edition at five francs a volume (Fr. 40 total). But in May the first of 100 *livraisons* appeared at 50 centimes apiece. Daniel Stern (pen name for Marie de Flavigny, comtesse d'Agoult) is supposed to have said that working-class families had their *Histoire des Girondins* next to Cabet's *Voyage en Icarie*. (For a comparison of formats and prices, see Appendix: Publication Figures.)

16. Jules Michelet, *Le peuple*, ed. Paul Viallaneix (Paris: Flammarion, 1974), 186.

17. Claude Lefort, "Penser la révolution dans la Révolution française," rev. of Furet, *Penser la Révolution française, Essais sur le politique (XIXe–XXe siècles)*, 134. Rpt. of "Pensons la Révolution française," *Annales Economies Sociétés Civilisations* (March–April 1980): 334–52.

We could debate with Lefort's binary opposition—the stable position
of the body versus the unstable position of language—and even with his
desire to historicize a philosophical and linguistic problem. But who
knows? Perhaps we can reflect upon literary questions only in a dialectic
or on a kind of Möbius strip with questions of history and society, all
inseparable from each other. Can we talk about figurative language and
intertextualities without both the concepts and realities of revolution
and public opinion—and vice versa?

In spite of his preponderant *I*, the author-Michelet never comes to
identify himself with the narrator or with the narratee. The one who
best develops the writer-reader symbiosis—the slyest or most instinctive
of all? — Lamartine, in part owing to his market-wise editor Gosselin,
finds the scheme needed to take advantage of the situation. An erotico-
political glue — definition of Romantic text and society — fuses writer
and narrator, narrator and narratee, narratee and reader, enunciation
and story, and then story and History. In the poem "Ischia," the narratee
is the pronoun *tu*, referring to different images of saccharine virgins à la
Lamartine (as opposed to the virgin-meat of Michelet). The I-narrator,
also ambiguous because he is both seductive and virginal, falls at her
feet in a swoon. At last this narratee takes on a name. It is the name of
Lamartine's wife, *Elyse*, which rhymes with *élysées*, paradise of the
gods, the *Champs Elysées*. The name suggests an outrageous pun — to
which I'll add the future seat of the French president, the Elysée Palace.
Elyse could be a form of the verb *élire*, to elect, as in "qu'on m'élise" (let
them elect me, if only you would elect me). *Elire* also adds a prefix to the
verb *lire* so that reading is already a major step toward election (*Elyse et
moi, élisez-moi, et lisez-moi*).

Matrix of the poem and base of its authority, the subliminal syllables,
the word *Elyse*, repeating like the wash of waves in the moonlight, whis-
pers to the couple, poet and lover, writer and reader, till they merge into
that one sound, more breath and music than meaning. The couple, including us now, all subsumed under the one proper name, turns into the
verb, the actual performance of the communal act of unity, intimate and
public, reading and voting. It is all one. In his poem, a popular Book-of-
the-Month Club selection, Lamartine urges you to vote in the next election for him as president.

Unexpectedly, Michelet of all people comes up with an entirely different relationship to the reader in one particular passage of the preface.

Instead of being involved, even fused with the reader, he separates himself and becomes the ironic observer of the reception of his text. In a sober, almost chilling passage, he writes from a perspective—author of his author, though never becoming a meta-author—through which even his beloved Church seems irrelevant: "If some of us tear into each other [*s'acharnent*] during these debates, on the other hand, a great France, born in '48, half a million men, who read, think, and are the future, regard all this as a curious thing, but outside of all interest, under circumstances that are completely different" (1:10).

This latest (last?) in a line of readers—the people, the reader-people, and finally the future reader-people—also has to be paradoxically conceived as both literal and figurative, represented and unrepresentable; ironic, in short. This double reader keeps interrupting its own representations, misinterpreting here and there, and worse, changing the conditions of interpretation such that notions like progress, consensus, cause and effect, realism, even representability and readability dissipate in a preface that must also set these same standards up as law, so that the text can proceed from there. It is hard to imagine how anybody could write such a text, but the Romantic historians did. On the other hand, it is hard to imagine how anybody, including modern social scientists, could write any differently.

IV The Freedom and Terror of Unknowable History: A Reading of Tocqueville

L'Ancien Régime et la Révolution (1856) is a classic in the different disciplines of history, literature, sociology, and political philosophy.[1] It immediately stands apart from its Romantic contemporaries because of its short length and its analytical chapters: "Why feudal rights became odious ... ," "How almost all Europe had the same institutions. ... "

1. Although one of the major books on Tocqueville is Richard Herr's *Tocqueville and the Old Regime* (Princeton: Princeton UP, 1962), most of American writing on Tocqueville is from the point of view of political philosophy and sociology: Louis Hartz, *The Liberal Tradition in America: An Interpretation of American Political Thought since the Revolution* (New York: Harcourt, Brace, 1955), Jack Lively, *The Social and Political Thought of Alexis de Tocqueville* (Oxford: Clarendon, 1962), Robert A. Nisbet, *The Sociological Tradition* (New York: Basic Books, 1966), Gianfranco Poggi, *Images of Society: Essays on the Sociological Theories of Tocqueville, Marx, and Durkheim* (Stanford: Stanford UP, 1972), and Marvin Zetterbaum, *Tocqueville and the Problem of Democracy* (Stanford: Standford UP, 1967); also his article in Leo Strauss and Joseph Cropsey's *History of Political Philosophy* (Chicago: Rand McNally, 1963), 657–78. Seymour Drescher, *Dilemmas of Democracy: Tocqueville and Modernization* (Pittsburgh: U of Pittsburgh P, 1968), relates Tocqueville's work to the institutions and mentalities of his society. Hayden White's chapter in *Metahistory: The Historical Imagination in Nineteenth-Century Europe* (1973) breaks with these general tendencies that explain Tocqueville's content; White brings out formal tensions without regard for intentionality. Irving Zeitlin's *Liberty, Equality, and Revolution in Alexis de Tocqueville* (Boston: Little, Brown, 1971) should be compared to Claude Lefort's close reading of *De la démocratie en Amérique* in *Essais*. Raymond Aron, *Les étapes de la pensée sociologique: Montesquieu, Comte, Marx, Tocqueville, Durkheim, Pareto, Weber* (Paris: Gallimard, 1967), has been especially influential in the United States. Though it is impossible to avoid the ideological implications of Tocqueville studies, it is hoped that they will not predetermine a rereading of his text.

But it shares with them a deeply contradictory discourse on the possibility of historical knowledge, and it resorts to a similar rhetoric for its own subtle self-defense. Tocqueville's text is full of wildly imaginative moments and ideological passion. The usual three chronological periods —Middle Ages, Old Regime, and Revolution—do not ostensibly order his history. They do, however, jostle just beneath the surface. In fact, Tocqueville's history is also obsessed with how one can order history in the first place, what separates out periods, and whether historical periods can ever be seen or read in such a clear order. What astounds me the most in this book, so commonly read and used even for a textbook, is how difficult it is. When I sat down and tried to make sense of some of Tocqueville's incredible sentences, my head started to spin.

THE INCOMPREHENSIBLE BEGINNINGS OF HISTORY

Tocqueville's avant-propos to *L'Ancien Régime* is an unabashed discourse of lucidity and revelation, concluding with that curious mixture of prophecy and martyrdom ("I alone saw . . . ") one usually associates with Michelet's preface to the *Histoire de France* or even with Nietzsche's *Ecce Homo*. The first chapter, on the other hand, echoes the modesty it advocates: "No great historical event is better calculated than the French Revolution to remind political writers and statesmen to be modest in their speculations."[2] This chapter develops the thematics of obligatory obscurity, which Tocqueville's own text, however, would seem to escape. The usual repetitions of the word *véritable*, a necessary strategy of the historian's rhetoric, mark the penultimate paragraph of the first chapter. But are Tocqueville's questions that lead to his answers —"What was its true significance, its real nature, and what were the permanent effects of this strange and terrifying revolution?"(4)—so different from Louis Blanc's subtitles: "True character of these events," "True meaning of this intervention," "The truth of this"?

After reading Tocqueville's forgotten contemporaries, one takes the rhetoric of truth not only with a grain of salt but as a sign that there is

2. Alexis de Tocqueville, *Oeuvres complètes,* ed. J.-P. Mayer (Paris: Gallimard, 1952), vol. 2, 1:79. Subsequent references to this work will be in the text. For longer passages, a reference will also be given to the English translation by Stuart Gilbert, *The Old Regime and the French Revolution* (New York: Doubleday, 1955). However, except in rare instances, Susan Weiner and I did not use Gilbert's translation, because it is not literal enough for close readings and in particular neutralizes Tocqueville's metaphors.

more going on in this canonized text than meets the eye. The last paragraph of the first chapter both reestablishes and complicates the
outlandish claims that precede it:

> It seems that the moment to research and say it [this true sense] has
> come, and that we are situated today at the precise point where one can
> better perceive and judge this great object. Far enough from the Revolu-
> tion to barely feel the passions which disturbed the view of those who
> made it, we are close enough to be able to enter into the spirit which
> brought it on and to understand it. Soon we will not be able to do this,
> since the great revolutions that succeed, making the causes that produced
> them disappear, thus become incomprehensible as a result of their suc-
> cess. (81–2; see Eng. 4–5)

The timing of true history is based on a kind of double *chairos*: "The
moment . . . has come," when the historian is at "the precise point where
one can better perceive." Historical subject and object are held suspended in just the right relationship for a moment; it is not a matter of
finding a stable vantage point, for the coincidence is temporary, like an
eclipse of the sun. The historian supposedly stands just far enough away
from the volatile object and yet not too far, at the edgy transition where
the passion that comes from being too close curves into analysis before
the desire and need for knowledge fade away and are forgotten. Instead
of achieving a proper separation from the historical object, the historian
is involved in the process that keeps creating both the object of observation and the historian as observer.

Two points simultaneously constitute themselves: one becomes the
"point of view" and the other the object. One does not exist without the
other, nor are they thinkable outside of this rhetorical act of comparison. This instance of comparison is another example of mutual self-constitution. Neither identical nor different, the points so constituted hold
within themselves the inevitable teleological system (of time and science)
and—here it comes again—open a space for history. In the way in which
the differentials of a signifying chain designate a signified in terms of a
signifier and vice versa, so that sense can proceed from there, the two
points can be named a *present* and a *past*. Then, like a sharpshooter lining up the points of aim, a third point is required, and a fourth, and so
on, so that the *arche-* and *telos* multiply ad infinitum in the same stabilized order. The third term might be called *future,* or one can say that a
desired future calls up from the present a desired past as history; or that

a past projected toward a future gives a notion of where one stands in the obscurity of the present. Et cetera. This basic duplicity of the system is what Tocqueville is trying somehow to describe. It is hard, however, to know what to name this duplicity: the self-constitution of the society of the *énonciation* (the time of the historical subject, the writer) and the society of the *énoncé* (the time of the historical object)?[3] Metalepsis and prolepsis? Allegory? Simply the double implied in figure itself? Actually separating the points to such an extent as to name them, as oppositions (*énonciation/énoncé*) or as "sides" of the sign, is to falsify their delicate relationship—as if they are both always on the edge of being confused and yet are mutually exclusive, unthinkable together.

The last sentence in the last paragraph of the first chapter, already quoted, does more than contradict the perfect alignment of two points from which unfolds the rhetoric of historical optics and objectivity;[4] it renders that rhetoric inoperable, by substituting another definition of history. "Soon it will be very difficult" to write the history of the Revolution, because, one assumes, the events will have faded away from memory, but on the contrary: "the great revolutions that succeed" have to prove that they are radically different from what went before, that they are new as opposed to old. So they have to erase the logical steps they took to gain power, for otherwise they would simply be continuity and not revolution. They deprive themselves, then, of a history, because, once in power, they can stay there only if they go back and make themselves incomprehensible, unrecognizable. A similar paradox from the first page of the avant-propos echoes this notion and becomes a little clearer: "In the end they [the revolutionaries] forgot nothing in order to make themselves unrecognizable" (69). A break in history is a reversal that calls attention to what can no longer be known. And the archetyp-

3. See the entry "Enunciation" in Oswald Ducrot and Tzvetan Todorov, *Encyclopedic Dictionary of the Sciences of Language*, trans. Catherine Porter (Baltimore: The Johns Hopkins UP, 1979), 323–33; *Dictionnaire encyclopédique des sciences du langage* (Paris: Seuil, 1972), 405–410. The *énonciation* (or even Benveniste's "metasemantics") will not serve here as the long-sought point of articulation between the text and history. The *énonciation* is a place where context breaks into the text, but text and history are not separate entities with something like a bridge connecting them. I keep the French because the English translation, more commonly "utterance" or "statement," has no good equivalent for *énoncé*.

4. It is hard to avoid metaphors of visual perception when discussing epistemology, although they are part of the problem. We expect the real to be visible, not just "intelligible." See Barthes, "Historical Discourse," 155.

ical break of history is the one between the Old Regime and the Revolution.

Rather than teleological stages, history superimposes one incomprehensible revolution upon another (which is not to say "one damn thing after another"). When Tocqueville set out to write his history all he saw was the Revolution, because the revolutionaries had supposedly obscured the rest. And the history in between Tocqueville and the Revolution, Jacobin-Romantic history, only duplicates the original opaque Jacobins (Furet). Tocqueville started, then, either in the void or the blockage of this totalizing *imaginaire*: "The radical revolution which separates us [from the Old Regime] produced the effect of centuries: it obscured everything that it did not destroy" (102). One can continue the argument by saying that Tocqueville's history, by necessity, had to be written within the revolutionary *imaginaire*. First he has to pretend that the Revolution is not there, that it did not destroy all that led up to it. In the process of doing so, he takes a step backward. But then what he has is the Old Regime or centralized monarchy, that succeeded as well by erasing how it got there (destroying charters between king and people, the self-rule of cities, the Middle Ages). Et cetera. History would then be as much a regressive obscuring as a progressive elucidation, and one would never have the end of Jacobin discourse, whose latest practitioner would be Tocqueville himself.

At the very least, these repressive layers create an impression of depth that we associate with history. Knowability is an illusion or, more precisely, rhetorical effect produced by the historical text. Tocqueville figures out a couple of tricks by which the historical text makes the reader think he or she knows directly the historical object: "We imagine we know all about the French society of that period, because we clearly see what was shining on its surface, because we have in our possession the history of the most famous characters who lived then down to the last detail, and because ingenious or eloquent critics managed to make familiar to us the works of the great writers who illustrated it [that history]" (69–70; see Eng. vii–viii). It is not just that we do not know the historical object or that we have been stunned by brilliant historical writing. We do not even read the great histories (Michelet, Tocqueville). Instead, we think we know history because we are familiar with certain quotations, clichés, passages, dates and facts that have been handed down without explanation, in anthologies of the critical literature.

Our knowledge amounts to a few bright pictures, illustrations, *images d'Epinal*.

The revolutionaries did not, therefore, become unrecognizable simply because they stripped away the past, but because they did not leave even their effaced traces, the trace of no-traces, but effaced their effacement by filling in their own brilliant version of the story. The more clearly, brightly, history is written, the more blinding it becomes, so that nothing behind the convincing depth of surface is imaginable, for one does not feel its lack. This constant replacement of the surface would seem to complicate the notion that revolutionary (Jacobin) historiography represents the Revolution as rupture, whereas Restoration historiography, whose tradition Tocqueville extends and twists, seeks to re-establish the continuity of French history. It should rather be said that any history operates by both radical unrecognizability and a complete refamiliarization; it is at the same time disjointedness and re-identity. If for the Russian and French formalists metaphor could be defined in terms of defamiliarization and the consequent necessity for refamiliarization, such a process, informative for thinking history as well, might be reformulated without the "historical" prejudice. That is to say, the defamiliarization does not necessarily precede refamiliarization: though mutually exclusive, both must take place simultaneously. But, although Tocqueville introduces the concepts of the unrecognizable or unfamiliar into the study of history, he prefers, for the success of his own history book, to underplay those difficulties in favor of the familiar, the re-knowable: "My intention is ... to trace this long revolution through its vicissitudes, to trace these same Frenchmen with whom I have just lived on such familiar terms under the old regime ... to see them modifying and transforming themselves along with the events, without however changing their nature, and constantly reappearing before us with a physiognomy that is slightly different, but always recognizable" (72; see Eng. x).

Tocqueville eventually substitutes his familiarity for the Revolution's, his history for Jacobin history. He clears the way for his interpretation by undermining the strategies of his competitors, but he does not, for obvious reasons, imply that his strategies will be similar.

But the discourse of the objective, knowable truth seems (always?) to generate a rather surprising and self-contradictory portrait of the historian-at-work, which would suggest that the first impression is perhaps

not sufficient. Tocqueville's avant-propos develops the troubling caricature of the (archetypical) historian (reminiscent again of Michelet, instead of the analytical Tocqueville) who, once on the search for truth,
cannot rest assured with the visible, knowable object (and perceiving
subject) but must accompany it, support it, motivate it once again by the
thematics of the descent into history's Hell and complicity with the entire social machinery of panoptic erotics.

The task of history that emerges from the avant-propos is ambiguous: on the one hand, the Revolution is an ideological block as heavy as
a tomb to overturn, where one collects the testament of the dead; on the
other hand, the tomb is a fake, a flimsy veil to be lifted, revealing a sleeping beauty who still lives and waits to reveal her secrets for the first time
in history. First, however, the historian must repress the present and take
on an Orpheus-Aeneas role: "In order to get a true understanding of
both the Revolution and its results, one has to forget for a moment the
France that we see, and go back and question [*interroger*] the France
which is in its tomb and no longer exists" (69). The historian then feels
pride (as usual) at having the very documents that transcribe the voice
of the times, authentic because it is dying. For Michelet it was the record
of the Sections, for Tocqueville the *cahiers de doléance*: "the last will
and testament of the old French society, the supreme expression of its
desires, the authentic demonstration of its final requests" (70). But
Tocqueville's vocabulary already begins to compromise the historian,
because, as he openly admits, he is privileged to be able to spy on his
object: "One was not afraid to let himself see all the way to the most
secret debilities [*infirmités*]" (71). There's something as sexual about
these exposed infirmities as the ones in Michelet's *Sorcière*. "Infirmities" was the euphemism that described the little wounds Father Girard
inflicted on the body of the unconscious LaCarrière, which he could
then discover as examples of her diabolical possession. Michelet, terrified by his own complicity with the priest-scribes of history, disclosed by
his very nervousness the inevitability of such complicity. Tocqueville (as
nervously?) recognized the advantages of using records from the Min-
istry of the Interior and central administration: "There are few interests
or passions that do not come to show themselves sooner or later, nude,
before it [*l'administration publique*]" (70). A disguised version of
(Barthes's) Michelet's lesbianism, and Foucault's panopticon, "Tocque-

ville" (any historian?) becomes automatically the voyeur of the State-Voyeur; this intimate vantage point alone secures whatever "sincerity" there is: "Every man freely spoke there and let his most intimate thoughts be known [*pénétrer*]. Thus I managed to acquire many notions of the old society that my contemporaries did not have" (71). The historian occupies, therefore, a position of double superiority. But his identity necessarily waffles between these two extremes: either he collaborates with the police state, going one better, or he repeats, commemorates the confusion of blinded Jacobin discourse (another police state). In this way the portrait of the professional historian ("le statut et le lieu de son énonciation")[5] already inscribes the ambiguity of the basic question the historical quest of *L'Ancien Régime* is meant to solve: "It [the central government] was usually astounded to find dead the people whose lives it had taken" (186). That is, what kind of transition is history anyway? And who or what is behind it?

It is at this point by the end of the avant-propos that Tocqueville, convinced of his own lucidity, promises to try to "entrevoir l'avenir." Here, too, he takes on the tone (later much more moving) of the martyr of liberty: "Several people will perhaps accuse me of showing in this book an unbridled taste for liberty, which people tell me no one really cares about anymore in France" (73). Instead of reading history or sociology, we associate these pleas more readily with the *Souvenirs*, in which Tocqueville begins by saying that no one ever understood (understands) how right he was (is) and ends by admitting that the book was written in order to induce within himself the self-confidence needed to write the book. The avant-propos ends with several direct quotations from *De la démocratie en Amérique* to demonstrate, before going any further, that the subject of this history, the author himself, has a familiar face after all his revolutions. If his own history is comprehensible, so is the history of his Revolution. Authenticity in history would finally seem to be more complicated than a simple prefatory statement of the importance and verification of sources. Tocqueville uses various ploys while pointing out how much historical truth depends on rhetoric, since this truth may be difficult to know.

5. See Michel de Certeau, "L'opération historique," *Faire de l'histoire*, ed. Jacques Le Goff and Pierre Nora (Paris: Gallimard, 1974), 1:3–41.

THE MONOLITH AND THE UNREADABLE REVOLUTION

From the beginning, nevertheless, Tocqueville asserts the modulation of the two "poles" that construct his text: "I confess then that while studying our old society in each one of its parts, I never entirely lost sight of the new one" (73). History demands, so to speak, one eye to *louche*, to be on each point at once, but Tocqueville implies that the object dominates or that the society of the *énoncé* has priority and that the society of the *énonciation* is a point of reference so the historian does not lose his balance (of objectivity). Tocqueville's text would tend, therefore, to privilege realism or metonymy (like Barthes's Thierry),[6] so that the object functions as the signified (*signifié*) and the figure of history is ultimately meaningful. Still, it is the very comparison between the Old Regime and the new society that makes the text of history possible. The Second Empire runs like a shuttle[7] throughout Tocqueville's text. The modern system resembles the old one with something added: "I suddenly saw a glacial body, more compact and homogeneous than any that had perhaps ever been seen in the world before" (143). Or the old system is said to be diminished in terms of the new: "The art of stifling the noise of all resistance was then a lot less perfected than today. France had not yet become the deafened place [*lieu sourd*] where we live" (173). These connections would seem coincidental if the signs of the *énonciation* did not begin to increase in density (especially in chapter 11, book 2, in which one paragraph has, for example, two references to "today" and one to "nowadays.") Comparisons proliferate until a new power, more "compact," "homogeneous," "perfected," and "more extensive, detailed, and absolute" (248) than any former social organization, appears in scattered passages as the end point of the comparisons but nonetheless dominates the textual horizon. "The object, despite its grandeur, was then still invisible in the eyes of the crowd; but little by little time exposed it to all gazes. Today it looms especially in the sight of princes" (86). The telos of Tocqueville's history, invisible at the "beginning," slowly reveals itself until it is right on top of the society of the

6. Barthes, "Historical Discourse," 72. Besides Gossman on Thierry, see also Jacques Neefs, "Augustin Thierry: Le moment de la 'véritable histoire de France,' " *Romantisme* 28 (1980): 289–303; and Pierre Barbéris, *Le prince et le marchand: Idéologiques: La littérature, l'histoire* (Paris: Fayard, 1980).

7. See Geoffrey Hartman, "La voix de la navette," *Poétique* 28 (1976): 398–412. See also Hayden White's use of the term *diatactical* in his introduction, *Tropics of Discourse: Essays in Cultural Criticism* (Baltimore: The Johns Hopkins UP, 1978), 4–5.

énonciation (Napoleon III). The reversal of perspective shrinks the Old Regime as the Empire grows until one feels that the *énonciation*, instead of the *énoncé*, acts as the signified; that meaning is given to the Old Regime only by virtue of this final revelation, without which the essence of the Old Regime would never be seen. The book on the Empire Tocqueville wanted to write but abandoned because Thiers's history preempted it wrote itself anyway, under a pseudotitle. Instead of *L'Ancien Régime et la Révolution* (since the Revolution falls out) one might title Tocqueville's book *Les anciens régimes et les empires*, if not *L'Empire*. The book seems to be an excuse for biting contemporary political critique. Neither imperial nor Restoration historiography, in this way, it is reminiscent of republican-socialist writing. One might suggest again that *L'Ancien Régime* — and *De la démocratie* — are also *Souvenirs*. "The only essential difference between the two eras is this: before the Revolution, the government could not cover for its agents except in resorting to illegal and arbitrary measures, whereas it has since been able to let them violate laws legally" (126). In other words, there was a purely formal difference between the two times, meaning that form differentiated the time.

The point of departure seems, then, to be not the Old-Regime-cum-Revolution but the Second Empire, a kind of 2001 Space Odyssey monolith that makes possible the recognition of, behind it, another shadow of the same (Empire I) and behind that, the Old Regime. Neither organic continuity nor rupture, this history of repetition is based on a teleology of clarity: "Its forms are less defined than today … but it is the same thing. Since them, nothing essential has had to be added or taken away" (127). The end point is not a perfection of the species but the unrecognizable made progressively sharper, made knowable.

History from the point of view of the Empire reverses the initial perspective set up by the "successful Revolution." There was, then, no terrible blockage to be overturned at all; that was all revolutionary rhetoric — which enhanced, however, the prestige of the anti-Jacobin historian who pretended to overturn its tomb. Tocqueville was not writing as a lone eye in the midst of neo-Jacobin blindness; he was necessarily blinded by the successful revolution of the Empire which, by definition, could not let him see the Revolution (of 1848/1830/1793/1789) and perhaps made the brilliant surface of the (Empire's) Old Regime seem like the depth of its own truth. *L'Ancien Régime et la Révolution* illus-

trates the specular displacements of the Second Empire. A history of the
Revolution (a history of anything?) would, then, be impossible except as
the sporadic critique of the Empire within its own *institution imaginaire*.[8]

It would be easy to say that the "only essential difference" between
the "then" (Old Regime) and "now" (Empire) of the text is the Revolution—and this would be true, except that the Revolution would be seen
only as an imperceptible step toward the Empire or the displacement between two historical objects (Old Regime and Empire) that are almost
identical. The Revolution would then be defined as the invisible difference between two similar moments. The metaphor of an empty space
would fit this figure of the Revolution: "Between it [the central power]
and particular individuals, nothing more existed than an immense and
empty space" (135). One might say, in this case, that writing a history
of the Revolution implies evoking that empty space over and over, not
letting it be collapsed by the two sides of resemblance (Old Regime/Em-
pire), keeping the resemblance imperfect enough to make an invisible
displacement almost visible.

But the Revolution was not as pure or clean, not so *propre*, as an absence. *L'Ancien Régime et la Révolution* was written to answer the
question: "What was the particular result [*l'oeuvre propre*] of the
French Revolution?" The book was supposed to characterize the "specific character" (*génie propre*) of the Revolution, "to consider it only in
and of itself" (95). As it turns out, these are the very tasks Tocqueville
cannot do. The Revolution does not disappear, but is incorporated fully
into the Old Regime. It is important to see the difference between this
transference of power and the two competitive histories of the Revolution as either rupture (republican) or continuity (Restoration). Whereas
Restoration histories closed in the gap of the Revolution, passing from
Louis XVI to Louis XVII and Louis XVIII, Tocqueville retains the Revolution, "improperly" united with the Old Regime. This fusion accounts for the frustration and confusion that must accompany any reading of Tocqueville's text: the only combinatory possibility that does not
exist, it seems, is the one expressed by the title. Two distinct terms cannot be read separately as *L'Ancien Régime et la Révolution*: the only
way the title can be read is *L'Ancien Régime* est *la Révolution*. And yet
the whole point of history is to keep the two apart, no easy undertaking,

8. Castoriadis, *L'institution imaginaire de la société.*

for one constantly reads the tautological repetition of either two revolutions or two old regimes.

In the new amalgamated society that Furet calls "centralized-democratic," either one emphasizes the principle of centralization associated with the Old Regime and the Revolution becomes an extension of its predecessor; or one reads the "substance" (84) of the Revolution ("the natural equality of men") back through the Old Regime, so that the latter drops out in favor of a long revolution: "This revolution's only effect was to abolish these political institutions ... which one ordinarily calls feudal, in order to substitute in its place a social and political order at once more uniform and simple, which had the equality of social conditions as a base" (95; see Eng. 19). As a result of this strange logic, the reader comes upon awkward tautological passages: "The Revolution's genius for unification [*génie unitaire*] was already tightly holding this old government that the Revolution was going to topple" (237). The repetition of the word *Revolution*, instead of using a pronoun, suggests that these might be two different revolutions with the same name. As a last hope for sense, Tocqueville himself (and readers thereafter) speaks of several "first" and "second" revolutions, meaning, not the republican pure-Revolution of 1789 followed by 1793, but growing centralization in Paris or the reorganization of the public adminstration (1787) as the first moment of important change, followed by the Revolution itself. This structural realignment smoothes over the accepted abyss of 1789 between Old Regime and new and promotes Tocqueville's own historical thesis, the Revolution as continuity.

So intricately related are the Old Regime and the Revolution, divisible neither as chronological breaks nor as absences of one another, that a history of the Old Regime would have to double as a history of the Revolution and vice versa. Only one history can be written, not two. Arriving at the end of Tocqueville's *Ancien Régime et la Révolution* is like finishing Proust's *A la recherche du temps perdu*: Proust's narrator says that he is finally ready to write the book the reader has just completed. In the same way, Tocqueville's reader realizes at the end that the Revolution has indirectly already been explained, though chronologically its history is just being promised. Since a direct or proper (*propre*) history of the Revolution is impossible, the only possible one, though improper, inauthentic, is none other than the repetition of the history of the Old Regime that has just been written. Not that Tocqueville's death was timely because he could not write his history of the French Revolution, but he would have written either an equally duplicitous text called *La Révolution (L'Ancien Régime)* or the narrative supplement of seven to twelve volumes that his republican brothers kept producing, like obsessions.

Finally, it does not matter so much whether Tocqueville speaks about the Old Regime or the Revolution; what matters is the formulaic relationship that emerges: "The Revolution created this new power, or rather, this power arose as if from itself [*est sortie comme d'elle-même*] from the ruin that the Revolution made" (85). If one continues to try to make logical-historical sense of this sentence, one fails to see the dynamic at work in Tocqueville's text, for can something emerge as from itself after having destroyed itself? It would be a constantly suicidal phoenix. But this phrase *X est sortie comme d'elle-même* both opens the book, included in the avant-propos, and closes it, as the title of the last chapter. If Tocqueville's sociocultural dynamic has been hard to name, if it has been as convincingly read by both (diachrony) historians and (synchrony) sociologists, it may have something to do with this enigmatic definition. That the text stumbles on language at this point is both a coincidence and not; the Old Regime is the "sign" of the Revolution, which, in turn, is the sign of the Old Regime:

> If I am asked how this portion of the old regime was able to be transferred in one whole piece and incorporated into the new society, I will answer that, if centralization did not perish in the Revolution, this is because it was itself the beginning and the sign of this revolution; and I will add that, when a people has destroyed inside itself the aristocracy, it rushes toward centralization as if by itself [*comme de lui-même*]. Much less effort, then, is needed to push a people in this direction than to keep it in place. Within them all powers naturally tend toward unity, and it is only with much skill that one can manage to keep the people divided.
>
> The democratic revolution, which has destroyed so many of the old regime's institutions, thus had to consolidate this one, and centralization found its place so naturally in the society formed by this revolution that one was easily able to take it for one of the revolution's results. (129; see Eng. 60)

Trying to reconstruct the figures of passage in this text is not easy. Centralization, which is hardly remarked among the other institutions of the Old Regime that fall with feudalism, is transported "in one whole piece" into the body of the Revolution that gives it a solid form. The Revolution does not add anything but consolidates what was shapeless and liquid. And the giving of solid form gives as well the effect of naturalness, of cause and effect. What is troubling is that, just before the solidification, the social stabilizer or the aristocracy was destroyed, creating a runoff, down a slope, where everything comes to a center and is alike. Though centralization appears to be the effect of the Revolution, it is hard, in turn, to say that it should be read as the reverse, as the cause of the Revolution. Invisible, without solid form, centralization is called a *sign*, almost, it seems, as a safer, more neutral term for *cause*. It would be possible to read *sign* as meaning prefiguration or portent of the readable sense to come, except that the Revolution will, in turn, be read solely in terms of that other sign of itself. *Comme de lui-même* midway in the passage complicates the transition by using the formulaic figure that usually describes the Revolution's emergence from itself, by transferring that figure to another object, and by suggesting that it can be generalized. "The Revolution arose as if from itself" implies that it emerged as from itself, but not really. The same expression, transferred to the people who are moving toward centralization, something like themselves, disrupts the other "pole" of movement, the arrival as well as the departure. The phrase "Il court vers la centralisation comme de lui-même" is more ambiguous than "sortie comme d'elle-même," for do the people run toward centralization as of their own accord, as if toward something made of their same substance, or as if away from themselves? Finally, all one can say is that something emerges from something like itself, but not itself, and runs toward something like itself, but not itself, in fact perhaps in opposition to itself. No wonder, then, (optical) rhetorical illusions of reversed cause and effect happen; the wonder is that we do not wonder whether that reversal is the rule, rather than the exception.

At this point, I could shift the definition of the dynamic of history, this figure of history, by saying that it paraphrases as well the definition of figurative language. Words or morphemes can be defined only in relation to one another through the rhetorical structure of comparison. And because comparison never completes itself, never stops in literal meaning, language constantly deals in figures. The way we talk about history —the people, societies, historical periods, similarities and differences— is also the way we talk about language. But having said that, the same questions start over again. The most one can say is that this movement forced on language by comparison, if that concept is magnified to an incredible degree, becomes an image of time. Time is an effect of language we organize into history. This integral participation of language does not rule out the process in which reference and linguistic signs, sticky reality and text, constantly turn one into the other.

What is left is to work back up to facts with this linguistic twist as both an undermining and the ground that fixes history. Is figure metaphor or metonymy, a casual coincidence or a causal link?[9] Or is it the impossibility of proposing links at all? A double that will never decide which it is? And we think we can find out by consulting authoritative texts in a historical tradition (Fontanier, Nietzsche). One is stating no more than a truism, another tautology, by saying that history, not meta-history, speaking always about itself, speaks (figurative) language and that language trying to figure itself out does no more than tell a history. Again this does not mean that either has priority, and that the semiotician has a last word over the historian. One might say that language is related to history as the Old Regime is related to the Revolution.

OUTSIDE THE EMPIRE? THE LITTLE CONSTITUTIONS

If the real opposition cannot be located between *L'Ancien Régime et la Révolution* but in some kind of diabolical dialectic, Tocqueville's history has a chance to set itself right by displacing the traditional break. For ideological reasons, Tocqueville chases it from the Revolution to have it reappear, for reasons of intelligibility, between the feudal period and the Old Regime. This binary, defined, for instance, by Furet as "the nobility's caste spirit" and "democratic individualism,"[10] retrieves, if one looks solely at content, the possibility of reconstructing a readable history. But the binary is strange since the term represented by the Old Regime-(Revolution)-Empires expands with hardly any opposition that the remains of a dying aristocratic caste, or a lost feudal world, might mount. It is, rather, the possibility of an alternative sociopolitical organization that Tocqueville evokes, in contrast to the Empires, with a proliferation of old constitutions (lower case *c*) associated with (Burke's) common law. One might call this alternative organization a theory of

9. See, for instance, Genette, "La rhétorique restreinte" and "Métonymie chez Proust," *Figures III*, and de Man, *Allegories of Reading*, ch. 3.

10. Furet, *Interpreting the French Revolution*, 156; *Penser la Révolution française*, 203.

the organic body of the law, opposed to the superimposed, abstract "machine"[11] of rules. The imperceptible confrontation of the two social systems tells, then, another story that mimes its object in the disparate, figurative manner of its presentation. *L'Ancien Régime et la Révolution* may have been the only way Tocqueville could have written a celebratory *History of the Old Constitutions.*

It is possible, just as the history of Revolution was written as absence, that the history of the old constitutions is written as the limit, both theoretical and historical, of this monolithic state that keeps expanding. But the Empire-(Old-Regime-Revolution) cannot do without its limits, for it needs some point of comparison, some difference, in order to see and write its own history. And that difference even goes so far as to suggest the distance that appears like objectivity, that breaks down into cause and effect.

Naming the binary terms of opposition is less urgent here than asking whether opposition is possible against or from within the over-centralized power. Tocqueville analyzes the way in which the Old Regime usurps custom and "supplants" the organic, but somehow he catches what escapes the slide into the homogeneous society: those old constitutions, ambiguous, nevertheless, in his text. One might even say that such a possibility reflects upon a "terror" that is working itself out figuratively in the text, although only once, at the end, is the capital *T* employed.

A scattered debate with Burke structures this history of the old constitutions within *L'Ancien Régime et la Révolution*: " 'Or, if it was impossible for you to remember the physiognomy of the constitution of your fathers, why did you not look over here? Here you would have found European common law of the past.' Burke did not see that what was in front of him was a revolution which had to abolish precisely this former [*ancienne*] common law of Europe; he does not realize at all that this is exactly what is going on, and nothing else" (96; see Eng. 21). The special emphasis of "this is exactly what is going on" makes one wonder what Tocqueville means here. First Tocqueville seems to be saying that Burke's advice to the French was beside the point. The revolutionaries were not interested in finding either their own French common-law tra-

11. Tocqueville refers to the Old Regime as a machine (165, 214, 222). The expanding monolith of repetition is related to the reading-writing guillotine machines of Jeffrey Mehlman's *Revolution and Repetition.*

dition or someone else's. But maybe Tocqueville goes further by suggesting that the whole purpose of the Revolution was to bring into being a new form of social constitution and to destroy both the history of common law and its very existence as legitimating principle.

The careful suffixing of all feudal politico-sociabilities by the word *constitution* deserves attention in Tocqueville's text. The way the eighteenth-century definition and prestige of the capital *C* Constitution is relegated to a note and used specifically only once contrasts with "revolutionary" histories that traditionally begin with the *Constituante*. This gerund might have been, for Tocqueville, almost a joke, for everything was already constituted by the time a formal Constitution appeared. But upon a closer reading, his text proliferates with constitutions — often *ancienne* (5 times), *vieille* (3), or *antique* (1) — and the word, associated not only with all of Europe or the Church but with each parish and village, extends to include as its object the vaguest of terms (*la constitution du pays*). It appears finally as if everything social that is imaginable has always already been constituted,[12] but perhaps in the (literal? figurative?) sense of the general physical health of a body. When Tocqueville speaks of "the maladies that attacked the constitution of the old regime," he means both the body and the political system. So if the accepted (revolutionary) interpretation of the Revolution determines, for instance, the statement from Littré, "The era of political constitutions opens in 1789,"[13] Tocqueville would have said that 1789 closed that era.

However, in the context of the new constitutional history, Tocqueville can only suggest the lost garden of the law in (under) the house of history. He takes from Burke the theory of common law that was developed in seventeenth-century England. When one examines British his-

12. In the thirteenth century, "to constitute" already meant to establish some kind of community (*s'établir dans une cité*). Then it referred to the act of setting up a whole of which all the parts were necessarily constituent (sixteenth century) and, finally, to the desire to be represented (eighteenth century). Suggesting Rousseau's process of self-constituting societies, it became common to write "L'Assemblée qui se constitue." This warning: *constitute* in juridical and journalistic language "is most often, when not taken in the literal sense of 'to found solidly,' a pompous equivalent of the verb to be." Paul Imbs, *Trésor de la langue française: Dictionnaire de la langue du XIXe et du XXe siècles (1789–1960)* (Paris: Editions du Centre national de la recherche scientifique and Klincksieck, 1971), 6:5–11.

13. Emile Littré, "constitution," *Dictionnaire de la langue française* (Paris: Pauvert, 1956), 2:730. See the *Oxford English Dictionary* for a different ideological perspective on constitutions.

tory more closely, common law does not, in fact, offer the clear alternative to the kind of legitimation practiced by the Old Regime that it is supposed to. Subject to various historical uses and abuses, the common-law tradition proves to be no less ideological, no more timeless and natural, than the Revolution. In the twelfth and thirteenth centuries, common law was royal law, not local institutions, not the thickness of an everyday life, what it becomes in Tocqueville and Burke, and Furet. By the fifteenth century, displaced by statute law, common law, as practiced by the Inns of Court, had defensively developed into "a wonder and a terror to everyone outside the legal fraternity."[14] Artificially revived in the seventeenth century to keep the king from proving original sovereignty and used later to combat the notion of popular sovereignty or to assure the sovereignty of Parliament, common law represented the opposite of what it actually was. The British believed (believe? and what about the Americans?) that common law is a happy coincidence that weathers the test of time and naturally grows up in the habits of the population until, without their noticing, the comfortable custom has become law.

Here is a notable example of this mythic definition from the seventeenth century: "For a Custome taketh beginning and groweth to perfection in this manner: When a reasonable act once done is found to be good and beneficiall to the people, and agreeable to their nature and disposition, then do they use it and practise it again and again, and so by often iteration and multiplication of the act it becometh a *Custome*; and being continued without interruption time out of mind, it obtaineth the force of a *Law*."[15] Already shifting the meaning from common (royal) law to the French term *loi coutumière,* Sir John Davies (1612) describes this perfect identity between *constituant* and *constitué* where a constitution is unthinkable, much less necessary. *Jus non scriptum,* such a permanent constituting/*constituante* has no origin, and consequently there is no possibility of undoing it. Challenging it would again be unthinkable.[16] The law resulting from this confirmation by custom must be not

14. Albert Beebe White, *The Making of the English Constitution, 449–1485,* 2d ed. (London: Putnam, 1925), 235.

15. Quoted in J. G. A. Pocock, *The Ancient Constitution and the Feudal Law: A Study of English Historical Thought in the Seventeenth Century* (Cambridge: Cambridge UP, 1957), 33.

16. See the legal discussions of this complex referent, absent yet present, in both the English and American systems of law: Ronald Dworkin, "Hard Cases," *Harvard Law*

only just but popular. Its paradoxical qualities of being both "in perpetual adjustment" or "unchanging and immemorial"[17] enhanced, by then, its rightness, instead of calling into question the whole reasoning.

Tocqueville adopted the organic, labyrinthian figure of (seventeenth-century) common law (*ces bizarreries des anglais*) but could see it only as fragmented or pushed "below," into the ground, by the neater structure of the new society: "Above real society, whose constitution was still traditional, confused and irregular, where laws remained diverse and contradictory, social ranks clear-cut, conditions fixed and feudal dues unequal, little by little an imaginary society was being built, in which everything seemed simple and ordered, uniform, fair, and conforming to reason" (199; see Eng. 146). The ancient constitutions formed a kind of infrastructure and could be designated as the real, for they looked as natural as the real was supposed to—confusing, irregular, diverse, contradictory, and unreasonable with rigidities and inequalities. Above this "foundation," which is more like a subterranean Id or Hugo's Vendée in *Quatrevingt-treize*, the house of society builds itself like a castle (in the *imaginaire*) where everything is expected to be the opposite of what is lying in disarray below. Not in shame, but rather in martyred pride. For the English believe that the common law kept away (French) despotism,[18] totalitarianism.

Here is where Tocqueville's language becomes possessed by a physiology as gruesome as Michelet's. On the one hand, the political liberty of the ancient constitutions is "stamped with sterility everywhere" (93), nothing but "vain appearances," "a few rags" (116) saved miraculously from the "ravages of time" (93). The old life was "snuffed out completely" (245); it happened almost intransitively, as without an agent or a reason: "One saw local liberties disappear. Everywhere the symptoms of independent life were ceasing; the very features of the physiognomy of different provinces were becoming confused; the last trace of pre-

---

Review 88 (April 1975): 1057–1109; Kent Greenawalt, "The Enduring Significance of Neutral Principles," *Columbia Law Review* 78 (1978): 982–1021.

17. Pocock, *Ancient Constitution*, 235.

18. "Thus England was spared an absolutism nurtured by the legal maxims of Roman Law." Bryce Lyon, *A Constitutional and Legal History of Medieval England* (New York: Harper & Row, 1960), 438. See also Pocock, *Ancient Constitution*: "This is certainly a deplorable attitude, and there is something peculiarly unpleasing about the spectacle of Bolingbroke blotting out vast tracts of human experience as unworthy of serious attention" (246).

vious public life was erased" (140). On the other hand, a violent struggle was in process, but invisible, because there was no confrontation, but rather numerous forms (deformations) of imperceptible "substitution": "The new spirit transforms the government on the inside without changing anything on the outside" (219). Chapter 5 (book 2) studies the insidious replacement of one power for another — "a work of patience, deftness and length of time ... built another structure from underneath [*en sous-oeuvre*]" (127). The most violent images of its consequences are only found scattered in Tocqueville's text, miming the dismembered body, *corps morcelé*, that society mourns. The slow substitutions of chapter 5 are unreadable to society (and history), and so do not meet with complaint: "It [The old regime] had left to the previous powers their old names and honors, but little by little had taken away [*soustrait*] their authority. It had not chased these powers away, but edged them out [*éconduits*] of their domains. Profiting from the inertia of some and the egotism of others in order to take over their places, availing itself of all their vices, never trying to correct them, but only to supersede [*supplanter*] them, it had ended up by replacing almost all of them" (128; see Eng. 58).

None of these apparent forms changes, none of the names, and the change that occurs is ambiguous. Are the tenants led liquidly away (*éconduire*) or dragged out from under where they hide (*soustraire*)? The height of the violence is hardly noticed, because it appears surprisingly early in the book, before one recognizes it for what it is (the text again mimes its object): "A frightful convulsion was needed to destroy and remove at once from the social body a part which was so attached to all its organs" (95). In fact, the aristocracy was far from dead, or even withered or isolated, but "its body was in a way stuck to everything" (96). Only the future can tell if these murdered old constitutions ever did die.

Yet despite the lack of external difference, "almost everything" is replaced; the transformation is complete. As the title of the chapter ("How centralization had been able to insert itself like this in the midst of the old powers and supplant them by destroying them") emphasizes, this change is a perversion of the ideal organic variety, for it gives the effect of being organic, identical to the organs: it plants itself under the present vegetation and works from there, or (using the other metaphor) it replaces like Frankenstein one set of organs with the other. But nothing grows naturally in those parts. The use of the word *supplanter* enacts what is happening in the text of society by trying to translate into organic language another synonym for metaphor (to trans-fer, carry elsewhere). *Supplanter* attempts to naturalize a self-constituting system so as to give it unquestionable legitimacy. And the horror of the situation is that such a transfer can ultimately work a shift in nature so that the body becomes someone else's, or so that the machine becomes the legal body-earth (mother and father).

The point of English common law was to make the two most distant connotations of the word *constitution* correspond in the body of the law. The point of the Old Regime administration was to give the effect of having both seeped down from reason and arisen from the body politic, but neither the figure from above nor the one from below could guarantee habeas corpus. Both figures fit the body they engender.

The distinction begins to break down between body and machine, the underground (garden) and the house, the real and the imaginary, the old constitutions and the Old Regime. The reader is surprised to notice that the (propaganda) description of the administration and *philosophes* as adhering to simple, clear, symmetrical, rational, natural (as in natural rights), transparent, logical values does not correspond to the sinuous practice that emerges. When the peasants take over the language of the *philosophes*, when the house sinks into the subterranean passages that are rising up, the new society looks more like the old constitutions than like itself: "However, the ideas of the time already penetrated these vulgar minds from all sides; they entered there by twisted and subterranean paths, and took strange forms in these narrow and dark places. Still nothing yet appeared changed on the outside" (188; see Eng. 134). Instead of straightening out the irregularities of the old society, the "new" ideas take the same conduits. The process is far from the clean change where a new house is built on a vacant lot. And even farther from the growth to perfection.

The reader forgets, as does history, the origin (according to Tocqueville) of the common law, which then strangely resembled the uniformity of the Old Regime and the new monolith of the Empire: "And yet from the midst of this incoherent mass there arose all of a sudden uniform laws" (91). *Lois uniformes* is the last phrase one would expect in a description of common law. In addition, basing society on custom does not bring about the harmonious society governed by the rule of law, but encourages a kind of unthinking obedience: "But the obedience [of the people] is an effect of custom rather than free will; because if they happen by chance to become emotional, the smallest emotion leads them right to violence, and almost always it is also violence and chance occurrence [*l'arbitraire*], and not the law, which suppresses them" (135; see Eng. 68). When something goes wrong, custom is too vague to stop the arbitrary violence.

Does Tocqueville mean there is a cycle of the same thing: from monolith to labyrinth to monolith, and so forth? And that the common-law constitutions took over using the same superficial coverup as the Old Regime? That there is no such thing as a common law growing like the body of the people itself? That custom or the effect of naturalness (history even) as a value in society's self-constitution is more than deceitful? Custom carries out an insidious destruction in the guise of organic, logical, and happy history. Something is always living there to be supplanted and transformed, which custom obscures and pretends to predate. And when total change imperceptibly occurs, it appears to fit itself smoothly into the existing social space, no matter how many contortions got it there — until another change, using the same strategies, starts to dig away at power again.

Finally one comes to a moment, in the reading of Tocqueville's text, when one establishes a limit of intelligibility or when one reads, as well, a provisional conclusion to the different impossibilities encountered, especially when a history of the old constitutions fails to inscribe the "revolution" Tocqueville means. One might maintain that the old constitutions *habent* the real *corpus* (Furet speaks of the society of corporations), and that the new is an imaginary (symbolic) usurpation of the body — as one can argue that Tocqueville sets history right by opposing one apparent but false change (Revolution) to an unreadable but real change (old constitutions to new society). "This is exactly what is going on. ... " The old must, by definition, have the body; and the new (the impossibility of incarnation, as Michelet called it) constitutes that (symbolico-real) place of struggle where the social body is reborn over and over again. Working from both ends, by the "rigid rules" on top and the "sinuous practice" on the bottom, by the imaginary and real, by the straight and by the perverse, a change introduces itself into the only social space there is where power resides and tries to eradicate that power, always holding on and responding in ever more subtle forms to the endless challenge. Therefore, apparent change is error and illusion, and real change unreadable. That is what terrifies.

After Toqueville repeats the adjective *terrible*, mocks the revolutionaries' view of themselves in chapter one, morphological forms of *terreur* (4 lower-case *t*'s; 2 more *terribles*) return toward the end of the book. Though once referring to the Old Regime *collecteur* or to the power of the *hommes de lettres*, the word usually evokes an effect of the Revolution with the (literal and figurative) Terror behind it as a necessary connotation. Although Furet brings a specificity and completion to the problem of the Terror by supplementing Tocqueville with Cochin and Furet's theory of the revolutionary *symbolique,* the *béance* or figurative slipperiness of Tocqueville's terror is worth preserving — but in organizing my own reading, do I already incorporate too much? *Le propre* of the Terror is not to be read so that, like the Empire, the more it invades history the less of it is noticeable because it appears so natural that nothing about it stands out. Perhaps the subtitle for *L'Ancien Régime et la Révolution* should be *La Terreur.*[19]

Although the tactics of supplanting the organic *symbolique* were displaced with slight variation from the old constitutions, to the Old Regime, and onto the Revolution as Terror, it is true that such a variant, always slighted, meant the difference in capitalizing the *T*. It is not just that the Convention came upon a power vacancy (which is not even certain) nor that it was any less confused or ordered or centralized than its predecessor, nor perhaps that the content of the social (civil administrative) networks switched to the political. It was the twist of the switch that made the difference:

> We shall see what results from the other alternative [to separate, without distinguishing, the power which must execute from the one in charge of surveillance and interdictions], when, transporting administrative procedures into politics, and following the tradition of the old regime, detested though it was, the system practiced in the provincial Estates and small urban municipalities was adopted by the National Convention. Thus what had formerly been no more than an impediment to public affairs suddenly gave rise to the Reign of Terror. (238; see Eng. 195 – 196)

The revolutionaries made two moves that looked relatively simple. First, they reversed the Old Regime's way of organizing the three

---

19. *L'histoire de la Terreur,* by Mortimer-Ternaux, would be published in 1868.

branches of power, executive, legislative, and judicial (*exécuter, prescrire, surveiller*). Whereas the Old Regime joined the three branches but could tell them apart, the Revolution separated them without distinguishing among them. This first move could have just repeated the bungling nature of Old Regime administration. But at the same time, the Revolution moved these functions of government from regional and local bodies to the National Convention. This second move was enough to make the former disorder dangerous. It looked like a simple transfer: "transporting administrative procedures into politics." But this new form of politics, or the realm of the political, was hardly imaginable under the Old Regime. Larger and more complicated than what takes place in the National Convention, it became that locus of symbolic popular struggle. So simply shifting power from one place to another meant creating havoc, a monster: the Terror. The form of Tocqueville's long sentence says as much as the content, maybe more. At the end of sinuous phrasing, as shifty as metaphor, the Terror emerges all of a sudden full-blown.

TERRIFYING LIBERTY

If such a history makes terror possible, it also has an effect on that equally difficult term in Tocqueville: *liberty*. At first it seems that the fate of liberty depends upon the ambiguous fate of the old constitutions; the two plural concepts, always torn and ravaged, mutually evoke one another in *The Old Regime*. At times, the aristocracy is what escapes substitutions: "Nothing could replace it completely; it would never know how to revive itself" (170). And this destiny accompanies liberty as well: "Liberty received a wound that would never heal" (170). But then bizarre resurrections happen, or excesses of the monolith of repetition itself produce a side effect of political guarantee: "It was a kind of irregular and badly constructed dike which divided the force of the central power and slowed down the impact of its shock" (169). But none of these deformed manifestations seems, in the last analysis, linked to what Tocqueville really means by freedom: "But if this kind of unregulated and unwholesome liberty prepared the French to be able to overthrow despotism, it made them less able than perhaps any other people to found in its place the peaceful and free empire of laws" (177; see Eng. 120).

Nevertheless, this "unregulated and unwholesome liberty"—which leads *away from* the desired goal — begins, it too, to proliferate in Tocqueville's text, to a point where one could extract a modern theory of dispersive liberties. The way nothing is really lost (the "aristocracy," the old constitutions), but rejoins the unrecognizable, means that liberty always has the potential for a zombielike return: "On several occasions, from the beginning of the Revolution up to our time, we find the passion for freedom succumbing, then reviving, then succumbing again, and yet again reviving; liberty will continue to do this for a long time, always inexperienced and unruly, superficial and short-lived" (248; see Eng. 209). Not growing from a permanent depth like the common law, liberty is also untried (unex*peri*enced as in unem*pir*ical) and disorderly, unlike the principles of a "new" society. And has it a source? Can it ever root? Can it never grow? "I often wondered from where the source of this passion for political freedom comes ... in what feelings it takes root and grows" (217). Can liberty ever generalize into organic history; or can, for instance, common law generate liberty? Tocqueville can find no "birthplace" for liberty, and suggests finally that its *propre* is to be completely self-referential: "These are its own pleasing qualities, its very charm, independent of its benefits. ... Whoever looks for something else in liberty besides liberty itself is made to serve" (217). After undergoing a transformation, the famous beginning of the fourth chapter of Constant's *Adolphe* reads: Charms of freedom, who could possibly depict you? Or Mallarmé's "Un coup de dés": A move of the empires (Old Regime – Revolution) will never abolish liberty. For no matter how complete and devious repression becomes, it never annihilates liberty.

Since liberty, like terror, is determined by not being dependent or caused or called forth by a reason, it could occur only in such an arbitrary system. And precisely in such a system, over- and under-determined, liberty is terrible. Tocqueville does not predict, as the Jacobin-Romantics seem to do, a second revolution. And yet finally his discourse is not so different from theirs for having tried to inscribe an alternative social figure in history (and therefore not in some utopian space), for having tried to experience liberty.

Tocqueville comes as close as he (anyone) will ever come to writing the figure of the impossible revolution, in the first chapter of *L'Ancien Régime*. He begins by making fun of all the people who neglected to see the Revolution that stood before them. Frederick the Great "does not recognize it at its approach" (79). The English, whose revolutionary fathers should have made the son more recognizable — for they had no trouble seeing the effaced face — "saw clearly, as if through a thick veil, the image of a great revolution advancing; but they cannot make out its form, and the action that it will soon exercise on the world's destiny and on their own is hidden to them" (80). The coalition of enemies fears what never comes: "There is almost nothing they are not prepared for, except what comes" (80). And by the time the Revolution finally arrives, it is the object of (Tocqueville's) parody. He imitates the hyperbole of the original revolutionary discourse as practiced by his Jacobin-Romantic contemporaries: especially the particular use of the Michelet-Hugo words *monstre* and *terrible* (empty *mots de clivage*):

> At the same time as one sees the head of the monster appear, its unique and terrible physiognomy unveil itself, when, after having destroyed political institutions it abolishes civil institutions, after laws changes customs, habits and even the French language; when, after having ruined the structure of the government, it shakes the foundations of society and seems finally to want to fight God himself; when soon this same Revolution overflows outside, with practices unknown until now ... an unheard-of power that breaks down the barriers of empires, smashes crowns, tramples the masses underfoot, and, strange affair [*chose étrange*]! at the same time wins them over to its cause while everything explodes, the point of view changes. What first seemed to the princes and statesmen of Europe like an ordinary accident in the lifetime of a people, appears to be a fact so new, so contrary even to everything which had previously happened in the world, and yet so general, so monstrous, so incomprehensible, that in perceiving it human understanding remains dumbfounded [*demeure comme éperdu*]. (80–81; see Eng. 3–4)

In this, one of the most tortuous and most comical paragraphs of the book, interrupted by the strange, uncharacteristic "*chose étrange!*" Tocqueville is not only miming the way history, always revolutionary, passes from one hyperbole (figure) to another, from one *incompréhensible* to another. He is deconstructing as well the notion of the incomprehensible. He is not only parodying Romantic historiography, but through this language of the other, he is operating his own self-parody. History is *incompréhensible* in proportion to how proud or ashamed the historian feels who has seen nothing. Developments anticipating the Revolution are nowhere to be found in the paragraph, which is, from the beginning, under the influence of a prior reversal and exaggeration. Is the Revolution destroying, abolishing, ruining, shaking foundations, challenging God himself, an unheard-of power? Or is this hyperbolic presentation of the Revolution already the reaction of those people and princes who changed the point of view and produced a Revolution to cover up their blindness, who invented the new, the monstrous, even the general, because, *éperdus*, they needed to explain their *éperdument*?

So what the reader gets is overreaction to the Revolution, instead of the event.

Is Tocqueville's method any more valid? He turns an overreaction into an underreaction. Whereas the others implied that the Revolution was overwhelming, he suggests that it was not all that important. Nothing new happened anyway. Is he covering up his own nervousness about interpreting this complex historical moment?

In the same way that Quinet does not write a theory of abortive history, Tocqueville does not generalize his observations of incomprehensible history. The Revolution inside the Old Regime, the little constitutions inside the empire, liberty inside the Terror, all of these remain viable and potent, though unreadable — maybe because they *are* unreadable. Tocqueville's metaphors, parodies, long sentences, and aphorisms do not add up to a theory of history, although they lead the reader to reflect over and over on the process of making and writing history. "We do not judge events any better up close than farther away" (80). "If by chance they [princes and ministers] speak the truth about it [the Revolution], it is without their knowing [*c'est à leur insu*]" (79). If we — is Tocqueville included in his own "they"? — say something insightful or theoretical about history, we do not know what or where that something is in the history we have written.

V The Blind Spot of History: Writing or Logography

The situation of the logographer's box on August 10, 1792, is one of those typically charged, symbolic moments in Romantic history of the Revolution. It has the advantage of being neither too blatantly symbolic (like the fact that Robespierre is shot in the mouth) nor, at the other extreme, too trivial, however uncanny, like the king's flattened wig or leaves already falling in August. When I was first drawn to the image of the Reporter's-Box, it was partly from a knee-jerk impulse to examine anything that focused on writing per se. But that interest corresponded to a theoretical motivation that steadily clarified itself: stenography is one of our major modern myths about writing history. Then the subject of my chapter took the lead and I became the willing victim of what Paul Veyne calls "pure curiosity for the specific,"[1] a motivation as strong as the desire for truth, if not stronger. Coming upon the self-effacing logographers, I felt the awe one feels on stepping into a quiet corner of rare books that everyone has noticed but no one has entered. I added a self-righteous ideological justification of my own. Historians had all abandoned the ungainly monstrous, monumental histories of the nineteenth century, implying that they were useless, if not silly. Some of these same contemporary historians were off writing social or labor history, even a version of the history of everyday life, as if they had found the place where a proper history would speak at last. They were still pursuing the stenographic myth of history: the coincidence of historical subject and object. No less heroic, I would go back myself—correct them and find the magic they missed.

THE LOGOGRAPHER'S BOX: AUGUST 10, 1792

The Bastille has fallen (July 1789); the women have walked to Versailles, shouting for bread (October 1789); the king has fled to Varennes

1. Paul Veyne, *Comment on écrit l'histoire* (Paris: Seuil, 1971), 63.

(June 1791). The new Legislative Assembly (October 1791), elected after the National Assembly has set up the constitutional monarchy and
bowed out, has an unsuccessful war effort on its hands: the *peuple* are
afraid and want the king where he can no longer betray them so they
march to his palace, the Tuileries, on August 10, 1792. However it happens, some of the people lie slain after shots ring out. Furious, their com-
rades invade, destroying and preserving the furniture, rescuing and kill-
ing the Swiss Guard.

That morning, just before the people arrive at his palace, the king finally agrees to leave and with his family makes his way across the Carrousel to the Salle du Manège, where the Legislative Assembly is in session. His flattened wig suggests that he has slept, despite the danger; it
also reveals how much the king depends upon his coiffure, as well as divine right. The chestnut trees in the Carrousel are prematurely turning
yellow, thus fulfilling the prophecy of the revolutionary Manuel, who
said, "The Royalty won't make it past the autumn leaves."

When the royal party enters the chamber of the Assembly, a man
named Rocher (the names are always perfect) either props the dauphin
on the secretaries' desk to unanimous applause or (depending upon
whom you read) snatches the trembling boy away from his mother to
display him. The king says he has come to avoid a crime and to seek security among the representatives. Vergniaud, president of the Assembly,
says they have sworn to die for the people's rights and the Constitution.
The royal group occupies the spot where the ministers usually sit and
then the king climbs up to take his place beside Vergniaud. His action
causes consternation, because the Constitution forbids the Assembly to
deliberate in the presence of the king. "And so King Louis sat him down,
first here, then there; for a difficulty arose. ... Finally he settles himself
with his Family in the '*Loge* of the *Logographe*,' in the Reporter's-Box
of a Journalist; which is beyond the enchanted Constitutional Circuit,
separated from it by a rail. To such Lodge of the *Logographe*, measuring
some ten feet square, with a small closet at the entrance of it behind, is
the King of broad France now limited."[2]

When Louis XVI moves into this mysterious box, he transgresses perhaps more than when he enters the great hall. History follows Louis off
the usual track to discover, as if by accident, a place that we can well

2. Thomas Carlyle, *The French Revolution: A History* (New York: Colonial Press,
1900), 2:95–96.

imagine having existed but that would ordinarily never come to light, and the indigenous life that works there. It is like scrutinizing an old photograph for someone, caught in the background, who is now more important than the picture's apparent subjects. The king is relegated to a peripheral zone just outside the enchanted circle, and separated from it by a railing: perhaps, in fact, that circle derives its power from this refusal to allow the (evil) presence in its midst. It is as if the king for the first time takes a step into real life, forecasting the days to come. The *loge* could imply an old idea of prestige and security associated with the medieval Church, for nobles reserved their elevated boxes just as they will later do at the opera. Instead, Carlyle emphasizes the absurd contrast between this tiny room and the huge country Louis singly owned. The British historian does not mention the former inhabitants of the *loge*, as will his contemporaries Michelet, Blanc, and especially Lamartine. Michelet mentions, though in passing, the name of the eye witness from whom he got his information about the queen:

> The Assembly designated, therefore, the *loge du logographe*, which was only separated from the room by an iron grating, and was located at the level of the upper rows of the Assembly. The King moved there with his family; he placed himself up front, indifferent, impassive; the Queen, slightly to the side, able to hide in this position the terrible anxiety in which the combat placed her. ... The Queen did not say a word, her lips were closed tight, said an eye-witness (M. David, later consul and député); her eyes were blazing and dry, her cheeks burning, her hands gripped her knees. (1:999)

It is not clear from Michelet what David is doing there, if he is a logographer, guard, or whatever. Even if Michelet disliked history focused on royal individuals, he is not above the usual dramatic Romantic portrait of the queen, that Fury, enemy of the people. Lamartine, who is more drawn to the queen, repeats the same information, at times verbatim, but takes time to notice the inconvenience caused by the king's arrival:

> This *loge*, ten feet square, behind the president, was level with the upper rows of the Assembly. It was separated from the room only by an iron grating sealed into the wall. The king was led there. The young secretaries who took down the speeches in order to reproduce literally the sessions, moved over [*se rangèrent*] a little to make room for the family of Louis XVI. The king sat in the front of the *loge*; the queen, at an angle, in order to veil her face in the shadow of the alcove. (3:187)

A little farther in the text, Lamartine gives more open recognition to M. David, using his description of the king instead of the queen:

> In this very *loge* of the logographer, a man, young at the time, recognized since then for his services, M. David, later consul-general, and deputy, respectfully noted for history the posture, physiognomy, gestures, tears, complexion, breathing and even the involuntary palpitations of the face muscles that the emotions of these long hours imprinted on the features of the royal family.
>
> The king was calm, serene... he ate, drank, tore apart his chicken with as much calm as if he had done so at a gathering after the hunt. (3:189–190)

The logographers could get more of a closeup shot than they must have been used to, contributing not to the humanity of the king, but to his caricature.

Lamartine explains the special nature of the secretaries or journalists who supposedly reproduced "literally" the Assembly sessions. And Blanc, who suggests that they are logotachygraphers instead of logographers, goes into more technical detail about these proto-parliamentary stenographers:

> Behind the president's chair there was a recessed room [*un réduit*] twelve feet square by six feet high, where the journalists usually sat who claimed to have found the means of writing as fast as one speaks. This recess, that an iron grille which was sealed into the wall separated from the hall, is called the lodge of the *Logotachygrapher* [*la loge du Logotachygraphe*].
> ... The lodge of the Logotachygrapher was designated for the king and his family. (1:706)

Although for Blanc the journalists have vanished as if by magic, they are precisely associated with stenography since he uses the cliché found as the subtitle to almost every manual of the "art": the means of writing as fast as one speaks. Blanc's *loge* is two square feet larger than Carlyle's or Lamartine's but it realizes the metaphor Carlyle suggested in opposition to the enchanted circle. A corner or nook, the *réduit* can also refer to a humble, if not poor, dwelling, and the adjective leaves no doubt that like Alice in Wonderland the king must undergo a reduction in size to fit in.

An illustration from a popular edition of Blanc's history gives us the picture suggested by the text, focalized from the point of view of the logographer (David?). The spectator is inside the *loge* with the king, looking out on the turmoil of the Assembly from a kind of window. The atmosphere inside the *loge* is quiet, though tense. At the far left of the engraving a shadow is cast upon the door, slightly ajar; it is certainly that of a guard standing in the hallway, but suggests as well that the angry crowd might penetrate at least that far. Although the royal family occupies the interest of the picture, everywhere there are signs of another absent presence, that of the logographer. Quill pens are left on the "sill," bookshelves line the wall next to the queen (assuming it is Madame Elizabeth who comforts the dauphin on the other side). Stacks of the newspaper *Le logographe* lie in the bottom left corner with one copy open, as if serving as the signature for the entire scene (In fact, the engraver chooses this open page for his own signature). It is as if the contents of the page have been projected as the scene before our eyes. Has the logographer disappeared, leaving metonymic signs in the hope of some remembrance? Or is his perspective so perfectly identified with ours, with that of the historian copying from him, with that of the narration itself, that he always remains invisible?[3] (see fig. 1)

The mystery of this absence animated my research: like wanting to know who "Anon." is.

I hesitated to abandon, in favor of the dubious logographer first, the people storming the palace and, next, the heroes of the Assembly, who finally suspended the monarchy. After all, it was clear from the beginning that he (David) would end up among the bad-guy bourgeoisie: consul-general, deputy. But the impasse reigning in the larger event justifies my treating *it* as the digression, returning shortly to the story of logography. First, though, let me go over once more the strategies that repress or deform popular expression, no matter how repetitive through history. To do so means looking at a history that is centered on the dominant

3. In *La Révolution* (Paris: Hachette, 1965), 1:226–27, François Furet and Denis Richet reproduce Gérard's drawing titled "The Assembly invaded by the crowd which heaps invective on the royal family who has taken refuge in the *loge du logographe*." The petitioners erupt into the space between the secretaries' table or president's desk and the *barre* (not shown); they gesticulate toward the royal family (especially the sneering queen, who alone faces them). The main light, eerie, emanates from the cell (still with bars) in which the family is located.

Figure 1. Le Roi se réfugie au sein de l'Assemblée. (Blanc, 1:705)

symbolic institution of power. The new social, cultural, or labor histories have struggled to get out from under the monolithic and limited vision of political history, so that going back to those overemphasized events appears regressive. The scene of the Assembly is not, then, a historical has-been because it fails to correspond to the fashionable object of history. The parliament serves as a major modern metaphor for social discourse, whether it is studied firsthand in the assemblies or in levels of displacement: the clubs, the sections, the secret societies, the cafés, or the street. A researcher cannot get around "parlia-ment" or social discourse to an "outside," except as the discourse coded as "outside" in terms of that same pervasive state institution. Although almost all of the nineteenth-century historians, especially the republicans, complained about the impotence of the Assembly, revolutionary history could not (then and now) be written otherwise than blocked through that mass, not necessarily corresponding to the other mass of popular unrest. As much can be done by reading with these structures as by pretending that popular society can be isolated from them in a pure form of self-reflection.

The Assembly was the place or operation by which the act of the people, as insurrection, came into being in the act of its representatives, as legislation. We might define this founding, if not slippery, principle of the Revolution as the speech-act of democracy, its political performative. Like the two sides of the linguistic sign, each mutually constitutes the other. The 10th of August, one of the first and most archetypal of these legitimating instances, demonstrates the metaphorical quality of the perfect correspondence required by democracy. The event itself both celebrates and belies the unity of the people and its representation, the fragile discursive coherence of that society. Romantic historiography makes its mark by seizing upon this irony, in horror, analysis, and confusion — which is why it unnerves us.

As fast as society was torn apart, it was implicitly restructured by the Legislative Assembly, through its form as much as through its legislation, by its rules and procedures, even the floor plan of its hall. The raised tribune from where the *tribuns* or deputies spoke (for the benefit of the *tribunes* or galleries as much as their colleagues) was across from the president's desk (behind which sat, unseen, the royal family and logographers). Just under the tribune, at floor level, and across from the president's secretaries (where documents were deposed), was the *barre* to which the outside petitioners presented themselves. Their designated speaker would then be recognized in the proper order. Although this "bar" referred to the idea of tribunal (as in the word *barrister*), its other meaning, related to *barrier,* was not lost (see fig. 2).

The 10th of August is structured by the repeated popular cry or petition for the king's removal, to which the deputies, satisfied that they have already removed him, turn a deaf ear. The people, who also seem not to be listening, make the same demand ad nauseam, as if it has not yet really been met. The impasse is tricky, for who is right? The revolutionary tribunal will insist that Vergniaud, intentionally or not, destroyed the monarchy with his right hand but restored it with his left by naming a tutor for the dauphin. The Romantic histories already read the contradiction of the event. Lamartine, for instance: "Vergniaud had hardly finished reading, when more demanding petitioners presented themselves at the *barre* and called for the Assembly to pronounce the demise of the perfidious king" (3:240). Influenced by the Romantics' account and curious to compare it with an eye-witness record, I was even more struck by the pattern of repetition in the *procès-verbal* or official minutes of August 10, 1792. Whereas Michelet writes that the petitioners "went away silent, but not satisfied" (1:1001), the *procès-verbal* paints a formal, almost ritualistic scene, like ancient Japanese warriors dropping their anger in the sacred temple of freedom and leaving like lambs. All they want is their names in the public record: "All the Citizens, satisfied at having been introduced to the Assembly, and at having faithfully returned the different objects that they found at the château, have the modesty of not doubting that the National Assembly would experience on its part a great satisfaction at knowing and publishing their names" (12:20).[4] Was that promise of gaining a historical identity

---

4. *Procès-verbal de l'Assemblée nationale* (Paris: Imprimerie nationale, 1792), 12:20. When you compare the form of how the *Procès-verbal* and *Le moniteur universel* record the same sessions, you notice immediately an important difference—which may have had an uncalculated effect on future history. The *Procès-verbal* notes the session in prose paragraphs, often using an indirect style to record the discussion, and refers to the deputy simply as a "member": e.g., "a Member asks the Assembly to pronounce the annulment of the nomination.... Another one observes that they..." (1). *Le moniteur,* on which most later historical narratives were based, uses a dramatic form, as if the occasion were a play, and identifies each deputy by name. Oddly enough, one finds the list of petitioners' names in the *Procès-verbal* without the names of the deputies and (chiasmus) the names of the deputies in *Le moniteur* where the people no longer appear by name. *Le moniteur universel* or *Gazette nationale; ou, le moniteur universel (réimpression de l'An-*

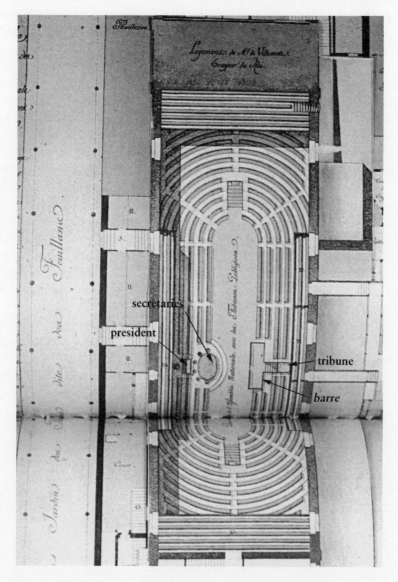

Figure 2. Floor plan of the Salle du Manège. (Shaded areas are second-floor galleries.)

enough to make the petitioners forget why they had come? The petitioners appear in history in order to be politely turned away from it: they
come, both to speak and to learn the lesson of the bar's revolving door.[5]

While the bar between the Assembly and the people was repeatedly
reinstated (undermining the victory outside?), the bar between the logographer's box and the enchanted circle was removed. This information, of interest to these Romantic accounts,[6] provides the main focus in
Thiers's version of the scene in the logographer's box: "The king... was
removed to the office of the clerk of the journals, and the iron railing
which separated it from the chamber was torn down, so that, in case the
chamber should be attacked by the multitude, he could, with his family,
take immediate refuge among the deputies."[7] An impassioned open appeal was, I assume, expected to work better than leaving the king cring-
ing in his dark lair. Carlyle interprets the gesture of pulling down that
barrier as another sign of the Legislative's dependency on the monarchy:
"Tear down the railing that divides it [the *loge*] from the enchanted Constitutional Circuit! Ushers tear and tug; his Majesty himself aiding from
within: the railing gives way; Majesty and Legislative are united in
place, unknown Destiny hovering over both" (2:96). Michelet clarifies
the irony that Carlyle alludes to: Louis XVI has a hand in his own un-
making, for he practiced ironwork as a hobby: "The King got busy himself, with... his arms of a blacksmith" (1:1000).

One of the first in a long line of democratic misrepresentations, if not
impasses, the 10th of August also dramatizes the social circulation set
up in this back room, as if the enormous pressure exerted by the popular
insurrection on the institution had sprung a tiny leak in the *loge*. History
is crossing paths in this small box: the artisan-king is descending and
joining fates with the artisan-scribe. One enters into passivity, while the

cien Moniteur depuis la réunion des Etats-Généraux jusqu'au Consulat) (Paris: Au bureau central, 1842), 13:378–84.

5. For another semiotic interpretation of the parliamentary political system based
on cybernetics, i.e., open channels of communication, see Pierre Avril, *Les français et
leur parlement* (Paris: Casterman, 1972), especially 37.

6. Along with Carlyle, Michelet, Lamartine, Blanc, and Thiers, Cabet includes the
detail about the iron grillwork even in a very condensed version of the scene: "[The king]
arrives, with his family, through an almost impenetrable crowd, and is placed in the *loge
du logographe*, from which the *grille* separating it from the Assembly is removed" (3:55
–56).

7. Adolphe Thiers, *Histoire de la Révolution française*, 2:251.

other waits to emerge from it. Whereas the petitioners could in theory participate in the official social discourse and the spectators in the tribunes gained power through their techniques of disruption, the logographers were socially and theoretically mute. They had no words of their own, but silently recorded those of others. Lamartine was the only historian (melodramatic enough, or open to the symbolic) to exploit that mythic resonance of the potentially powerful scribe:

> For several hours now the silence of the tomb reigned in the lodge of the logographer. Only the noise was heard of the hurried pens of the clerks [*rédacteurs*] which ran along the paper, inscribing minute by minute the words, gestures, emotions of the hall. The lurid light of candles which shone on their table, showed the young Dauphin in the lap of the queen and sleeping to the sound of the decrees which lifted both empire and life from him. (3:253)

The space of the box completes its transformation: the small step outside the magic circle leads in a slide from *loge* to hovel to tomb. The innocent bystanders, the logographers, assume a more threatening demeanor. The scratching pens make a tormenting noise, indicating what actually kills the dauphin, death-by-quill, or at least what conspires with its own prediction of violence. Impassive, more than passive, the scribes take on an uncanny grandeur: *plumes* suggesting birds, Egyptian falcon-gods, otherworldly judges. If the people were not satisfied that the king had fallen once and for all, the pens already inscribed both his overthrow and death, along with the execution of many others who, unsuspecting, thought on the 10th of August that they had won the day (e.g., Vergniaud). Their words copied so diligently would be used against them.

A HISTORY WITHIN A HISTORY: THE MUTE EATS THE
WORD, THE MUTE SPEAKS THE WORD

My narrative now abandons center stage to set up operation in the *loge*. But here we will not find a different history; rather, the same history from another angle. The circulation released here takes on the same shape and flow of story (constantly threatened, as ever, by impasse). The history of stenography can fall into the usual organic plot of rise and fall or even a circle or spiral of a return-to-beginnings (with-a-difference).

The stenographers move from muteness to possibilities of speech and back to silence, from the social ranks of the powerless to power and back again.

In our tradition, stenography culminates with the parallel growth of eighteenth and nineteenth-century parliamentary institutions, although modes of abbreviation have existed as long as writing itself. Prerevolutionary stenographers in France, "tachygraphers," led a life reminiscent of the itinerant artisan but lacked the organization of a guild and knew hard times. The mini-biographies of Coulon-Thévenot and his student Dupont will illustrate the case. Not until the July Monarchy did its practitioners profit from the new networks of power. The men who inaugurated this creative period of the practice were both wild innovators (Grosselin is a good example) and sober builders of the new democracy (e.g., Flocon, Lagache). Energy was to peak in 1848, the desired conjunction of so many hopes, but it too was short-lived. Already a leading steno, Prévost, had proposed that his colleagues become a part of the government bureaucracy, a proposal he realized during the Second Empire, when politics did not stand in the way of nascent professionalism. Today in France candidates undergo tough national competition, but the job in the Senate and Assembly still carries a kind of prerevolutionary artisanal pride and sometimes stays within the same family.

If that is the story, here again is the impasse pursuing it. The democratic speech-act, difficult enough to achieve, is to no avail if no scribe is present to record it. All three elements are, therefore, mutually constituted to assure their common social existence: the representative (speaker), the represented (silent), and the historian (writer). History, like that fated tree falling in the deserted woods, might be happening off somewhere away from the nearest historian and would go unobserved, even unperceived. In fact the presence of a scribe defines the event, as well as vice versa. But often history and the historian are not together where they should be. One of the first stenographers to write about his profession, Delsart, complained in 1847 that "stenographers were lacking for Mirabeau, Barnave, Vergniaud, Danton."[8] Stenography would have enabled that democratic coincidence of the people with its speech to be caught and preserved, converted intact from (legislative) acts to written history. Thanks to stenography, no gap would exist, nothing

8. Albert Navarre, *Histoire générale de la sténographie et de l'écriture à travers les âges* (Paris: Librarie Ch. Delagrave, n.d. [1905]), 398.

would be lost. At last history would be both significant and faithful, loyal to its objects. Later, during the Restoration and July Monarchy, the scribe was there with his new tool, stenography, but history would not show up—until 1848. That year the eighteenth-century Revolution was finally supposed to realize itself, and this time history would be there to record it. The 24th of February, 1848, does come close to doubling the 10th of August since again the Chamber is invaded by the people, and the steno leaves an extraordinary testimony to the breakthrough, including his own, which accompanies — coincides with — that of the "people." And for a short while, stenography too shares in the euphoria of possibility, but already the promises fall short — and that legitimating correspondence no more works in stenography and historiography than in the Assembly, politics, and history.

But we will put the impasse aside and enjoy the story.

Although already historians, logographers (the word also refers to the first Greek writers of history before Herodotus) were not yet stenographers. The inhabitants of the box were probably not even Blanc's logotachygraphers. Thirty-eight members of the Société logographique, including M. David, had their own longhand method for getting out *Le logographe* from about April 1791 to August 10, 1792.[9] Few of the sessions were actually recorded *in extenso*; even so, the task was arduous. Twelve to fourteen journalists sat at a round table in what the historian of stenography Breton calls a "vast room behind the chair of the president"[10] (which must be our *loge* — vast for the little person, small for the big). Each logographer scribbles quickly on a numbered strip of paper, then gives his neighbor a shove with knee or elbow and this one takes over from there, and so on around the table. The strips of papers are reassembled and recopied by other sub-scribes in yet another backroom. Even the one person, Maret, who knew stenography and has the

9. Blanc's confusion, it turns out, was legitimate, for it is not clear whether the king sat in the gallery reserved for the journalists of *Le logographe* or their rivals, *Le logotachygraphe*. In *Histoire des édifices*, Brette goes into detail concerning the arguments for and against both propositions, concluding at last that we will never know exactly where the king sat (2:243–50). *Le logographe* was accused of "truncating facts, distorting our meetings and distilling the poison of *incivism* with a most perfidious art" (2:246, n. 1). It was closed shortly after the 10th of August. Armand Brette, *Histoire des édifices où ont siégé les assemblées parlementaires de la Révolution française et de la première République* (Paris: Imprimerie nationale, 1902).

10. Quoted in Navarre, *Histoire générale de la sténographie*, 398.

reputation of providing history (i.e., the future *Moniteur*) single-hand-
edly with most of our parliamentary documents, may not have used the
new method. The steno-historian Michelot (not Michelet) confesses that
"Maret could only meet the task thanks to stenography. But History
does not say what method he used."[11] Delsart says that Maret's notes
were taken "in ordinary writing." In any case, once copied, the notes of
the steno were destroyed, so that that text which comes closest to the
event is now lost.

The Legislative Assembly (1792) did not act upon a proposal to use
stenography, but Coulon de Thévenot finally persuaded the Convention
at the end of its career to consider using his "tachygraphy." The deputies
or Five Hundred actually took him up on his promise under the Directory but let the project languish, since Coulon's newspaper or bulletin
did not live up to expectations.

Coulon de Thévenot (the *particule* was made up by him) is the best
example of an unsung hero of the early prestenographic days. Although
he started in the potentially elite prerevolutionary artisan class of Paris
as a *maître d'écriture*, having attended the Royal Academy of Writing,
he could not make a living at his chosen profession. Even the interest
shown by d'Alembert at the Academy of Sciences did not help. Coulon
had to make ends meet by traveling the provinces, where he made pre-
sentations to the local learned societies and gave private lessons like a
music teacher. Records kept at Bordeaux show the difficult life both
Coulon and one of his converts led: they seemed to hover, holding to
their pride, between the working and unemployed (future
"dangerous"[12]) classes. When Coulon asked in Bordeaux for some more
"lucrative occupation" than his beloved tachygraphy, his only "re-
source," the Musée de Bordeaux gave him archives to copy. The same
fate awaited his student Dupont. Both returned to Paris, where two was
too much competition. Once they even performed a kind of public joust
or duel to prove who was the fastest tachygrapher in town. The old man
Coulon, now hard of hearing, ultimately triumphed by getting his student convicted of fraud, claiming that the young upstart advertised as

11. Marius Michelot, *Les systèmes sténographiques* (Paris: Presses univ. de France,
1959), 47.
12. See Louis Chevalier, *Classes laborieuses et classes dangereuses à Paris pendant la
première moitié du XIXe siècle* (Paris: Plon, 1958). See also William H. Sewell, Jr., *Work
and Revolution in France: The Language of Labor from the Old Regime to 1848* (Cambridge: Cambridge UP, 1980).

his own, new method one that was virtually no different from the master's original. Dupont in turn argued that Coulon's method was no more original than his, since the old man had only translated into French what he found already in English. (In this Coulon was no different from his rival compatriots.) On the eve of the Revolution, Dupont, like Coulon before him, ended up in Bordeaux, reduced to seeking gainful employment in business after living on the social fringe. He narrated his résumé ("précis de la vie") and job request, as was the polite custom, in the third person: "The scorn that this moving around brings, ordinarily associated with charlatans, is one of the powerful and important reasons which finally today make the sieur Dupont ardently desire to see his errant institution at an end, and which, perceiving no other means, persuade him (stomping out all manner of self-respect) to announce publicly for the first time his wish to occupy a place in commerce, finance or any other position... however modest."[13] As a clerk or *commis*, Dupont probably started out copying; after his dreams were dashed in Paris, maybe he went back to copying again. If only Coulon and Dupont had resolved their squabbles, they might have anticipated the joys of Flaubert's Bouvard and Pécuchet.

It is easy to imagine the itinerant tachygrapher displaying on his tours the miraculous properties of his trade as in a traveling medicine show. His method could cure the ills of writing. Whole passages of books could be compressed into a few lines so the reader could retain all the volumes he read. And nothing would escape the listener. Writing, that poor laggard cousin dragging behind swift sound, was finally catching up and flew side by side with melodious words. As phono-graphy or tono-graphy, written language could achieve that ambition of being perfectly coupled with speech (i.e., phonetic). Such general improvement would naturally carry over from writing to the mind: people would think more clearly, express themselves better. Lawyers would correct their logic, businessmen act more efficiently, poets capture their precious burst of inspiration. Stenography offered no less than a victory over space (steno: narrow) and time (tachy: swift). A report filed after Coulon's presentation to the Musée de Bordeaux repeats the salesman's

13. René Havette, *Deux sténographes à Bordeaux en 1784 et 1789 (Coulon de Thévenot et Dupont, de la Rochelle): D'après les manuscrits de la société littéraire du Musée de Bordeaux et les documents de l'auteur* (Paris: Revue internationale de sténographie, 1903), 25.

pitch: "The goal of the tachygraphic art being especially one of serving
to economize time, to multiply so to speak, the hours, to follow the ra-
pidity of the imagination, ... to come finally to the aid of men of letters
and scholars, before whom time seems to fly ... it is enough that this
method be a mirror in which their genius again finds just in time and
appropriately all the objects whose image it has once received."[14]

Tachygraphy could not only save time, but gain it, make it, reproduce
it. Everything received by the brain, if only subliminally, would be fixed
there, fulfilling, in lieu of the computer, the dream of total recall. The
writing-magician wowed his audience with his feats, for there was
something awe inspiring about what could also serve as cryptography
as well as tachygraphy. However, it did not pay to emphasize that angle
too much, for, as Dupont put it, many potential students "trembled at
the mere view of the characters"[15] and considered the art too hard to
master. It paid rather to emphasize its simplicity: anyone could learn it,
quickly. It is even easier than ordinary writing (because phonetic), un-
contaminated by classical vestiges. Stenography could moreover answer
to that dream of a common, universal language that intrigued the eighteenth century and modified itself to meet the aspirations of the Revolution. The subtitle of a typical manual published in 1793 *Chez le ci-
toyen Charon* by a certain Armand confirms these values: *The Art of
writing as quickly as one speaks, or tachygraphy applicable to all idioms
and founded on such simple and easy principles to seize, that one can
know in a day the elements of this art and put oneself in the position, in
very little time, of following the speech of an orator.*[16]

Coulon saw the Revolution as his big chance, and he showed zeal taking notes at the Jacobin Club. But unfortunately a practitioner of a rival
system brought his past as holder of the (empty) title *secrétaire-tachy-
graphe du roi* to the attention of a local committee, and Coulon had to
lie low. He copied for the "administration" and later worked for the War
Office. He had to eat the grandiose words of his promises and support
himself on pedestrian fare, biding his time. I imagine him at this stage
as one of those seedy but heroic copiers in Abel Gance's *Napoléon*, sto-
ically chewing the convictions of prisoners.

14. Ibid., 11–12.
15. Ibid., 27.
16. René Havette, *Bibliographie de la sténographie française* (Paris: Dorbon-Aîné,
1906).

But Coulon did not profit from the circulation opened up by the fall of the king. Both Michelet and Lamartine laud the success of M. David (Lamartine sets up the echo with the better-known David, another painter of revolutionary scenes). Maret, steno with *Le moniteur*, also made it big: Bonaparte noticed him and named him "secretary of the Consuls" and then "secretary of State." He will become a peer in the July Monarchy.

Although *Le moniteur* hired three stenographers (Delsart, Lagache, Prévost) to cover the Chamber of Deputies during the Restoration, stenography came into its own during the July Monarchy and profited from the growing impulse toward democracy. In 1833 the Chambers first subsidized the service provided by *Le moniteur*, which hired eleven *réviseurs* and *rouleurs*, who worked not unlike the present-day parliamentary team. (Even today in France *rouleurs*[17] stand at a desk so they can turn, look, and listen while writing by hand, not using a stenotype machine. *Réviseurs* give a summary analysis, which is then used to check the verbatim account of the *rouleurs*.) Two notable examples of this more fortunate generation of stenographers include Augustin Grosselin (1800–1870), who was swept up as much as anyone in the inventions that stenography stimulated at the time, and Célestin Lagache (1809–1895), for whom stenography became a political act in itself. The latter passed almost imperceptively from silence into speech on the 24th of February, 1848.

Grosselin had the advantage of being from a family of the legal profession. He started, like many a stenographer, by publishing his own manual at an early age and by taking down the courses of Guizot and Cousin at the Ecole normale. From 1820 to 1851 he worked for *Le moniteur* in the Chambers. But the coup d'état forced him, like Victor Hugo, to develop his more independent pursuits. Already in 1836 he had published a system of universal language in which 1500 general ideas, organized into fifteen tableaux, each received a number. (I assume you could then communicate with anyone in the world simply by a combination of these numbers.) Besides producing what the historian Navarre called "curious atlases," Grosselin created in 1861 a "phonomimic"

17. For an entertaining, illustrated description of the French parliament, see François Muselier [pseudonym for Bernard Pingaud], *Regards neufs sur le parlement* (Paris: Seuil, 1956). An illustration on p. 23 shows (from behind) a *rouleur* at work in the almost empty room of the modern Assemblée nationale, in the Palais Bourbon.

method for communication with the deaf. He also perfected a way of including, along with the words of a speaker, those all-important inflections of voice he called *tonography*. With three hundred variations possible on thirty basic signs, Grosselin could express "the least nuances of feeling."[18] For instance, a heart with a point under it represented goodwill; an upside-down heart, hate; one with a grave accent, affection; with an acute accent, love. Today's French parliamentary stenographers also choose from among a code of possibilities, a finite number of emotive formulae, what is called the *mouvements de séance*, for they have no time to linger over how they might personally express the various forms of disruption practiced by the legislators.[19]

The career of Célestin Lagache, who published his method at eighteen, represents the height of a certain kind of sociopolitical mobility. After working for *Le moniteur* in both the Chamber of Deputies and *Pairs* for almost twenty years, he was first elected as a deputy to the Constituent Assembly of 1848, and after a distance from public life during the Second Empire, returned to head the parliamentary stenographic service from 1861 to 1879, when he again made the transition to public life as a Senator until his retirement (1892). Before knowing that Lagache was its author, I had admired the *procès-verbal* of the 24th of February, 1848, as one of the mythical texts which, along with the 10th of August, 1792, can pretend to have caught the word of the people in action. I was aware of the odd, dramatic sense of that text, for the narrative voice is present when the eerie, empty Chamber first starts to fill up and stays until it seems that the scribe is the very last person to lock up and go home after the crowd has left to follow the Pied Piper of the day, Lamartine, to the Hôtel de Ville. An audacious narrator, he does not hesitate to enter illegal voices into the official record, to recognize not only the anonymous "voice from the gallery" or even the symbolic and real "voice of the people," but the names of those who speak after the president has fled and the Assembly is supposedly no longer in session. A moment occurs in his text like the one when the logographers make room for the king in 1792 and the reader catches a glimpse of them. It is as if the stenographers appeared in 1792 but waited to speak until 1848. As

18. Navarre, *Histoire générale de la sténographie*, 217.
19. In addition to an interview with Pingaud (see n. 17), much of my information concerning contemporary French parliamentary stenography comes from an interview with the Chef du service sténographique of the Senate in the fall of 1976.

the Provisional Government is being named, the stenographers participate along with everyone else, the deputies and crowd they also give voice to:

> M. DUPONT (DE L'EURE). We're proposing to you that we form the provisional government (Yes! yes!—Silence!)
>
> *The Stenographers*. Silence! We'll call out the names!
>
> M. DUPONT (DE L'EURE). Here are the names!
>
> *Numerous voices*. Names! Names![20]

The stenographer enters his own voice into history.

When I was reading along in Albert Navarre's voluminous *Histoire générale de la sténographie*, there was Lagache, hero of the day, according to Navarre, along with Lamartine and the "people":

> On the 24th of February, 1848, Célestin Lagache, at the time *réviseur* of the stenographic service, was at his desk, when the *Chambre des deputés* was invaded by the riot, and everyone fled, preoccupied with the general every-man-for-himself. Concerned about duty and unconcerned about danger, remaining alone at his bench, he recorded, impassive and faithful witness, down to the least words pronounced, the least incidents taking place, from the moment of the first dramatic entrance of the Parisian people. It is thanks to his courageous composure [*sangfroid*] that the authentic proceedings of the first hours of the revolution have been conserved for history.[21]

For Navarre, Lagache is a brave, impassive soldier at his post, his desk. Lagache cannot, however, have been so disinterested if, when the Assembly reconvenes, he will find himself on the other side of the line he had already transgressed in his text.

Whereas the nineteenth century of French government is referred to as the Republic of deputies,[22] 1848 might be especially called the Republic of secretaries (or even stenographers). Flocon, who began his journalistic career as a stenographer, was included with Blanc, Albert, and

20. E. Laurent, ed. (with L. Lataste and C. Pionnier), *Archives parlementaires* (Paris: Librarie administrative de P. Dupont, 1862–19–), 2d series (1848), 501.

21. Navarre, *Histoire générale de la sténographie*, 219.

22. For the rise and fall of speech-making and parliamentary prestige, see Roger Priouret, *La République des députés* (Paris: Grasset, 1959).

Marrast on the list of the provisional government, but possessing only the status of secretary. After complaining, they all were eventually promoted to full membership, including the worker Albert. For Flocon, stenography was an inseparable part of the new republican program. He believed that the Second Republic would not only educate all citizens but give them that means of universal, simple, and complete communication. One of his early speeches to the Assembly alluded to this expectation and must have struck his colleagues as a little strange. Or is that my interpretation of the ambiguous *mouvement*? The word indicates the basic *mouvement de séance* or some kind of general agitation. "I would like stenography to be an integral part of the education of all French citizens (agitation, movement). A word: what I say may seem strange, but believe a man of experience ... that there is no easier, simpler study, which puts more clarity and order in ideas."[23] At last that message Coulon struggled so hard to deliver from the sidelines was close to being championed by the institutions of power itself. Like the Revolution, nothing could stop the inevitable spread and triumph of stenography. Victor Hugo, for one, prophesied that it "would be the popular writing of the twentieth century."[24]

Stenography was indeed eventually instituted in Europe and the United States and throughout the world. The practice was so familiar and universal that it served as a metaphor outside of the context of parliament—while parliament too, and the political metaphors associated with it, functioned as a basic, if not the basic, cultural reference during the nineteenth century and even into the twentieth. Freud, for instance, wondered in *The Interpretation of Dreams* if the repeated dream symbols did not "occur with a permanently fixed meaning like the 'grammalogues' in shorthand [*wie die 'Siegel' der Stenographie*]."[25] (Freud will ultimately reject this tempting stenography of the unconscious in lieu of the concept of overdetermination. Even so, he is again unable to come up with this new concept without the help of another parliamentary metaphor, the *scrutin de liste*).[26] But as stenography grew in popu-

23. Quoted in Navarre, *Histoire générale de la sténographie*, 267.
24. Ibid., 283: an apocryphal quote?
25. Sigmund Freud, *The Interpretation of Dreams*, ed. and trans. James Strachey (New York: Basic Books, 1958), 351. *Die Traumdeutung, Gesammelte Werke* (Frankfurt am Main: S. Fischer, 1976), 2/3:351.
26. Representation in dreams is no more "just" than parliamentary representation:

larity and spread into certain educational institutions and bureaucracies, something paradoxical happened: instead of gaining, it lost prestige. The magic was gone. While being extended and diffused, it was at the same time cut off from the real centers of power. Although until relatively recently a lawyer might have been trained as a court stenographer (e.g., James Francis Byrnes, 1879–1972), the case is rare today. The women graduates of the once-prominent secretarial schools (now technical colleges?) are less likely to become secretaries of state than members of one of the least well-paid and organized sectors of the working class, in which the self-image of being a white-collar modern artisan sometimes helps and sometimes does not.

PETTY THEFT IN THE MONUMENTS

Stenography participated in the general disappointment when democratic history failed to realize its identity. Instead of closing that gap between word and act or between text and event, stenography continued to throw language back on itself. At such a point one might elevate frustration to a poem or theory, or pick up again with fresh recruits in pursuit of a new insurrection, another political performative. As the forms of history evolve or revolve, the spinoff histories in their wake, which do not seem to fit anywhere, have their own energy: sometimes they end up explaining, even changing the direction of the rest, sometimes they do not mean much to anyone beyond what they are, curious and specific.

One of the most (unintentionally?) humorous books that "deconstructs" stenography *avant-la-lettre* happens to have been published in 1849. Scott de Martinville writes a history of stenography that is really

---

"Thus a dream is not constructed by each individual dream-thought, or group of dream-thoughts, finding (in abbreviated form) separate representation in the content of the dream—in the kind of way in which an electorate chooses parliamentary representatives; a dream is constructed, rather, by the whole mass of dream-thoughts being submitted to a sort of manipulative process in which those elements which have the most numerous and strongest supports acquire the right of entry into the dream-content—in the manner analogous to election by *scrutin de liste*" (284). Freud may have been referring to the controversial French elections of 1885 when the *scrutin de liste*, after short experiments in 1848 and 1871, was reinstated. On the second ballot, the republicans, who had won a majority of the votes but fewer seats that the conservatives (129 to 177) swept the seats, 240 to 25. *Scruta* are "old or broken stuff, trash, frippery, trumpery" (*O.E.D.*).

Jacques Derrida picks up this metaphor of stenography in "Freud et la scène de l'écriture," *L'écriture et la différence* (Paris: Seuil, 1967), 312, 321.

the chronological refutation of each method as it follows the other. Almost a litany, his *Histoire de la sténographie* ... shows how the perfection added to a system is just enough to undo it entirely:

> It appears, so I say, that signs provide the means of following without too
> much difficulty the orator who would speak a monosyllabic language. ...
> In order to obtain speech and to facilitate reading, you soon saw that
> when a word was composed of several syllables, you had to combine the
> signs which constituted it in order to form a monogram; but that cannot
> happen, in most cases, except by means of parasitic traits which neces-
> sarily augment the space covered, disfigure the signs some of the time but
> at the very least make them lose their first simplicity.[27]

In the beginning, you have no trouble, hints Scott de Martinville—as anyone knows who has tried to teach herself shorthand or any foreign language—if you stick to one-syllable words, that is, baby talk. When you get to normal speech, you start to lose it. There was some kind of mythical understanding in the literature that writing had to be cut by a sixth to reach the speed or narrowness of sound. Although stenographic manuals may start out with alphabetic or syllabic equivalents for natural language, that first step saves no time or space because you only end up translating from one code to another. So abbreviation is the first essential principle: reducing a word not only to its phonetic components but to the minimum number of sounds necessary to be understood (vowels, for instance, can be dropped). Speedwriting stops at this stage, whereas stenography succeeds only by trying to go further. The next strategy is the use of root signs to which "parasitical" marks are added to indicate, for example, prefixes, suffixes, or verb tenses. But even this important advancement of "parasitical traits" does not gain enough time: you can still only transcribe a drawl. The secret is found in the "monogram" (or "brief phrases," in the jargon of modern stenography): a single sign corresponds to certain clichés or frequently used combinations in the particular context, like business or law. Enough efficiency is finally gained. Except for one problem: the language that was to imitate the train, the new ideology of nineteenth-century industrial society valuing speed and

27. Edouard-Léon Scott de Martinville, *Histoire de la sténographie depuis les temps anciens jusqu'à nos jours; ou, Précis historique et critique des divers moyens qui ont été proposés ou employés pour rendre l'écriture aussi rapide que la parole* ... (Paris: Chez Charles Tondeur, 1849), 33.

efficiency,[28] had turned into a system of pictograms, into hieroglyphics. A secretary who does not use these phrases every day may look at notes from the day before with the bewilderment of someone surveying a Babylonian tablet. And who can resist adding one's own twist to the system? So that if one secretary is out sick, no one else can decipher what the boss said.

From Condillac to Mallarmé — which basically means Romanticism —theoretical work on language (or anything?) is said to have undergone an eclipse: did it retreat, disguised, into areas like Scott de Martinville's history of stenography? Stenography was supposed to be the language that would overcome language, or at least provide the mediation and conversion from nondiscursive reality into discourse. Instead of freeing itself from language, or even producing a new one, stenography kept reproducing the shadow of the old one in all of its complexity. It is no coincidence that such an ancient practice of abbreviation, which goes back most notably to the Romans, depends upon what are rhetorical devices: *apocope* (to cut endings: sigla or acronyms are radical examples) and *syncope* (to cut middles), forms of ellipsis — which only invite *augmentatio*. In essence, stenography rediscovered the figurativity of language, always double, or rather, shifting within itself. The operations of stenography represent how we manipulate time like an accordion or how language manipulates our contradictory sense of time. It highlights the obsession we cultivate, convinced, at each age, of the geometric progression of our own speed, the unique acceleration of our particular lives. We talk like journalists, speaking a slang of modern abbreviations. But at the same time we get bogged down, invent long neologisms (like *figurativity*) shaping concepts to embody our supposedly new complexities. The time we save, we waste. The time we gain, we kill. But ever-changing language gives us a sense of movement.

Stenography also calls attention to the ironies implicit in our history that aspires to be scientific. The early "positivist" history, as it was called in the 1840s instead of "Romantic," hoped that stenography would ensure its transition from the status of literature to science. Im-

28. Cf. the ideology of Michelot's *Les systèmes sténographiques*: "In modern Times, the development of parliamentary life in England and then in France and the economic takeoff resulting from the discovery of steam were necessary for the countries of western Europe to constitute, in the last century, the great stenographic systems securing a sufficient simultaneity between work and material notation" (8).

portant documents, at the center of this new parliamentary (as opposed
to royalist) history, would be both complete and objective. Not that deputies could not, cannot, cheat in the official record, but stenography
promised to give us the text that comes closest to reality — if we do not
lose that text or it is not always theoretically lost. We like to think of the
reality toward which we direct our (asymptotic) approach as a kind of
sound barrier (truth barrier) to break, instead of a barrier to be itself incorporated into our practice. Each time we appear to be getting closer,
because of a new method or materials, the bar springs back again to re-
confirm our distance. And perhaps we are approaching nothing more
than the reaffirmation of that bar, so that it and not the historical object
itself becomes the infinite or figurative limit against which history is
produced.

As historians and literary critics continue to study the tricky relationships and confusions between text and real, we are reminded of the double imperative of the linguistic sign, for which the bar between signifier
and signified remains a crucial element. Although text and reality seem
to advance and retreat in terms of each other, with one appearing at
times to capture the other, so that the bar looks mobile, uncontrollable
if not meaningless, it is also (arbitrarily) fixed so we escape madness and
continue to try to communicate with each other, make sense of ourselves
and our society, and live our everyday lives.

Around the wobbly yet stable bar between the angry masses and the
Assembly, a new postrevolutionary society has to organize itself.
Around the bar between the stenographer and the event, a history also
seeks its narrative coherence. The "people" cannot cross that bar, although individuals may; they are by definition the represented, not the
representatives. So, metaphorically, the stenographers too cannot cross
the bar from muteness to speech, writing to action, shadow to the light.
Roland Barthes speaks of that requirement in nineteenth-century history (succeeded by empirical-positivism and neorealism) to suppress the
signs of the *énonciation*. History depends theoretically on the silence of
the steno — and it is convenient that it also depends from a practical
point of view on keeping the population in the Pandora's box quiet.

You might guess that about the time stenography became well en-
sconced in the institutions of society — as both the state and its ideological apparatuses, courts, schools, offices — history decided that those
records, meticulous and complete as they were, no longer held any inter-

est. Aulard's *Histoire politique de la Révolution française* (1901) closes
the circle begun with Buchez and Roux's *Histoire parlementaire* (1834).
Social and labor history would precisely locate its object in the cracks
and gaps of the stenographed monuments if these monuments had not
already blocked out the details and the very notion of (everyday) life.
History would, therefore, seem to define itself not by its ability to coincide with the object it sought, but by its very fickleness. Give it the answer and it will change the question. No archive stays in place; characters jostle back and forth between foreground and shadow. Thus the
whole enterprise of history becomes problematic: we know that what we
carefully save will not interest posterity, which will want what we over-
looked and considered worthless instead. How can a museum be run under those conditions?

Baudelaire evokes an idea of history that tries to take into account
that paradox and has recourse, not surprisingly, to the metaphor of stenography. The poet was preoccupied with how to record modern life,
not in its traditions and institutions, but in its very evanescence. He de-
taches the most technically developed method of historical documenta-
tion, stenography, from its usual historical object, the Assembly, and lets
it loose in places one would least expect, in the street or park. His model,
Constantin Guys, a painter of modern life, worked like a kind of stenographer; his rapid sketches of a moving carriage or boat, more of movement than the object itself, resembled the traces with which the stenographer transcribed the *mouvements de séance*. "No matter what
position it is thrown into, with whatever speed it is launched, a carriage,
like a boat, borrows from movement a complex and mysterious grace
very difficult to stenograph. We can place a sure bet that, in a few years,
the drawings of M. G. will become the precious archives of civilized life"
(1191). Like an investor, Baudelaire lays his money on the future of
these apparently frivolous sketches. He anticipates the change in a definition of history.

Or we can interpret Baudelaire's sentence more theoretically, to mean
that whatever does not last long, whatever passes from fashion, com-
poses history, and not what remains. A contradiction in terms, a history
of modern life could perhaps not exist. Like Midas, history automatically converts its object, whether in movement or not, into a monument
that is, by definition, never modern. Maybe this threat is why historians
covet objects that are either fugitive or difficult to conceptualize (very

difficult to stenograph) like *imaginaires, mentalités, longues durées,* even nonhistorical thought: most likely to escape the fate of monumentalization. But just as the people can become as frozen as the king, the king can also become as elusive as the people.

Instead of always missing its appointed rendezvous with itself, perhaps history, on the contrary, can never go wrong no matter what it does or says. We talk as if whole populations have slipped through our nets, whole expanses of terrain lie undiscovered and virginal, or important details elude us as too subtle, but we also find that history seems to hold within it exactly what we need — if never knowing we needed it until it is given. Whatever scrap survives suits our history best. Even the social history of modern or everyday life is always present if we know how to read it. Whoever reports on Coulon's presentation to the Musée de Bordeaux (another secretary), as naive as Molière's M. Jourdain, thrills at the realization that what we respect as hallowed by history is what happened to be left around. He marvels that the lowly slave Tiron knew tachygraphy and took down what Cicero said. These casual notes become our classics. "Our enjoyment today is the daily larceny [*larcins journaliers*] that they [the ancient tachygraphers] made in their modesty."[29] Like Guys's sketches transformed as if by magic into precious archives, the little larcenies of these servants are later revered as treasures. Our national archives are stolen booty. And one gets the idea that the copyist took the words out of the orator's mouth, to sell to posterity. There is still something *louche,* even illegitimate, about the profession. One can see Coulon and Dupont, in their "modesty" (i.e., poverty), committing a little petty theft at the tables of the great. But their pilfering provides our plenty.

Romantic history should, according to our tradition, be the most monumental and deadly of narratives, and yet even it could not help but transport the history we desire. The metaphorical and empirical sense of the historical object in Baudelaire that he calls modern life is preserved, to take a contemporary example, in the notion of everyday life. In his *Critique de la vie quotidienne,* Henri Lefebvre also insists on the dialectic of practice and theory in the study of everyday life. If he returns to issues now common to contemporary social history like work, leisure, and family, he never forgets the paradox of his uncanny object, so

29. Havette, *Deux sténographes,* 10.

familiar as to be strange. The bizarre banal, it is everywhere the ground (*sol*) of history and nowhere, in no one privileged context. In the second volume of his *Critique*, Lefebvre erects a historian who raises "objections" to his program. This "historian" admits that the study of everyday life is interesting but frankly, "don't you return, for better or for worse, to the anecdotal ... to the marginal?"[30] In other words (though the historian does not go this far): you are going backward into Romantic historiography. In his defense, Lefebvre comes close to making the implication explicit: "Let's not fall into ethnographic romanticism." In fact, he then proceeds to conceptualize one of the most elusive contributions of Romantic history. Going beyond "historicism" (to be avoided, according to Lefebvre), in which everything becomes material for history, ethnography legitimately justifies its concentration on everyday life. Archaic societies fuse ordinary objects with culture itself, with the historicity of their culture—as opposed to Western capitalist societies, except in times of revolution, when the repressed daily life demands better representation. "The least usual object" is not "a product, even less a thing, but a work of culture and of art ... always bearing symbols and multiple signification!" (2:26). While attracted to the ethnographic program, Lefebvre makes a case for the specificity of his own investigation: "For us, here, it is a question of the modern quotidian"[31] — which only doubles the enigma.

Romantic historiography was supposedly mesmerized by the sense-making event. That event, besides eventually calling into question the sense it ostensibly supports, is eroded, moreover, by the elements proliferating around it, the marginalia: portraits, flashbacks, sub-mini-histories, digressions, and sidetracks like the visit to the *loge* of the logograph. Like the structure of postrevolutionary society itself, the event becomes a minimal narrative function holding together a constantly overflowing coherence. Reading these nineteenth-century histories, in

30. Henri Lefebvre, *Critique de la vie quotidienne* (Paris: L'Arche, 1967), 2:25.

31. Ibid., 2:26. The conceptual connection between ethnography and everyday life is also useful for Michel de Certeau. "This remnant left over by technological colonization acquires the value of purely private activity, becomes charged with the symbolic investments of daily life, ... is in short made over into something like the active and legendary memory of everything still stirring in the margins or interstices of the dominant scientific or cultural norms." But this "remnant" requires the "explanatory discourse" of science and culture to be "known." Michel de Certeau, "On the Oppositional Practices of Everyday Life," *Social Text* 1 (1980):28, 30.

which our sameness is returned to us as curious, if not outlandish, best approximates the ethnographic experience whose pleasures, however, provoke less guilt in us than the analysis of our own commonplace Romanticism.

VI   Conclusion: Inconclusive History

The texts of Romantic history generate diverse forms of both narrative and social change. I wanted to describe those innovative forms of history, not as circles or spirals, not as geometrical or even logical — but I could not set out to describe them directly. These alternative forms emerge only in relation to the traditional order of teleology and explanation. They appear in the cracks of a development that goes awry, almost by surprise.

Language is the metaphorical system of reference that I have used, both explicitly and implicitly, to say what I observe in Romantic history. Language has been the allegory of my explanations.[1] But even if I keep language and history turning like sides of a Möbius strip, it is still as dangerous to depend upon language as on any other interpretative system. For all aspire to be the sole means of explanation.

THE ALLEGORY OF LANGUAGE: THE TERROR OF LANGUAGE

Language is the concrete, material site of competition for power in a democratic society. Language, not only speech and writing, refers, in the largest sense of semiotic systems, to all kinds of symbolic expression: art, music, dress, gesture, body language. Any one of these forms of expression is only a theoretical — albeit crucial — hedge against the constant return of violence in society and against the rigidity of arbitrary hierarchies.

The function of language in the new postrevolutionary society may shed some light on why Romantic histories are so wordy. It is as if they

1. This chapter is a meditation upon Hayden White's statement, directed at the problem of historical writing, that "every discourse is always as much about discourse itself as it is about the objects that make up its subject matter." *Tropics of Discourse*, 4.

had to outdo the revolutionaries themselves, and the Revolution was, as
Furet and others have remarked, one of the most verbose, *bavarde*, periods in modern history. Is another definition of Revolution the explosion of language? In comparison, do we think of science as laconic?

The Romantic historians had an uncanny sensitivity to language,
even if they abused it. Lamartine's *Histoire des Girondins* runs the gamut of linguistic possibilities elaborated in response to the discursive bat-
tles of the Revolution. The poet-politician was paying close attention to
his models because he came to the history of the Revolution with specific, practical questions — not only how to avoid Quatrevingt-treize,
but how to get elected, how to make the entire nation cohere around his
speech, poetry or history.

Revolutionary language in Lamartine passed through a five-stage
spectrum extending from Mirabeau to Marat or the *crieur public*. Mirabeau organically corresponded with his referent and produced the harmonious sign of a unified France. He was France's mirror. Then with
Vergniaud and the Girondins the politico-linguistic sign began to break
apart. They projected the "natural" inspiration of oral rhetoric from the
Paris tribune toward their fictive constituency in Bordeaux and all of de-
centered France. Danton maintained and perfected the prestige of im-
provisation, begun with Mirabeau. Improvised speeches supposedly
best translated the popular will in its rising and falling inflections. But
Robespierre hit upon the most successful and paradoxical formula. He
wrote his speeches to make them appear spontaneous as he played to the
immediate, responsive audience in the galleries of the Convention and
Jacobin Club. His planned spontaneity appeared to embody the Revolution most fully. Robespierre became the sign of the Revolution. His
words coincided thereafter with the actual acts of the people.

But Marat went him one further. He too appeared to capture the language of the people, but he moved the nature of that language to the very
edge of words, next to inarticulate expression. Marat pushed language
to its limit. His performance was as paradoxical as Robespierre's and no
less successful: he wrote oral or street language. He wrote what should
have been unwritable speech. His *feuilles* — paper or "leaflets" — scattered like leaves, like natural objects. They were hawked by *colporteurs*
and read on street corners to those who could not read for themselves.
Marat and the other revolutionary journalists brought language to the
brink of "delirium," according to Lamartine. "[Language] borrowed

from the populace its proverbs, triviality, obscenities, uncouthness even including that swearing with which it interrupts its words" (1:247). If the people who do not speak or write express themselves in the interruptions of speech, then Marat's strategy best corresponded to them. The Thermidorians, those political realists, could either maintain or suspend the coincidence of language and reality, sign and referent, according to their needs. They claimed belief in a teleological system of progress, representation, God, good sense, and commerce while using to their advantage what we would today call the floating signifier or any rhetorical ploy (parliamentary rules of order), verbal and nonverbal methods of persuasion.

Not just the heroes of the French Revolution are touched by the power of the linguistic *symbolique*. By virtue simply of participating in the Revolution, everything is affected, as if the light of destiny transforms banal objects, everyday people whether famous before or not, chance occurrences, into messages laden with deep meaning. Maybe this automatically happens to anything as it enters history, and even more so in the case of the French Revolution, since history was finally not just the distant affair of royalty. Maybe this symbolic effect is connected to that equally curious phenomenon by which history retrospectively always appears inevitable, as if it knew all the time where it was going. So every little role gains that magic of having been in the right, or wrong, place at the right time.

Still, the texture of Romantic history seems overly saturated with symbolic resonances.[2] It is not enough to say that the authors were poetically inclined. Something else is going on.

Roland Barthes pointed to gratuitous details as the "reality effect" of both realism and history. But try as they might, details could not stay gratuitous in Romantic history (nor in realism). The unprepared king happened to fall asleep in his wig, and that half-flattened wig is the sign that the symbols of power have lost their aura. The kingdom was now out of kilter. Reading Michelet often gave me the strange impression of reading *Alice in Wonderland*, or a fairy tale — making the narrative no

2. See Lynn Hunt's chapter "Symbolic Forms of Political Practice" in *Politics, Culture, and Class in the French Revolution*, 52–86. It is hard to say whether the nineteenth century inherited a sensitivity to symbolic practice because of the eighteenth-century experience or whether we read back into the past that symbolic overload because the Romantic historians exaggerated it.

less serious, and even more powerful. Michelet's text adds an extra dimension besides analysis and narrative: one that touches upon dream and nightmare, childlike fears and passions. In his scene of the 10th of August (1792), Petion's carriage stands all night beside the Louvre palace, then leaves empty at 4 A.M., making an eerie sound. The vehicles of power were deserting their old boss for new ones. Already the burning forest of bayonets and pikes gathered in another part of town and started its march, "flaming with the fire of the morning sun" (1:984). The new dawn. Even that greasy chicken the king ate in Lamartine's logographers' lodge is not ordinary chicken. It is the gluttony of hundreds of years. Lamartine depicted the king in ever more uncanny situations. After Louis was arrested, he retired every night during his trial to read the history of England's Charles I, sensing that it would be his own (5:48). He and the queen played chess, capturing each other's "king" or "queen" (4:319). And finally the most uncanny detail of all: his prison cell was papered (*tenture en papier peint*) with pictures of prison scenes and instruments (4:310). How far can the *mise-en-abîme* go?

The names especially seem all too perfect, after the fact. The citizen who pursued a fleeing Swiss Guard into the Assembly on the 10th of August was named Clémens.[3] Michelet had a field day with Danton, how his whole rotund person and his voice boomed and barreled forth: *tonner*, the verb was unavoidable. Mirabeau, that mirror of France, true blue sky of the nation, reflected the harmonious beauty of the people — although he himself was ugly, his face pockmarked. Was Lamartine thinking of *Mire à beau*? And Robespierre. The reader cannot help but pay closer attention to the name when the revolutionary hero himself signed only one piece of it, Rob——. After his arrest on the 9th of Thermidor, Robespierre could not bring himself to finish the signature calling for the insurrection.[4] Rob——: was that his real name? *Robe/Dérober.* He was a man of the robe, a lawyer, and supposedly represented within him the solid foundation of the Revolution. Lawgiver (Moses), he was to bring forth the new commandments of the future society in stone. Or had he stolen the sacred symbols of popular power, stolen the rock and hidden it under his cloak, his disguise apparent only in his own name? The names of the historians themselves catch the contagion of

3. *Procès verbal de l'Assemblée nationale,* 12:22.
4. See Marie-Hélène Huet, "La signature de l'histoire," *Modern Language Notes* 100 (September 1985):715–27.

symbolism. Sentimental, effeminate La-martine, the erasures in Blanc, Thiers (Etat). But how appropriate finally is Cabet, because he takes an unthinkable revenge on Louis Capet, turning the old reign on its head in a book — worse than Napoleon I's fate as *Napoléon le petit* in Hugo? Contemporary French writer Castoriadis mentions in *L'institution imaginaire de la société* that history always comes up with the requisite perfect nose (Cleopatra), that is, the right object.

These strangely perfect details call attention to the way linguistic-social meaning is conferred. Meaning accelerates; its operation is exposed so that some symbols are deflated — the king's purple robe, his wig — while others are created, inflated — the pikes. The Revolution brings everything into bold relief, one way or another; up or down, power or impotence. The symbolic energy exists on both small and large scale. The heads on pikes represent literally what is symbolically happening in the headless society.

Then there is the coup de grâce of the symbolicized Revolution, the great triad or dialectic: the Constituent Assembly, the Legislative Assembly, and the Convention. This progression holds within it the story of language as the allegory of Revolution.

The new nation started down the logical path. First it called a constitutional convention and named it "la Constituante." This body was to set up the founding principles of the new society in a Constitution and inscribe the most sacred of concepts in the Declaration of the Rights of Man. Already those new leaders were attempting the impossible. Claude Mouchard asks, reflecting on Thomas Paine and the Rights of Man: "How could it [this human act of speech] pretend to engage men universally and for all time without falling into presumption, without becoming constraining itself, without denying something of that liberty it affirms?"[5] To write these rights down, to express them, both wrongs them, closing them into limits, and opens them up to any disuse and misreading. But founders, like Paine, could not afford to be so self-conscious. They needed to be swept up in the promise of possibility, not paralyzed. On the other hand, they could not afford not to be self-conscious either. It was too dangerous.

The Constituent Assembly stepped aside for the next stage. The Legislative Assembly was supposed to enact the laws that would logically

5. Claude Mouchard, introduction to Thomas Paine's *Les droits de l'homme* (Paris: Belin, 1987), 44.

follow from the founding principles so that the new society might unfold
its political, even its entire social life as desired. When do the cracks in
this perfect logic begin to show up? The Constitution did not manage to
balance powers—can it ever hope to do so without adding, subtracting,
too much here or there and never reaching a perfect equilibrium? But the
germ of failure, according to the revolutionaries, inserted itself into the
inoperable system when the hypocritical king took a false oath saying he
would abide by the Constitution. One of the first in a long series of false
oaths? Defenders of the king said that he could not have abided by the
Constitution even if he had wanted to. The document was stillborn:
Quinet's aborted Revolution. So the Constitution barely had time to
prove itself impossible before the Legislative Assembly was burst apart
by the invasion of the people on the 10th of August.

Then another "constitutional assembly" had to be convoked, but
since there had already been one, what would be the name of the second
one? Assemblée constituante II? But each time the revolutionaries
wanted new beginnings, not repetition, especially not so soon. Naming
was never a slight matter. No birth of a nation is innocent. The Convention took the second part of the name the Americans had used (having
already borrowed the first part of "Constitutional Convention") and
called it the Convention. Was the apparent success of the American Revolution any guarantee when transferred to France? There could be no
more suggestive word than "convention." It seems such a simple choice,
for it means nothing more than a general gathering. But it also refers to
that elusive Other of the Revolution: habit, universally accepted practices—what Burke threw up as the opposite of the French Revolution,
the old constitutions on which one could count, unlike the new one, for
the calm, time-tried decisions of the ages. Maybe the name could work
to bring about that impossible conjunction. The Revolution was supposed to descend from the abstract natural law of truth and justice and
rise from the equally "natural" liberties of everyday life and customs.
The French Revolution sought to embody both the naturalness of convention and man's innate humanity to man.

But what happened in the Convention? Instituting the Constitution
was indefinitely postponed. And the Revolution discovered something
else, neither constitution, institution, nor habit. A space appeared that
seemed exceptional, a space of formal delay and suspended suspension
where provisional daily solutions wrote themselves nonetheless deeply

into tradition with no more formal legitimacy than bargains, experiments, and creative gambles. The Jacobins, or any new group in power, thought that they were only taking immediate measures in extraordinary circumstances and would soon get down to instituting that society they proposed. But those first makeshift decisions stick, have their own unexpected lives and history. Postponement has monumental effects. The period of limbo inscribing the future of a society cannot be anything but terrifying. Is that one definition of the Terror? In *The Book of Laughter and Forgetting*, Milan Kundera compares a new love affair with "unwritten conventions"; spontaneous gestures that have not been thought out become the "fine print" of the contract, the rituals of years.[6]

The triad — from Constituante to Législative to Convention — tells two different stories, like the double story of Romantic history. In one story the Revolution constitutes its eternal principles, legislates the new society flowing from that constitution so smoothly that the new society fits into the old mold as easily as into a pair of worn shoes (or, using Tocqueville's image, as easily as one plant slips into the root tracks of another). The other story collapses that process almost from the beginning (always already?), so that the new government, looking forward to climbing la Montagne, is pulled back into the Plain of the Convention, or worse, the quicksand of the popular swamp, *marais* (where revolutionaries like *Marat* live).

The three stages of the historical or linguistic process tell the allegory of any attempt to say, to ground saying, to institute, to ground institutions. Whether the proclamation is a linguistic performative (like "We declare ourselves to be the National Assembly"), a definition, or any statement, the sayer wants it to be understood the way it was said, not to take off into multiple meanings. But what saying can be founded or grounded completely? "The Revolution is the advent of Justice" — no, that is not right; rather, "The Revolution is the reaction of Justice." Better qualify that too — "The Revolution is the tardy reaction of Justice" — and one's original premise/promise is nearly lost.

This triad of speech and revolution recalls old trinities and new ones. Hegel's thesis, antithesis, synthesis. Freud's superego, ego, id. Psychoanalyst Jacques Lacan's *symbolique, imaginaire, réel*. Linguist Fer-

6. Milan Kundera, *The Book of Laughter and Forgetting*, trans. Michael Henry Heim (New York: Viking Penguin, 1981), 36.

dinand de Saussure's referent, signified, signifier. Paul de Man's logic, grammar, rhetoric. Various terms fill in the three categories, but the basic tripartite structure stays the same. In terms of the Romantic or any historical text, one could construct: allegory, fictions, the archive; or The One Story, particular narratives, facts. Hayden White uncovered behind the traditional threesome the system of tropes, as already observed in Vico: metaphor, metonymy, synecdoche — and the collapse and beginning again that pass through irony (also see Northrop Frye, Kenneth Burke). The threes can reproduce and divide into fours, fives, sixes. They can also withdraw into binary oppositions and finally collapse back into the one.

THE HISTORICAL "SYMBOLIQUE": RETURN OF THE REAL (REVOLUTION)

But what happens when the one, the original or founding coincidence (of history and its meaning, of word and thing) is radically arbitrary or figurative itself? The coincidence is never perfect even though, in order for the system to unfold, retrospectively everything happens *as if* the word corresponds to the thing, expression to intention, subject to object, thought to history, law to popular opinion, as if nothing could be any other way. Here is the way Saussure expresses it in the field of linguistics. Instead of already formulated ideas listed in a rational column next to their proper names, two shapeless masses (like water and air) slice up arbitrarily into relative values that result "solely from the simultaneous presence of the others."[7] Moving out from Saussure's definition, de Man emphasizes that language depends upon comparison. Words or literal meanings do not exist on their own, but sense comes from relations between terms: "not this but that." Language is by definition figurative. Literal meaning results only after the figures sort themselves out. Literal meaning is the retrospective effect of a language that is always figurative. This language theory helped me conceive of what Rousseau and Montesquieu might have meant by the self-constituting legitimacy of society, in which society's sense of itself and the forms of its organization, that is, the represented (public) and representatives, work themselves out in a reciprocal relationship.

7. Ferdinand de Saussure, *Course in General Linguistics*, ed. Charles Bally and Albert Sechehaye with Albert Riedlinger (New York: McGraw-Hill, 1966), 114.

Historical interpretation works in a similar way. The historical object, the historian and historian's culture, and the textual explanation or narrative—all three come into being together through an interdependency. The historical object or event is not a ready-made reality that exists outside of the relationships of signification.

Seen from the hypothesis of figurative language, certain fundamental paradoxes of historical thought make more sense. In fact these paradoxes seem fundamental to any definition of history. They are not curious riddles or side effects in the problems of historical thought, or even impasses to be avoided at all costs. Irony, or forms of self-contradiction like paradox, play an integral part in historical understanding. Irony is always inside, twisting the historical dynamic into the set of threes that no longer correspond neatly with beginning, middle, and end. And particular ironic statements about history seem somehow related — as if there is one unstated law behind them that must nevertheless remain unstated. Here is an example that preoccupied many nineteenth-century political thinkers (Marx, Michelet): men and women make the history they (we) can never know.[8] Anyone or everyone can direct history in terms of her or his own desire. But remember that some other, unknown power also controls that desire, both its expression and its results. On the one hand, history is determined by us, and on the other, history is overdetermined and thus undeterminable. Or another way of coming at the same enigma: history is always right, but we can never get it right— in the sense both of historical action and of writing. In hindsight, history appears to be so right that it automatically becomes destiny; we imagine it as no other way than as we know it. But then, oddly enough, we cannot adequately explain to ourselves or to others what happened in our past, just as we cannot quite explain why that marriage did not work, what happened to make that particular child of those parents. We explain it over and over, never satisfied. Here is another one of these confounding paradoxes: history, like the popular will, always and yet never errs. History is errancy and uncanny coincidence.

Saussure spoke of the immutability and mutability of the linguistic sign; both conditions, although mutually exclusive, operate necessarily at the same time. "The signifier, though to all appearances freely chosen with respect to the idea that it represents, is fixed, not free, with respect

8. "Men make their own history, but they do not make it just as they please." Marx, *The Eighteenth Brumaire*, 15.

to the linguistic community that uses it. The masses have no voice in the matter."⁹ But then: "Language is radically powerless to defend itself against the forces which from one moment to the next are shifting the relationship between the signified and the signifier. This is one of the consequences of the arbitrary nature of the sign."¹⁰ It is striking that Saussure uses barely disguised metaphors of history and even of political struggle to define his linguistic concepts. He cannot tell us about language without comparing it to mass movements or revolution. Since the word *masses* often conjures up a scene from the French Revolution (at the Bastille) rather than the Russian or American revolutions, it is not farfetched to see the French Revolution as Saussure's allegory of explanation here. Saussure describes a strange predicament where there is total obedience and yet complete, unpredictable freedom. The institutions of everyday life are absolutely fixed and yet defenseless against linguistic and social change, complete reversals of meaning.

Sentences like these make it impossible to claim primacy for linguistics, language, or literature as an explanatory system for history, or for anything else. Someone else could use other fields of knowledge to come at the same problem: e.g., psychoanalysis (continental, more than Anglo-American?), rhetoric, philosophy, anthropology ("everyday life"), maybe even physics ("uncertainty principle"). Different disciplines need to borrow terms that are already metaphorical in order to define and tell about their own work, but sometimes in their borrowing they assimilate unwanted, even unapparent, baggage. For instance, historians use *graphs* and *figures* like a statistical *hors-texte* within their text that rises beyond narrative to a space of greater scientific precision. But both words, their etymologies, remind us that we are working within writing and fictive human shapings.

I have chosen to talk about the "historical symbolic" in order to keep a parallel with Furet's "political symbolic." The word *symbolic* has resonances both from psychoanalysis and rhetoric, and it sometimes has opposite meanings. In the French context of the 1960s, the word rings of Lacan's trinity. But it does not fit exactly with what Furet seems to mean. In Lacan the *symbolique* is that ever-unreadable structure of language into which we slip as into our own (father's) name and which orders, or disorders, us, like the unconscious. For Lacan we operate in the

9. Saussure, *Course in General Linguistics*, 71.
10. Ibid., 75.

realm of the *imaginaire* through which a third term, the real, equally unreadable as the symbolic, circulates in this stable and unstable relationship of the triangle. Different from Lacan's threes, symbol in de Man
participates in a binary opposition. Symbol is that illusory coincidence
which allegory interrupts.[11] De Man is closer to Saussure, who implies
that *symbol* is never totally arbitrary (Justice's scales), so if used in the
linguistic sense should be replaced by his more precise term, *signifier*.
Furet's concept, the political symbolic, seems to correspond less with
Lacanian terminology than with Roland Barthes's "floating signifier." If
we say here that the symbolic refers to the general semiotic system in
which we live and work, the word can retain its contradiction as both
coincidence and interruption, illusion and reality. Otherwise one has to
invent one of those maddening *porte-manteau* words like *symbolico-
real*.

The status of the political symbolic is ambiguous in the work of François Furet. For Furet, Jacobin discourse or revolutionary ideology is not
just "a transition, but a beginning and a haunting vision of that beginning [*fantasme d'origine*]." The Jacobin strategy of identifying their
own project with that powerful symbolic space, the origin or matrix of
society, "was to become universal: it was the first experiment with democracy."[12] On the other hand, that universal unravels into a state of delirium, a freak experiment in *surréalité*. The Jacobins act out one possibility of democracy, its pure, radical form, that locates the limit of its
excesses. Furet (taking one of Marx's cues in *The Holy Family*) interprets Thermidor as representative democracy put back on track: "[The
Thermidorians] rediscovered the independence and the inertia of society, the need for political trade-offs, and the compromises demanded by
the interplay of means and ends."[13] The Jacobin moment is an error, a
weakness, even an addiction that political actors give in to—like ex-al-
coholics, says Furet. In his work, the "political symbolic" of Jacobin discourse has the status of an accident and a relapse. On the one hand, the
Jacobins discover and define democracy; on the other hand, they distort

11. Paul de Man, "The Rhetoric of Temporality," *Interpretation: Theory and Practice*, ed. C. Singleton (Baltimore: The Johns Hopkins UP, 1969), 173–209; rpt. in *Blindness and Insight*, ed. Wlad Godzich (Minneapolis: U of Minnesota P, 1983), 187–228.
12. Furet, *Interpreting the French Revolution*, 79; *Penser la Révolution française*,
109.
13. Furet, *Interpreting the French Revolution*, 70; *Penser la Révolution française*,
98.

it beyond recognition. They start out as the rule of democracy and become its negation. Instead of asking Furet which they are really, we might consider the duplicity at the heart of Jacobin discourse as what defines democracy and not one side or another of the question.

A social system that constitutes itself, regenerates its own inside/outside "popular" referent, commands a tremendous energy by the fact of the uncertainty that inhabits it. A paradoxical grounding is what gives democracy its force. For the Jacobins came upon an unexpectedly dynamic body politic through the necessary illusion of a coincidence, always already imperfect, with the people. That belief of circulating the people's own identity through Jacobin discourse is not an ideal, abstract principle or distant goal but the reference or lens through which everything in a democracy takes on reality and legitimacy. Such an identity invariably turns out to be, to have been, a patchwork of compromises. Yet it is not those compromises but the constant reference to a popular authority that allows for the continuous possibility of radical social change.

There is no guarantee that this social change will be positive or negative, what was desired or not. The political symbolic of democratic society, the free signifier of democracy, describes a powerful open form that does not automatically fill with any particular ideological content, such as anarchy, liberal representative government, or totalitarian state. A democracy mediated by parties and pressure groups looks preferable to that terrifying vision sometimes given of revolutionary France. The revolutionaries were mesmerized by a direct source of magnetic power, people rising up as if out of themselves, refusing by definition to be mediated. It was an unlivable daily situation. As dangerous as it was liberating.

No one has the last word on revolution, just as no one has the last word on history — or on radical social change, if *revolution* is too difficult a word to use because of the different connotations and contexts attached to it. Checks and balances, trade-offs and compromises that appear to define social and political reality create a *surréalité* that gets more and more distant from the source of democratic legitimacy. A "balance of power" is just as illusory as total consensus. Take away or add a little here, so we have to take away or add a little over there, always too much so go back and correct it, ad infinitum. The subtle hegemony of a (Thermidorian) representative social system can exercise an effective and total social control—which does not mean that there is no difference between representative democracy and popular-democratic totalitarian systems. To see them as effects of the same problem, attempting to provide social meaning and identity, does not collapse their differences. Therein lies the hard work of living in a democracy: maintaining such differences in the symbolic and real density of everyday life. Romantic history offers this kind of training to the contemporary reader. The democratic system, which functions like figurative language, holds within it the greatest potential for both control and freedom. No wonder these possibilities evoke in some people fear, if not terror, and in others hope and exhilaration. But why does the problem of language stir up so much trouble when introduced into historical or social-science debates? Is there something terrifying about language itself, or literature, or the unconscious? Literature and history, language and science, could not survive each one on its own without the continual competition among them. History and literature are not defined independently of each other in the sense that one could be identified with fact and the other with fiction. Instead, they define themselves in relationship to each other, fluctuating the line of their division. The line varies according to the cooperation and antagonism between them. Retrospectively that line serves as the mutable and immutable bar between fact and fiction, truth and illusion, science and insanity.

My arguments here displace still further the idea of history as the investigation of truth. Political and professional debate, literary methods of rereading, any kind of discursive competition ground the practice of history that depends upon the "historical symbolic." These are not the offstage activities of a more professional endeavor still centered on that search for a progressive, if not total, objectivity. They are central and integral moments inseparable from the truth that one finally comes to. The truth is never an end (or beginning), but a constantly shifting middle that reconstitutes its own ends and beginnings. That is to say, truth is a loose symbolic space that historians must occupy as if they discovered it.

The bartering of Michelet and Blanc, Thiers and Cabet over the terrain of history (Furet and Mazauric, etc.) is both petty and completely serious; at stake are the nature and interpretation of reality. The historian's interpretation, if honored by tradition, takes on that monumental air of History that always comes out right. History-as-it-really-was (Ranke). One day the historian puts forth a fragile hypothesis; the next day or in a hundred years that hypothesis has the apparent solidity of truth, though it too can be overthrown in turn. Using Furet's binary oppositional terms, analysis and commemoration, but rephrasing the relationship: each historian must prove that he or she is practicing analysis, instead of repeating the inevitable commemorations. Or rather, each historian presents his or her commemoration as analysis and makes it stick.

We are always commemorating something, and not always what we think. In a theoretical sense, we are all Jacobin historians; we imply, if not say outright, that the new regime of analysis and maximum objectivity begins with us. We look back and find suitable heirs for the new history we rewrite from the moment of our new epistemological break, and everything before us, except what foreshadows us, automatically becomes the old regime.

In *L'Ancien Régime et la Révolution*, Tocqueville sets up the image of double blindness or double commemoration defining historical analysis from both "ends," subject and object. The subject or historian necessarily commemorates the ideological or cultural structures from which she or he speaks and writes, the presuppositions of the questions asked. This condition, which Furet calls the "optical illusion" of history, is more than subjectivity, more even than a cultural subjectivity that can be corrected. The form of our seeing and reading cannot be extracted from the content we find and invent there. And the historical object emerges from no less a contaminated process. It survives in the archive only by blocking out so much else, either by accident or its own violent strategies. The historian commemorates his or her own invisible structures and transports almost without knowing it the layered commemorations of the past. Analysis emerges, if at all, as if "on the other side" of these.

Nietzsche describes a similar double bind in *On the Advantage and Disadvantage of History for Life*. Either we see only ourselves projected wherever we go, repeating the mirror of our constant ethno-egocentric present, or we are all the reembodiment of some ghost living out an unforgivable past through us. We are all zombies. Instead of lifting ourselves into a synthesis of both, we often cannot separate out which is which. Yet we make these distinctions, as crucial and daring as origins and as banal and automatic as everyday life, all the time. In this book, I have isolated theoretical examples of this important gesture of arbitrary division—before/after; past/present; object of study/subject or author of study; text/nontext; sign/referent; private/public; historical/political; truth/people.

If some of the underlying premises of history change, historians and literary critics will also alter the questions they bring to their object. It seems less imperative to decide whether the Revolution is continuity or rupture and whodunit, whether the Terror was justified or not, whether the Revolution was tragic or comic, succeeded or failed and why. We might ask, instead, how, where, and why rupture is located in one place or erased in another. What are the implications of various explanations whether they solve the Revolution or dissolve it? History is not only the culture's way of making and remaking sense of itself, but an investigation into the mechanisms, the seductions of a specific logic or reasoning. It is also the challenge of unthinking the presuppositions upon which the acceptable explanations and interpretations of our culture are formed— "counterintuitive knowledge" or the historical imagination open to the possibility of difference and change. (Utropia ...)

I vowed that I would not end up with a definition of history, and now look what I've done. "Language made me do it." I have emphasized the process of making judgments, as if my own judgments, political, ethical, moral, wait patiently and emerge from the other side—but they are always present, all the time. I want to say who done it (language?) as much as anyone else. A narrative without a crime and a villain is unreadable.

While I introduced this book as a search for handles on a monstrous, shapeless object (water, air), I am aware of nudging forward what is just ahead of my writing, the temptation of defining the French Revolution or revolution in general, democracy, the people, and that enigma, the Terror. I admit to being pleasantly surprised when a kind of definition spun out of a development, as when that "bar" in the Legislative Assembly stood as the flexible limit around which history along with society sorts itself into "inside" and "out." I tried to imagine the different shapes of history that flickered each time in each individual text to see if they could be named in some category together, a Romantic epistemology or a Romantic theory of history—that swerve of repulsion that adds another smoke screen of history; the spirit of Justice rising from Michelet's protean Grace; Blanc's dis-appointment; Tocqueville's ever-renewable monolithic institution and the equally resistant subversive little constitutions. In the chapter about the logographers, what is essential flips with what is accidental, banal, anecdotal. It is hard to generalize. Something new both springs up as if from nowhere and always continues to dig there, circuitous and invisible (old), until it emerges, betraying itself in that coming to light and publicity, no longer itself but its other, the immutable institution. Often two mutually exclusive figures of history occupy the same terrain and must be "thought" together. *Headless History* is the only way I know how to describe "it": revolution, historical change, terror.

Every writer should leave space to show how undefinable and traumatic her or his objects of study are, before rushing to explain them. Every work of history needs a moment of uncertainty, a moment given over to the disarray, or rather, the still point of uncertainty.[14] Originally, in my project, I wanted to move through the Revolution and arrive somehow at making the Terror appear for what it really was. But I left the event of the 10th of August as the last chapter so that the book appeared to stop, confounded by the Terror that always looms ahead. In that last chapter, besides returning to the archive (researching each individual logographer), I ended up telling a kind of story. What is the status of story? —one of the best forms of explanation and definition after all.

TWO STORIES: MUTUALLY EXCLUSIVE BUT
NECESSARILY TOGETHER

The fall of the Bastille (July 14, 1789) and the 9th of Thermidor (July 27, 1794) are two stories constantly evoked in the history of the French Revolution, and in this book. They can become too symbolic in their opposition to each other—high point of the Revolution and its end (or the end of the betrayal of the Revolution). To put it another way, they are two possible figures of the Revolution always present, flip sides of the same sign. In one, the cycle of repetition has played itself out. Language, popular identity, political expression, that unpredictable dialectic with the real, have piled up their errors or worn themselves down to nothing but power's vacuum. The vision of impasse and frustration becomes con-

14. Stanley Mellon wrote that "what we have tried to do ... is to detraumatize the Revolution." ("Nineteenth-Century Perceptions of Revolution," *The Consortium on Revolutionary Europe, 1750–1850: Proceedings,* 1975 [Athens, Ga.: The Consortium on Revolutionary Europe, n.d.], 6).
See "Messages from the Unknown" in Reddy, *Money and Liberty in Modern Europe,* 46–51.

vincing and takes hold. Speech itself has drowned out the voice of the people.

On the other hand, at some point, no one knows exactly when, there is no single low point of frustration that automatically brings it on—at some point the unforeseeable, unsayable stirring takes form and is. There is not a word for it; all expression is nonverbal, even inarticulate. This burst of self-identity seems to exist in the realm of the inexpressible. Almost immediately, however, there is an explosion of words. Was all that new language repressed that now is released? And these words hover for a moment before they are susceptible to the inevitable wear and tear, repetition and cycle. This revolutionary moment cannot really motivate hope, for the revolution is both more unpredictable and more predictable than hope, that mediator which tides one over, waiting. No one even suspected that anything was coming—but everyone knew it all along. No one can stop it when it arrives.

These two stories, whose literal chronology I have reversed to give them that mirror effect, should be collective stories, but no doubt my own voice is all too present, much as I try to imitate the group of Romantic historians in the first case and Michelet in the second. In fact, it is hard to mime their mixture of passion and canniness, myth and manipulation, and I cannot resist, like Cabet or Michelet, interrupting with my own *mouvements de séance*, mutilating the phrases for my own purpose.

ROBESPIERRE'S DEMISE: THE BOOMERANG OF FREE
SPEECH (BY COLLECTIVE AUTHORSHIP)

The Jacobin power of terror had already begun to slip into farce. After the Festival of the Supreme Being, a witch, an ambitious hag, the "Mother of God" used Robespierre as a cult figure (says Michelet). This was the beginning of the end.

Everything went wrong for Robespierre, but it seemed so fatal, so necessary and allegorical that future historians still wonder whether he was not courting his own disaster. (Contemporary historian Bouloiseau notes: "Everything seemed like a set-up, even the awkwardness [*Tout parut truqué, même les maladresses*]."[15]) The scene was so staged that it appeared to follow some drama already written.

15. Marc Bouloiseau, *La république jacobine: 10 août 1792 – 9 thermidor an II*

Suspense, that masterful Jacobin talent, had been building. On the 7th of Thermidor (1794), Robespierre made a sentimental journey to Rousseau's old stomping grounds, the Ermitage, where he remained for hours in silent meditation. What would Robespierre say on the 8th of Thermidor in that long-awaited speech? Nothing. Nothing new. What a disappointment! (Lamartine). What a misjudgment in strategy (Blanc). The long speech, words crossed out and rewritten right up to the end, extended the same scare tactics that had already begun to break down.

Before Thermidor, Marat had been one of the few people brave enough to call Robespierre's bluff and demand "that one motivate these measures" (Lamartine, 6:51). Marat knew that Robespierre's power resided in the delay of motivating the politico-linguistic sign. But Marat's life was cut short even before the others'. Without hindrance, Robespierre was able to perfect an absolutely ambiguous discourse that worked on double entendre. A chosen few understood exactly who was being accused even though nothing was clearly said — so Robespierre himself could not be blamed. And those accused thought all the time they were being praised until too late. They were under arrest.

As usual, on the 9th, Robespierre had heated the audience up to fever pitch, with language both erotic and menacing. Each listener sat on the edge of his seat. Who would be accused this time? That floating signifier of the "enemy," flip side of the "people," passed over all their heads as they waited for it to stop, like some scary child's game where the unseen handkerchief drops behind anyone's back. Robespierre's speech was a long, tantalizing postponement of not-naming names. The problem now was that the linguistic sign had reversed its meaning, its connotations: everyone thought he was being accused, and not the other way around. So paranoia, "indignation," grew with impatience. In the middle of all the verbiage, Robespierre said: Pitt is the enemy and guess who else? then, almost coquettishly: "Ah! I dare not name them in this moment and in this place, I cannot decide myself to tear the veil covering the deep mystery of iniquities all the way off." This striptease of the word drove the Convention crazy.

In the discussion afterward, Charlier cried, "When one prides himself

---

(Paris: Seuil, 1972), 248. In my own account of the 9th of Thermidor, I have not given references for speeches of the revolutionaries common to all historical accounts and records, but I have for descriptions and commentaries quoted directly from Romantic historians.

on having the courage of virtue, he has to have that of truth too; name those you accuse!"

"Yes, yes, name them, name them!" (*Nommez-les, nommez-les!*) shouted a group of the Mountain, standing and shaking their fists. It is like the audience of the melodrama yelling for its villain. "It was necessary to name them, and, since one did not name them, the threat, even if it was addressed only to a few, seemed to hover over all" (Michelet, 2:531).

The next day, the 9th of Thermidor, Saint Just got up and actually admitted that the man he so admired, Robespierre, "did not explain himself enough yesterday." At last! the audience thought, now we'll finally have the answers and the terrible tension will be over. But no! Robespierre's right-hand man only exacerbated it further, beyond all bounds. "Saint Just's harangue had the form of an *énigme* [riddle or enigma?] whose answer was the death of Robespierre's enemies. But the orator wanted to let the Convention pronounce that answer" (Lamartine, 8:322).

Dangerous to leave the signifier open, both riddle with a tricky answer and enigma for which there is never any right response. The empty space of naming, if left running long enough, always turns and strikes back at its author. Robespierre left the space open for that one name everyone heard, without its being spoken, that was filled by euphemism after euphemism ("that man who ... ," "the tyrant over there ... ," Michelet's "one" in the quote above). The Thermidorians knew that they could not combat the word with the word, so they chose to "suffocate" Robespierre with all their noise and reduce him to silence. Then came the famous outcry: "May Danton's blood suffocate you."

"Noise submerges him. They hear only the bitter barking of a voice that rends the air. One sees only gestures at once supplicating or threatening, whose words can not be seized. The voice of Robespierre grows hoarse and chokes off completely" (Lamartine, 8:338–39). Then the unknown Louchet whispered the call for arrest, using Robespierre's name.

Robespierre knew that anyone who assumes the voice of the people for any amount of time undergoes a risk that few survive. That night he performed the symbolic gesture that saved the Revolution by ending it. He refused to authorize the insurrection in his favor. He signed Rob—, then stopped. Am I stealing that legitimacy which is not mine to own and is no one's? Who can sign for the people? *Mais au nom de qui?* Robespierre's question is the only answer the Revolution can give to future democracy.

The mad chaos of that night. Robespierre delayed, delayed, was surrounded at the Hôtel de Ville, where his friends had forced him to come hold out with them. When soldiers burst in, Robespierre's brother threw himself from the window. Robespierre himself was shot (suicide?) — where else but in the mouth? (like Goethe's Werther). In his speech he said, everyone says I talk all the time but I cannot get a word in edgewise. The word machine, backed up by the guillotine, was at last put to silence. Then came the worst torture. They carried him to the waiting room of the Convention and left him on his stretcher there. In pain, paralyzed and mute, he "saw and heard everything" (Lamartine, 8:369). He had to listen to the arguments, calumnies, without being able to object or even comment. A similar image returns to haunt the historian Michelet (in *La sorcière*) as the most horrible of torments: forced to witness (the rape or murder of the people) without being able to say a word.

On the platform of the guillotine, the executioner ripped the bandage off Robespierre's mouth, tearing from the condemned man a piercing scream of pain. "It was the cry of this poor people the peasant woman spoke about, the cry of millions of unfortunate ones they were going to drag back to the quarries. The blade descended, and, for a long time, all was said [*tout fut dit*]" (Blanc, 2:552).

THE SURRENDER OF THE BASTILLE: THE REVERSAL
OF MADNESS AND NORMS (ADAPTED FROM
MICHELET)[16]

On the 13th [of July 1789], Paris barely considered defending itself. On the 14th, it attacked. What happened to make this change?

The night before the 14th: doubt, trouble, a mad disorder. But "the morning was luminous [*le matin fut lumineux*]." Everyone saw the same light. And in every heart the tiny voice spoke: "Go, and you'll take the Bastille! [*Va, et tu prendras la Bastille!*]"

"What was impossible, insane, strange to say. . . . And everyone believed it anyway. And so it came to be [*Et cela se fit*]." [Just like "and so there was light" on that first morning of Genesis.]

16. My paraphrasing is not in quotation marks; direct quotations are from Michelet, 1:144–62.

The Bastille was armed to the hilt, enclosed in walls ten feet thick at the top, thirty or forty thick at the base; it could shrug off bullets and pummel the defenseless people from above, from the towers, iron-barred windows, and slits [*meurtrières*] in the stone.

"The attack on the Bastille was not reasonable at all. It was an act of faith."

No one proposed it. But everyone believed, and everyone acted. Along the streets, quais, bridges, boulevards, the crowd cried out to the crowd: To the Bastille! To the Bastille! Everyone heard.

Don't say the troublemakers at the Palais-Royal were behind it. And don't even suggest that the electors from the Hôtel de Ville had anything to do with it. On the contrary, they tried to stop the imminent confrontation, but they weren't traitors either.

So who did it? Who? The people. Everyone.

And what happened in that short night, when no one slept, so by morning all dissension, all uncertainty disappeared with the darkness and they all had the same thought?

We know what happened at the Palais-Royal and at the Hôtel de Ville; that's no help. But what happened in the homes [*foyer*] of the people, that's what we need to know.

And since I have no documents on this question—and who does, because the people left none, especially not on this night, how could they? Were their thoughts even formulated yet? So I'll use my intuition—"We can guess by what happened later" that each person thought back on the long past and judged it; each one condemned it as wrong. The ghost of the father who suffered and died in silence returned to his sons and spoke.

And you, strong men, you looked down on your sleeping children and decided to take up the fight of the future.

Both past and future said the same thing: Go!...

And Justice gave the troubled heart a solid center: Go ... I am with you. And finally that little voice, the voice of humanity, that seems so weak yet overturns towers, already had the Bastille trembling.

That intrepid woman [give us her name] who worked tirelessly to free Latude, she took the Bastille.

[Then Michelet tells about the people taking arms at the Arsenal and the various delegations, one from the Hôtel de Ville, but none so forceful as the mighty Thuriot alone, member of the Constituent Assembly. He forced the hated governor of the prison to turn the cannons back from the edge of the tower where they aimed on the mass that squeezed and swayed below.]

At this point the people naively believed they could walk right into the Bastille. But as they crossed the first bridge into the first courtyard, and then later into the second courtyard, both times they were fired upon. They thought they had been betrayed. Now no words could express what they were feeling. "The people's rage was inexpressible." They had waited long enough. Even though more and more of the bourgeois guard joined the people, no official order ever came down from the Hôtel de Ville to take the Bastille. It was talk, talk, and delay, "long speeches in vain." Horrifying rumors circulated about massacres of the people all over the city.

The crowd also filled the Place des Grèves, overflowed into the Hôtel de Ville, where the city government hedged. They forced the provost, whom they blamed most, and the rest of the electors to retreat into the hall of Saint Jean, where those officials trembled between life and death. The din and confusion continued to grow until the people forgot why they had come, forgot the provost and the Bastille.

Five-thirty in the afternoon. "A cry goes up from the Place des Grèves. A tremendous noise, at first far away, it breaks out, advances, grows closer, with the speed and explosion of storm. . . . The Bastille is taken!"

[Ah, but note that our narrator led us off to the Hôtel de Ville, himself forgot the Bastille, so that we are not present at that legendary moment. Who dares witness a legend? Would the bourgeois historian sully it if he were there, if he pretended to be where he could never be, dissolved in a crowd of people? We readers, and Michelet with us, are in the hall and hear the shouts outside. That is the only way we know that the Bastille has fallen. And the shouts of the people at the Bastille, where everyone fights, are even farther away. We experience this central moment in all of French history by hearsay through absence.]

No, Michelet insists, you cannot say the Bastille was taken, but instead, it gave itself up. "Its bad conscience got to it, drove it crazy, and made it lose heart."

Michelet leaves a place in his history for the amazement, the chaos, the inexplicable explosion of the Revolution — not the only dominant place, but crucial nonetheless. Even if he has to come upon that place from the sidelines of the Hôtel de Ville, the Bastille and all that it represents resonates throughout his work.

The "fall" — no, "surrender" — of the Bastille, is an icon of nonlogical forms of historical change. The people go to bed with the image in their heads of an invincible stone giant and wake up the next morning and realize on their own that the Bastille has nothing to stand on but thin air. What one day appears utter madness can reverse the next day into "the way things are." And the opposite reversal is just as possible. This view of history is more frightening than an evolutionary one. As Michel Foucault has written, we try to marginalize otherness as madness to quarantine in one institution or another (prison, asylum, university, theater). In vain we cordon it off as a not-us and construct fictive degrees of rehabilitations that will bring it back into our likeness. Radical difference is either too close to us or so inconceivable that either way we cannot recognize it at all in the framework of our knowledge. Like the Revolution that the nobles cannot see there in front of their faces and that the people cannot even imagine as being possible. Also like Romanticism that reveals too much about ourselves, so that we do not want to read it. Over and over in nineteenth-century histories the problem of social change comes up against this paradox that especially dismayed Louis Blanc: we cannot get there from here, and we are already there now by virtue of being able to conceive of ourselves differently.

Michelet allows the reader to contemplate an astounding moment in history that is theoretically and practically significant. This moment is the shock, good or bad, of realizing or thinking you see something, real or *imaginaire*: the promise of empowerment, emptiness of present power, demasking, confidence for the first time. Whether in revolution or in history, paradigms of knowledge flip unexpectedly (after the long travail). Each new interpretation, each new regime institutes its own madness or strangeness as truth, which only another inexpressible reservoir of justice and rage can confront from its place of ingenious resistance.

Appendix Publication Figures

The *Catalogue générale de la librairie française (1840–1865)* (Paris: Librairie Ancienne Edouard Champion n.d. [1867–?], ed. Otto Henry Lorenz), is probably incomplete and even inaccurate in places. The figures on Lamartine do not compare with Talvert and Place's. And Lorenz covers only the editions published between 1840 and 1865. Still, the relative comparisons made possible by figures from the Lorenz catalogue are interesting.

Author	Format	Dates of Publication	Publisher	Price
Blanc	12 vols. in 8	1847–62	Pagnerre	60F/set
Blanc	1–74 livraisons in 8	1865	Jondé	10c/livr.
Cabet	4 vols. in 8	1840 (orig. 1839)	Pagnerre	18F
Cabet	5 vols. in 8	1845–47	rue J-J Rousseau	20F
Lamartine	4 vols. in 8 or 200 livraisons	1847	rue du Battoir	10.50
Lamartine	8 vols. in 8	1848	Furne	28F
Lamartine	8 vols. in 8	1853	Furne	30F
Lamartine	4 vols. in 8	1858	Furne	24F
Lamartine	6 vols. in 12	1860	Hachette	12F
Lamartine	3 vols. in 4 or in livraisons	1865–66	Le Chevalier	21F 10c
Michelet	7 vols. in 8	1847–53	Chamerot	45F
Mignet	2 vols. in 8	1861 (orig. 1824)	Didier	12F
Mignet	2 vols. in 12	1864	Didier	7F
Quinet	2 vols. in 8	1865	Lib. Internat.	15F
Thiers	10 vols. in 8	1858 (orig. 1823)	Furne	50F
Thiers	8 vols. in 12	1858	Furne	28F
Thiers	4 vols. in 8	1858	Furne	40F
Thiers	2 vols. in 4 200 livraisons or 20 series	1865–67	Furne	21F 10c 1.10
Tocqueville	1 vol. in 8	1857	Lévy Frères	7.50

Author	Format	Dates of Publication	Publisher	Price
Tocqueville	in *O. compl.*	1860–65	Lévy Frères	6F
For the sake of comparison:				
Cabet	*Almanach icarien* in 16	1842	Mallet	50c
Cabet	*Voyage en Icarie* in 18	1848	Mallet	3F
Lamartine	*Méditations* p. in 12	1864	Hachette	3.50
Michelet	*Le peuple* in 12	1846	Hachette	3.50
Quinet	*Ahasvérus* in 12	1843	Comon	3.50
Thiers	"Discours..." in 8	1846	Paulin	50c

I did not note illustrations and atlases. The "popular editions" of the 1860s meant more illustrations, usually folio size, in *livraisons,* cheaper materials and production. Otherwise: the smaller the format, the less expensive, the more "popular." The in 12 for 3.50 is more or less equivalent to the standard good paperback of our time.

Bibliography

Allen, James Smith. *Popular French Romanticism: Authors, Readers, and Books in the Nineteenth Century.* Syracuse: Syracuse UP, 1981.

Aron, Raymond. *Les étapes de la pensée sociologique: Montesquieu, Comte, Marx, Tocqueville, Durkheim, Pareto, Weber.* Paris: Gallimard, 1967.

Avril, Pierre. *Les français et leur parlement.* Paris: Casterman, 1972.

Bann, Stephen. *The Clothing of Clio: A Study of the Representation of History in Nineteenth-Century Britain and France.* Cambridge: Cambridge UP, 1984.

Barbéris, Pierre. *Le prince et le marchand: Idéologiques: La littérature, l'histoire.* Paris: Fayard, 1980.

Barnes, Harry Elmer. *A History of Historical Writing.* 2d ed. New York: Dover, 1963.

Barthes, Roland. "Le discours de l'histoire." *Social Science Information* 6(August 1967): 65–75. Rpt. in *Poétique* 49 (February 1982): 13–21.

———. "Historical Discourse." *Structuralism: A Reader.* Ed. Michael Lane. London: Jonathan Cape, 1970. 145–55.

Baudelaire, Charles. *Oeuvres complètes.* Ed. Y.-G. Le Dantec and Claude Pichois. Paris: Gallimard, 1961.

Benjamin, Walter. *Illuminations.* Trans. Harry Zohn. Ed. Hannah Arendt. New York: Schocken, 1968. First pub. 1955.

Bernard-Griffiths, Simone. "Rupture entre Michelet et Quinet à propos de l'histoire de la Révolution." *Michelet cent ans après.* Grenoble: Presses univ. de Grenoble, 1975. 145–65.

Blanc, Louis. *Histoire de dix ans, 1830–1840.* 4th ed. 4 vols. Paris: Pagnerre, 1844.

———. *Histoire de la Révolution française.* 2 vols. Paris: Maurice Lachâtre, n.d.

———. *Histoire de la Révolution française.* 12 vols. Paris: Langlois et Leclercq, 1847.

Blanchot, Maurice. *La communauté inavouable.* Paris: Minuit, 1983.

Bloom, Harold. *Agon: Towards a Theory of Revisionism.* Oxford: Oxford UP, 1982.

Bouloiseau, Marc. *La république jacobine: 10 août 1792—9 thermidor an II.* Paris: Seuil, 1972.

Brette, Armand. *Histoire des édifices où ont siégé les assemblées parlementaires de la Révolution française et de la première République.* Paris: Imprimerie nationale, 1902.

Brooks, Peter. *The Melodramatic Imagination: Balzac, Henry James, Melodrama, and the Mode of Excess.* New Haven: Yale UP, 1976.

Bulletin du centre d'analyse du discours (La rhétorique du discours, objet d'histoire, XVIIIe—XXe siècles). Pref. by Jacques Guilhaumou. 5 (1981).

Cabet, Etienne. *Histoire populaire de la Révolution française de 1789 à 1830, précédée d'une introduction contenant le précis de l'histoire des français depuis leur origine jusqu'aux Etats-Généraux.* 4 vols. Paris: Pagnerre, 1839.

Carlyle, Thomas. *The French Revolution: A History.* 2 vols. New York: Colonial Press, 1900.

Carroll, David. "On Tropology: The Forms of History." *Diacritics* 6 (Fall 1976): 58–64.

Castoriadis, Cornelius. *L'institution imaginaire de la société.* 3d ed. Paris: Seuil, 1975.

Certeau, Michel de. *L'écriture de l'histoire.* Paris: Gallimard, 1975.

———. "On the Oppositional Practices of Everyday Life." *Social Text* 1 (1980): 3–43.

———. "L'opération historique." *Faire de l'histoire.* Ed. Jacques Le Goff and Pierre Nora. Paris: Gallimard, 1974. 1:3–41.

Chevalier, Louis. *Classes laborieuses et classes dangereuses à Paris pendant la première moitié du XIXe siècle.* Paris: Plon, 1958.

Conry, Ivette. *L'introduction du darwinisme en France.* Paris: Vrin, 1974.

de Man, Paul. *Allegories of Reading: Figural Language in Rousseau, Nietzsche, Rilke, and Proust.* New Haven: Yale UP, 1979.

———. Introduction. *Studies in Romanticism* 18 (Winter 1979): 495–99.

———. "The Rhetoric of Temporality." *Interpretation: Theory and Practice.* Ed. C. Singleton. Baltimore: The Johns Hopkins UP, 1969. 173–209. Rpt. in *Blindness and Insight.* Ed. Wlad Godzich. Minneapolis: U of Minnesota P, 1983. 187–228.

Derrida, Jacques. "Freud et la scène de l'écriture." *L'écriture et la différence.* Paris: Seuil, 1967. 293–340.

Duchet, Claude, and Françoise Gaillard. Introduction. *Sub-Stance* 15 (1971): 2–5.

Ducrot, Oswald, and Tzvetan Todorov. *Dictionnaire encyclopédique des sciences du langage.* Paris: Seuil, 1972.

———. *Encyclopedic Dictionary of the Sciences of Language.* Trans. Catherine Porter. Baltimore: The Johns Hopkins UP, 1979.

Dworkin, Ronald. "Hard Cases." *Harvard Law Review* 88 (April 1975): 1057–1109.

Flaubert, Gustave. *Bouvard et Pécuchet.* Ed. Jacques Suffel. Paris: Flammarion, 1966.

———. *Correspondance (juillet 1851 – décembre 1858)*. Ed. Jean Bruneau. Paris: Gallimard, 1980. Vol. 2.

———. *Correspondance, 1859 – 1871*. *Oeuvres complètes*. Ed. Société des études littéraires françaises. Paris: Club de l'honnête homme, 1975. Vol. 14.

Freud, Sigmund. *The Interpretation of Dreams*. Ed. and trans. James Strachey. New York: Basic Books, 1958. First pub. 1900.

———. *Die Traumdeutung*. *Gesammelte Werke*. Frankfurt am Main: S. Fischer, 1976. Vol. 2/3.

Furet, François. *La gauche et la Révolution au milieu du XIXe siècle: Edgar Quinet et la question du jacobinisme (1865 – 1870)*. Paris: Hachette, 1986.

———. *Interpreting the French Revolution*. Trans. Elborg Forster. Cambridge: Cambridge UP, 1981.

———. *Marx et la Révolution française: Textes de Marx présentés, réunis, traduits par Lucien Calvié*. Paris: Flammarion, 1986.

———. *Penser la Révolution française*. Paris: Gallimard, 1978.

Furet, François, and Denis Richet. *La Révolution*. Paris: Hachette, 1965.

———. *French Revolution*. Trans. Stephen Hardman. New York: Macmillan, 1970.

Gaillard, Françoise. "An Unspeakable (Hi)story." *Yale French Studies* 59 (1980): 137 – 54.

Gearhart, Suzanne. *The Open Boundary of History and Fiction: A Critical Approach to the French Enlightenment*. Princeton: Princeton UP, 1984.

Geffroy, Annie, Jacques Guilhaumou, and André Salem. "L'histoire sur mesures ou pour une statistique du discours." *Bulletin du centre d'analyse du discours de l'Université de Lille III (Sur la Révolution française)* 2 (1975): 15 – 60.

Genette, Gérard. *Figures III*. Paris: Seuil, 1972.

———. *Narrative Discourse: An Essay in Method*. Trans. Jane E. Lewin. Ithaca: Cornell UP, 1980.

Gérard, Alice. *La Révolution française, mythes et interprétations (1789 – 1970)*. Paris: Flammarion, 1970.

Gershoy, Leo. "Three French Historians and the Revolution of 1848." *Journal of the History of Ideas* 12 (1951): 131 – 45.

Giesey, Ralph E. "The King Imagined." *The Political Culture of the Old Regime*. Ed. Keith Michael Baker. Vol. 1 of *The French Revolution and the Creation of Modern Political Culture*. Oxford: Pergamon, 1987. 41 – 59.

Gossman, Lionel. "Augustin Thierry and Liberal Historiography." *History and Theory* 15 (1976): 1 – 83.

———. "History and Literature: Reproduction or Signification." *The Writing of History: Literary Form and Historical Understanding*. Ed. Robert H. Canary and Henry Kozicki. Madison: Wisconsin UP, 1978. 3 – 39.

———. "History as Decipherment: Romantic Historiography and the Discovery of the Other." *New Literary History* 18 (Autumn 1986): 23 – 57.

Gramsci, Antonio. *Selections from the Prison Notebooks of Antonio Gramsci*. Ed. and trans. Quintin Hoare and Geoffrey Nowell Smith. New York: International Publishers, 1971. First pub. 1948 – 51.

Greenawalt, Kent. "The Enduring Significance of Neutral Principles." *Columbia Law Review* 78 (1978): 982–1021.

Guéhenno, Jean. *L'évangile éternelle.* Paris: Grasset, 1927.

Guilhaumou, Jacques. *La langue politique et la Révolution française: De l'évènement à la raison linguistique.* Paris: Méridiens Klincksieck, 1989.

———. "Première partie: Le rapport des forces (1792–1794), Sur le jacobinisme à la lumière de quelques remarques de Gramsci." "Deuxième partie: Premiers jalons pour une étude des discours révolutionnaires." *Dialectiques* 10–11 (1975): 34–57.

Guilhaumou, Jacques, and Régine Robin. Avant-propos. *Bulletin du centre d'analyse du discours de l'Université de Lille III (Sur la Révolution française)* 2 (1975):1–13.

Hartman, Geoffrey. "La voix de la navette." *Poétique* 28 (1976): 398–412.

Havette, René. *Bibliographie de la sténographie française.* Paris: Dorbon-Ainé, 1906.

———. *Deux sténographes à Bordeaux en 1784 et 1789 (Coulon de Thévenot et Dupont, de la Rochelle): D'après les manuscrits de la société littéraire du Musée de Bordeaux et les documents de l'auteur.* Paris: Revue internationale de sténographie, 1903.

Herr, Richard. *Tocqueville and the Old Regime.* Princeton: Princeton UP, 1962.

Huet, Marie-Hélène. *Rehearsing the Revolution: The Staging of Marat's Death, 1793–1797.* Berkeley: U of California P, 1982.

———. "La signature de l'histoire." *Modern Language Notes* 100 (September 1985): 715–27.

Hugo, Victor. *Oeuvres complètes.* Ed. Jean Massin. Paris: Club français du livre, 1967–71. Vol. 10.

———. *Quatrevingt-treize.* Paris: Garnier-Flammarion, 1965.

Hunt, Lynn. *Politics, Culture, and Class in the French Revolution.* Berkeley: U of California P, 1984.

Imbs, Paul. *Trésor de la langue française: Dictionnaire de la langue du XIXe et du XXe siècles (1789–1960).* Paris: Editions du Centre national de la recherche scientifique and Klincksieck, 1971.

Jameson, Fredric. "Figural Relativism, or the Poetics of Historiography." *Diacritics* 6 (Spring 1976): 2–9.

———. *The Political Unconscious: Narrative as a Socially Symbolic Act.* Ithaca: Cornell UP, 1981.

Johnson, Christopher. *Utopian Communism in France: Cabet and the Icarians, 1839–1851.* Ithaca: Cornell UP, 1974.

Kantorowicz, Ernst Hartwig. *The King's Two Bodies: A Study in Medieval Political Theology.* Princeton: Princeton UP, 1957.

Kaplan, Edward K. *Michelet's Poetic Vision: A Romantic Philosophy of Nature, Man, and Woman.* Amherst: U of Massachusetts P, 1977.

Kellner, Hans. "A Bedrock of Order: Hayden White's Linguistic Humanism." *History and Theory* 19 (1980): 1–29.

———. *Language and Historical Representation: Getting the Story Crooked.* Madison: U of Wisconsin P, 1989.

Kundera, Milan. *The Book of Laughter and Forgetting.* Trans. Michael Henry Heim. New York: Viking Penguin, 1981. First pub. 1978.

LaCapra, Dominick. *Rethinking Intellectual History: Texts, Contexts, Language.* Ithaca: Cornell UP, 1983.

LaCapra, Dominick, and Steven L. Kaplan, eds. *Modern European Intellectual History: Reappraisals and New Perspectives.* Ithaca: Cornell UP, 1982.

Lamartine, Alphonse de. *Histoire des Girondins.* 8 vols. Paris: Furne, 1847.

Laurent, E., ed. (with L. Lataste and C. Pionnier). *Archives parlementaires.* Paris: Librairie administrative de P. Dupont, 1862–19–. 2d series (1848).

Lefebvre, Henri. *Critique de la vie quotidienne.* 3 vols. Paris: L'Arche, 1958–81.

Lefort, Claude. *Essais sur le politique (XIXe–XXe siècles).* Paris: Seuil, 1986.

———. Préface. Edgar Quinet, *La Révolution.* Paris: Belin, 1987. 7–28.

Littré, Emile. *Dictionnaire de la langue française.* Paris: Pauvert, 1956. Vol. 2.

Lorenz, Otto Henry. *Catalogue générale de la librairie française (1840 – 1865).* Paris: Librairie Ancienne Edouard Champion, n.d. (1867–?). Vols. 1, 3, 4.

Louandre, Charles. "Statistique littéraire de la production intellectuelle en France depuis quinze ans." *Revue des deux mondes* 20 (1847): 255–86, 416–46.

Loubère, Leo A. *Louis Blanc: His Life and His Contribution to the Rise of French Jacobin-Socialism.* Evanston, Ill.: Northwestern UP, 1961.

Lyon, Bryce. *A Constitutional and Legal History of Medieval England.* New York: Harper & Row, 1960.

Marx, Karl. *Der 18. Brumaire des Louis Bonaparte. Gesamtausgabe (MEGA).* Berlin: Dietz, 1985. Vol. 11.

———. *The Eighteenth Brumaire of Louis Bonaparte.* New York: International Publishers, 1963.

Marx, Karl, and Frederick Engels. *The Holy Family; or, Critique of Critical Criticism: Against Bruno Bauer and Company.* Trans. Richard Dixon and Clemens Dutt. Moscow: Progress Publishers, 1975.

———. *Manifest der Kommunistischen Partei. Frühe Schriften.* Ed. Hans-Joachim Leiber and Peter Furth. Darmstadt: Wissenschaftliche Buchgesellschaft, 1975. Vol. 2.

———. *Manifesto of the Communist Party.* New York: International Publishers, 1948.

Mehlman, Jeffrey. *Revolution and Repetition: Marx/Hugo/Balzac.* Berkeley: U of California P, 1977.

Melchior-Bonnet, Alain. "Histoire et littérature." *La grande encyclopédie.* Paris: Larousse, 1974. 29: 5939–40.

Mellon, Stanley. "Nineteenth-Century Perceptions of Revolution." *The Consortium on Revolutionary Europe, 1750 – 1850: Proceedings, 1975.* Athens, Ga.: The Consortium on Revolutionary Europe, n.d. 1–12.

———. *The Political Uses of History: A Study of Historians in the French Restoration.* Stanford: Stanford UP, 1958.

"Metahistory: Six Critiques." *History and Theory* 19 (1980).

Michelet, Jules. *Histoire de la Révolution française.* Ed. Gérard Walter. 2 vols. Paris: Gallimard, 1952.

———. *La montagne. Oeuvres complètes.* Ed. Paul Viallaneix. Paris: Flammarion, 1987. Vol. 20, ed. Linda Orr.

———. *Le peuple.* Ed. Paul Viallaneix. Paris: Flammarion, 1974.

Michelot, Marius. *Les systèmes sténographiques.* Paris: Presses univ. de France, 1959.

Le moniteur universel or *Gazette nationale; ou, Le moniteur universel (réimpression de L'ancien moniteur depuis la réunion des Etats-Généraux jusqu'au Consulat).* Paris: Au bureau central, 1842. Vol. 13.

Mouchard, Claude. "Déchirer l'opinion." *L'arc* 79 (1980): 69–76.

———. Introduction. Thomas Paine, *Les droits de l'homme.* Paris: Belin, 1987.

Mouchard, Claude, and Jacques Neefs. *Flaubert.* Paris: Balland, 1986.

Muselier, François. [Pseudonym for Bernard Pingaud]. *Regards neufs sur le parlement.* Paris: Seuil, 1956.

Navarre, Albert. *Histoire générale de la sténographie et de l'écriture à travers les âges.* Paris: Librairie Ch. Delagrave, n.d. (1905).

Neefs, Jacques. "Augustin Thierry: Le moment de la 'véritable histoire de France.' " *Romantisme* 28 (1980): 289–303.

Orr, Linda. "Le discours jacobin de l'historiographie romantique." *Sédiments 1986.* Ed. Georges Leroux and Michel Van Schendel. Québec: Hurtubise HMH, 1986. 133–43.

———. "Outspoken Women and the Rightful Daughter of the Revolution: Madame de Staël's *Considérations sur la Révolution française.*" *Women and the French Revolution.* Ed. Sara E. Melzer and Leslie Rabine. Forthcoming.

———. "The Revenge of Literature: A History of History." *New Literary History* 18 (Autumn 1986): 1–22.

———. Rev. of Stephen Bann, *The Clothing of Clio: A Study of the Representation of History in Nineteenth-Century Britain and France. History and Theory* 24 (1985): 307–25.

———. "The Romantic Historiography of the Revolution and French Society." *The Consortium on Revolutionary Europe, 1750–1850: Proceedings, 1984.* Athens, Ga.: The Consortium on Revolutionary Europe, 1986. 242–47.

Ozouf, Mona. "L'opinion publique." *The Political Culture of the Old Regime.* Ed. Keith Michael Baker. Vol. 1 of *The French Revolution and the Creation of Modern Political Culture.* Oxford: Pergamon, 1987. 419–40.

Pachet, Pierre. *Le premier venu: Essai sur la politique baudelairienne.* Paris: Denoël, 1976.

Petrey, Sandy. *History in the Text: "Quatrevingt-treize" and the French Revolution.* Amsterdam: John Benjamins B.V., 1980.

———. *Realism and Revolution: Balzac, Stendhal, Zola, and the Performances of History.* Ithaca: Cornell UP, 1988.

Pocock, J. G. A. *The Ancient Constitution and the Feudal Law: A Study of English Historical Thought in the Seventeenth Century.* Cambridge: Cambridge UP, 1957.

Priouret, Roger. *La république des députés.* Paris: Grasset, 1959.

Procès-verbal de l'Assemblée nationale. Paris: Imprimerie nationale, 1792. Vol. 12.

Quinet, Edgar. *La Révolution*. 2 vols. Paris: A. Lacroix, Verboeckhoven, 1865; Belin, 1987.

Reboul, Fabienne. "Histoire ou feuilleton? La Révolution française vue par Lamartine." *Romantisme* 52 (1986): 19–33.

Reddy, William M. *Money and Liberty in Modern Europe: A Critique of Historical Understanding*. Cambridge: Cambridge UP, 1987.

Réizov, B. *L'historiographie romantique française (1815 – 1830)*. Moscow: Editions en langues étrangères, n.d. (1950?).

Rigney, Ann. "Toward Varennes." *New Literary History* 18 (Autumn 1986): 77–98.

Robin, Régine. *Histoire et linguistique*. Paris: Armand Colin, 1973.

———, ed. *Langage et idéologies: Le discours comme objet de l'histoire*. Paris: Editions ouvrières, 1974.

Rousseau, Jean-Jacques. *On the Social Contract*. Ed. Roger D. Masters. Trans. Judith D. Master. New York: St. Martin's Press, 1978.

Saussure, Ferdinand de. *Course in General Linguistics*. Ed. Charles Bally and Albert Sechehaye, with Albert Riedlinger. New York: McGraw-Hill, 1966. First pub. 1916.

Scott de Martinville, Eduard-Léon. *Histoire de la sténographie depuis les temps anciens jusqu'à nos jours; ou, Précis historique et critique des divers moyens qui ont été proposés ou employés pour rendre l'écriture aussi rapide que la parole. . . .* Paris: Charles Tondeur, 1849.

Sewell, William H., Jr. *Work and Revolution in France: The Language of Labor from the Old Regime to 1848*. Cambridge: Cambridge UP, 1980.

Soboul, Albert. Avant-propos. Claude Mazauric, *Sur la Révolution française: Contributions à l'histoire de la révolution bourgeoise*. Paris: Editions sociales, 1970.

Staël, Madame de [Germaine Necker]. *Considérations sur la Révolution française*. Ed. Jacques Godechot. Paris: Tallandier, 1983.

———. *De la littérature considérée dans ses rapports avec les institutions sociales*. Ed. Paul Van Tieghem. 2 vols. Geneva: Droz, 1959.

Taine, Hippolyte. *Les origines de la France contemporaine*. 25th ed. Paris: Hachette, 1906. Vol. 5.

Talvart, H., and J. Place. *Bibliographie des auteurs modernes de la langue française*. Paris: Editions de la Chronique des lettres françaises, 1928.

Terdiman, Richard. *Discourse/Counter-Discourse: The Theory and Practice of Symbolic Resistance in Nineteenth-Century France*. Ithaca: Cornell UP, 1985.

Thiers, Adolphe. *Histoire de la Révolution française*. 6th ed. 10 vols. Paris: Furne, 1837.

Tocqueville, Alexis de. *L'Ancien Régime et la Révolution*. Ed. J.-P. Mayer. *Oeuvres complètes*. Paris: Gallimard, 1952. Vol. 2, pt. 1.

———. *The Old Regime and the French Revolution*. Trans. Stuart Gilbert. New York: Doubleday, 1955.

Veyne, Paul. *Comment on écrit l'histoire*. Paris: Seuil, 1971.

Vigny, Alfred de. *Cinq-Mars. Oeuvres complètes*. Paris: Gallimard, 1948. Vol. 2.

White, Albert Beebe. *The Making of the English Constitution, 449 – 1485*. 2d ed. London: Putnam, 1925.

White, Hayden. *The Content of the Form: Narrative Discourse and Historical Representation*. Baltimore: The Johns Hopkins UP, 1987.

———. *Metahistory: The Historical Imagination in Nineteenth-Century Europe*. Baltimore: The Johns Hopkins UP, 1973.

———. *Tropics of Discourse: Essays in Cultural Criticism*. Baltimore: The Johns Hopkins UP, 1978.

Woloch, Isser. *Jacobin Legacy: The Democratic Movement under the Directory*. Princeton: Princeton UP, 1970.

Zeitlin, Irving. *Liberty, Equality, and Revolution in Alexis de Tocqueville*. Boston: Little, Brown, 1971.

Index

Library of Congress Cataloging-in-Publication Data

Orr, Linda, 1943–
    Headless history: nineteenth-century French historiography of the
Revolution / Linda Orr.
        p.   cm.
    Includes bibliographical references.
    ISBN 0-8014-2379-1 (alk. paper)
        1. France — History — Revolution, 1789 – 1799 — Historiography.
2. Historiography — France — History — 19th century.   3. France —
Intellectual life — 19th century.   4. French literature — 19th
century — History and criticism.   5. France — History — Revolution,
1789 – 1799 — Influence.   6. Literature and revolutions.   7. Literature
and history.   I. Title.
    DC147.8.O77   1990
    944.04'072 — dc20   89-22140